WRITING SPACES: READINGS ON WRITING

Series Editors, Charles Lowe and Pavel Zemliansky

WRITING SPACES: READINGS ON WRITING

Series Editors, Charles Lowe and Pavel Zemliansky

Volumes in *Writing Spaces: Readings on Writing* offer multiple perspectives on a wide-range of topics about writing. In each chapter, authors present their unique views, insights, and strategies for writing by addressing the undergraduate reader directly. Drawing on their own experiences, these teachers-as-writers invite students to join in the larger conversation about the craft of writing. Consequently, each essay functions as a standalone text that can easily complement other selected readings in writing or writing-intensive courses across the disciplines at any level.

Writing Spaces

Readings on Writing
Volume 2

Edited by
Charles Lowe and Pavel Zemliansky

Parlor Press
Anderson, South Carolina
www.parlorpress.com

Parlor Press LLC, Anderson, South Carolina, 29621.

Printed in the United States of America
S A N: 2 5 4 - 8 8 7 9

Library of Congress Cataloging-in-Publication Data

Writing spaces : readings on writing. Volume 1 / edited by Charles Lowe
and Pavel Zemliansky.
    p. cm.
  Includes bibliographical references and index.
  ISBN 978-1-60235-184-4 (pbk. : alk. paper) -- ISBN 978-1-60235-185-1
(adobe ebook)
  1. College readers. 2. English language--Rhetoric. I. Lowe, Charles,
1965- II. Zemliansky, Pavel.
  PE1417.W735 2010
  808'.0427--dc22
                              2010019487

Cover design by Colin Charlton.
This book is printed on acid-free paper.

Parlor Press, LLC is an independent publisher of scholarly and trade titles in print and multimedia formats. This book is available in paperback and Adobe eBook formats from Parlor Press on the World Wide Web at http://www.parlorpress.com and from the Writing Spaces website at http://writingspaces.org. For custom editions including selections of essays from all volumes, please contact Parlor Press. For submission information or to find out about Parlor Press publications, write to Parlor Press, 3015 Brackenberry Drive, Anderson, SC, 29621, or e-mail editor@parlorpress.com.

Contents

Acknowledgments   *vii*

Ten Ways To Think About Writing: Metaphoric
   Musings for College Writing Students   *3*
      E. Shelley Reid

Composition as a Write of Passage   *24*
      Nathalie Singh-Corcoran

Critical Thinking in College Writing: From
   the Personal to the Academic   *37*
      Gita DasBender

Looking for Trouble: Finding Your Way into
   a Writing Assignment   *52*
      Catherine Savini

How to Read Like a Writer   *71*
      Mike Bunn

Murder! (Rhetorically Speaking)   *87*
      Janet Boyd

The Complexity of Simplicity: Invention
   Potentials for Writing Students   *102*
      Colin Charlton

Writing "Eyeball To Eyeball": Building A
   Successful Collaboration   *122*
      Rebecca Ingalls

On the Other Hand: The Role of Antithetical Writing
   in First Year Composition Courses   *141*
      Steven D. Krause

Introduction to Primary Research: Observations,
    Surveys, and Interviews   *153*
        Dana Lynn Driscoll

Putting Ethnographic Writing in Context   *175*
        Seth Kahn

Walk, Talk, Cook, Eat: A Guide to Using Sources   *193*
        Cynthia R. Haller

Reading Games: Strategies for Reading Scholarly Sources   *210*
        Karen Rosenberg

Googlepedia: Turning Information Behaviors
    into Research Skills   *221*
        Randall McClure

Annoying Ways People Use Sources   *242*
        Kyle D. Stedman

Everything Changes, or Why MLA Isn't (Always) Right   *257*
        Janice R. Walker

Storytelling, Narration, and the "Who I Am" Story   *270*
        Catherine Ramsdell

The Sixth Paragraph: A Re-Vision of the Essay   *286*
        Paul Lynch

Why Blog? Searching for Writing on the Web   *302*
        Alex Reid

A Student's Guide to Collaborative Writing Technologies   *320*
        Matt Barton and Karl Klint

Beyond Black on White: Document Design and
    Formatting in the Writing Classroom   *333*
        Michael J. Klein and Kristi L. Shackelford

Contributors   *351*

Acknowledgments

We would like to thank a lot of people who contributed to this project. First of all, we are very grateful to all the contributors for their hard work, their willingness to listen, and their ability to work with our reviewers who suggested numerous changes to their drafts. Without the enthusiasm and expertise of our contributors, this project would not exist.

Next, we would like to thank the members of our editorial board who also served as chapter reviewers. No doubt, you have put countless hours into the job of helping the authors make their chapters better. We know that the contributors have really enjoyed the collaborative and supportive review environment which you created.

We also want to acknowledge the immense amount of work of the editorial staff. Matt Barton, Colin Charlton, Craig Hulst, Terra Williams, and Elizabeth Woodworth—you did everything from copyediting chapters to graphic design and visual editing, to editing and proof reading contributors' bios and chapter descriptions. Your contributions have been vital to this second volume of Writing Spaces, and it would not have been possible without you.

Finally, a thanks to our partners at Parlor Press and the WAC Clearinghouse for their continued support of this open textbook series for first year composition.

WRITING SPACES

Ten Ways To Think About Writing: Metaphoric Musings for College Writing Students

E. Shelley Reid

1. A Thousand Rules and Three Principles

Writing is hard.*

I'm a writer and a writing professor, the daughter and granddaughter of writers and writing professors, and I still sit down at my keyboard every week and think, *writing is hard.*

I also think, though, that writing is made harder than it has to be when we try to follow too many rules for writing. Which rules have you heard? Here are some I was taught:

> Always have a thesis. *I* before *E* except after *C*. No one-sentence paragraphs. Use concrete nouns. A semi-colon joins two complete sentences. A conclusion restates the thesis and the topic sentences. Don't use "I," check your spelling, make three main points, and don't repeat yourself. Don't use contractions. Cite at least three sources, capitalize proper nouns, and don't use "you." Don't start a sentence with "And" or "But," don't end a sentence with a preposition, give two examples in

---

every paragraph, and use transition words. Don't use transition words too much.

When we write to the rules, writing seems more like a chore than a living process that connects people and moves the world forward. I find it particularly hard to cope with all those "Don'ts." It's no wonder we get writer's block, hands poised above the keyboard, worried about all the ways we could go wrong, suddenly wondering if we have new messages or whether there's another soda in the fridge.

We can start to unblock the live, negotiated process of writing for real people by cutting the thousand rules down to three broader principles:

1. Write about what you know about, are curious about, are passionate about (or what you can *find a way* to be curious about or interested in).
2. Show, don't just tell.
3. Adapt to the audience and purpose you're writing for.

When we write this way, we write *rhetorically:* that is, we pay attention to the needs of the *author* and the needs of the *reader* rather than the needs of the *teacher*—or the rules in the textbook.

Everything that matters from the preceding list of rules can be connected to one of those three rhetorical principles, and the principles address lots of aspects of writing that aren't on the list but that are central to why humans struggle to express themselves through written language. Write about what you know about *so that you can* show not just tell *in order to* adapt to your audience's needs and accomplish your goals. (Unless you do a good job showing what you mean, your audience will not understand your message. You will not meet their expectations or accomplish your goals.) Make clear points early *so that* your audience can spot your expertise or passion right from the start. Write multi-sentence paragraphs in which you show key ideas in enough detail that your audience doesn't have to guess what you mean. Use a semi-colon correctly *in order to* show how your carefully thought out ideas relate to one another—and to win your reader's confidence.

Writing will still be hard because these are some of the hardest principles in college; they may be some of the hardest principles in the galaxy. But if you write from those three principles, and use some of the strategies listed below, your writing will finally have a fighting chance of being *real,* not just *rules.* And that's when writing gets interesting and rewarding enough that we do it even though it's hard.

2. Show & Telepaths

What does that "show, don't just tell" idea really mean? Let's try some time travel to get a better idea. Can you remember being in kindergarten on show-and-tell day? Imagine that a student gets up in front of you and your fellow five-year-olds, empty-handed, and says, "I have a baseball signed by Hank Aaron that's in perfect condition, but I can't bring it to school." You're only five years old, but you know that she's got two problems, right? Not only can you not *see* the ball to know exactly what "perfect condition" looks like, to eyeball the signature and smell the leather and count the stitches, but you have no reason to *believe* this kid even if she describes it perfectly. If you tell without showing, your reader might not only be confused but might entirely disbelieve you. So you're two strikes down.

Another way to explain show vs. tell is with a story. There is a very, very short science fiction story in a collection of very short science fiction stories entitled "Science Fiction for Telepaths."

This is the entire story, just six words: "Aw, you know what I mean" (Blake 235).

"Wah-ha-ha!" go the telepaths, "what a great story! I really liked the part about the Martian with three heads trying to use the gamma blaster to get the chartreuse kitchen sink to fly out the window and land on the six-armed Venusian thief! Good one!" Since the telepaths can read the storyteller's mind, they don't need any other written details: they know the whole story instantly.

This story is a little like when you say to your best friend from just about forever, *you know what I mean,* and sometimes she even does, because she can *almost* read your mind. Sometimes, though, even your best buddy from way back gives you *that look.* You know *that look:* the one that says he thinks you've finally cracked. He can't read your mind, and you've lost him.

If you can confuse your best friend in the whole world, even when he's standing right there in front of you, think how easy it could be to confuse some stranger who's reading your writing days or months or years from now. If we could read each other's minds, writing wouldn't be hard at all, because we would always know what everyone meant, and we'd never doubt each other. If you figure out how to read minds this semester, I hope you'll tell us how it works! In the meantime, though, you have to *show* what you mean.

3. The Little Green Ball and Some People: Doing Details Right

Now we know: I can read my own mind, and you can read your own mind, and this self-mind-reading is even easier to do than breathing in and out on a lovely April morning. When I write something like "I have a little green ball" on the whiteboard, I read my mind as I read the board, so I understand it—and I'm positive, therefore, that you understand it. Meanwhile, you read my sentence and your own mind together and the meaning is so perfectly clear to you that it's nearly impossible to imagine that you're not understanding exactly what I intended.

I have a little green ball. Even a five-year-old could read this sentence and know what I mean, right?

Try something. Bring both hands up in front of your face, and use each one to show *one* possible size of this "little" ball. (You can try this with friends: have everyone close their eyes and show the size of a "little" ball with their hands, then open their eyes, and look around.) Hmm. Already there's some possible disagreement, even though it seemed so clear what "little" meant.

Maybe "green" is easier: you know what "green" is, right? Of course. But now, can you think of two different versions of "green"? three versions? five? In the twenty-five minds in a classroom, say, we might have at least twenty kinds of little, and maybe a hundred kinds of green, and we haven't even discussed what kind of "ball" we might be talking about. Those of you who are math whizzes can see the permutations that come from all those variables. If I sent you to Mega Toyland with the basic instructions, "Buy me a little green ball," the chances are slim that you would come home with the ball I had in mind.

If I don't care about the exact ball—I just need something ball-like and not too huge and somewhat greenish—then it doesn't matter. I can leave it up to you to decide. (Occasionally, it's effective to avoid details: if I were writing a pop song about my broken heart, I'd be deliberately vague so that you'd think the song was about *your* heart, and then you'd decide to download or even buy my song.) But the more

I care that you know exactly what I'm thinking, the more the details matter to me, then the more information I need to give you.

What information would you need to write down so that someone would buy the exact little green ball that you're thinking of while he or she is shopping at Mega Toyland?

If you're going to *show* me, or each other, what you're thinking, using only language, it will take several sentences, perhaps a whole paragraph—filled with facts and statistics, comparisons, sensory description, expert testimony, examples, personal experiences—to be sure that what's in your mind is what's in my mind. After my students and I finish examining my ball and choosing rich language to show it, the whiteboard often reads something like this: "I have a little green ball about an inch in diameter, small enough to hide in your hand. It's light neon green like highlighter ink and made of smooth shiny rubber with a slightly rough line running around its equator as if two halves were joined together. When I drop it on the tile floor, it bounces back nearly as high as my hand; when I throw it down the hallway, it careens unpredictably off the walls and floor." Now the ball in your mind matches the ball in my hand much more closely.

Showing is harder than just telling, and takes longer, and is dependent on your remembering that nobody reads your mind like you do. Can you think of other "little green ball" words or phrases that you might need to *show* more clearly? How do you describe a good movie or a bad meal? How would you describe your mother, your hometown, your car? Try it on a blank page or in an open document: write one "you know what I mean" sentence, then write every detail and example you can think of to make sure that a reader *does* know what you mean. Then you can choose the most vivid three or four, the ones that best show your readers what you want them to understand.

There's another kind of description that requires mind reading. If I write on the board that "some people need to learn to mind their own business sometimes," would you agree with me? (By now, you should be gaining some skepticism about being able to read my mind.) In my head, I'm filling in "some people" and "their business" and "sometimes" with very specific, one-time-only examples. It's like I have a YouTube clip playing in my head, or a whole season's worth of a reality TV show, and you don't have access to it yet. (I might as well be saying "I have cookies!" but not offering to share any of them with you.)

If I give you a snapshot from that film, if I use language to pro-vide a one-time-only example, I *show* you: "My ninety-year-old grand-mother needs to stop calling up my younger cousin Celia like she did last night and telling her to persuade me to move back home to Lara-mie so my mom won't get lonely and take up extreme snowboarding just to go meet some nice people." Does that help you see how the one-time-only example *you* were thinking of, when you read my boring sentence along with your own mind, is different from what I wanted you to think? As writers, we need to watch out for the some-people example and the plural example: "Sometimes things bother me" or "Frederick Douglass had lots of tricks for learning things he needed to know." If an idea is important, give an exact one-time snapshot with as much detail as possible.

In a writing class, you also have to learn to be greedy as a reader, to ask for the good stuff from someone else's head if they don't give it to you, to demand that they share their cookies: you have to be brave and say, "I can't see what you mean." This is one of the roles teachers take up as we read your writing. (One time during my first year teaching, one of my students snorted in exasperation upon receiving his essay back from me. "So, like, what do you do," he asked, "just go through the essay and write 'Why? How so? Why? How so? Why? How so?' randomly all over the margins and then slap that 'B–' on there?" I grinned and said, "Yep, that's about it.")

It's also *your* job as a peer reader to read skeptically and let your fellow writer know when he or she is assuming the presence of a mind reader—because none of us knows for sure if we're doing that when we write, not until we encounter a reader's "Hunh?" or "Wha-a-a-?" You can learn a lot about writing from books and essays like this one, but in order to learn how *not* to depend on reading your own mind, you need feedback from a real, live reader to help you gauge how your audience will respond.

4. Lost Money and Thank-you Notes: What's in an Audience?

Writing teachers are always going on and on about *audience,* as if you didn't already know all about this concept. You can do a simple thought-experiment to prove to them, and to yourself, that you already fully understand that when the audience changes, your message has to change, sometimes drastically.

Imagine that you've done something embarrassingly stupid or impulsive that means you no longer have any money to spend this semester. (I won't ask you what it is, or which credit card or 888 phone number or website it involves, or who was egging you on.) You really need the money, but you can't get it back now. If I just said, "Write a message to try to get some money from someone," you might struggle a bit, and then come up with some vague points about your situation.

But if I say, "Ask your best friend for the money," you should suddenly have a very clear idea of what you can say. Take a minute and consider: what do you tell this friend? Some of my students have suggested, "Remember how you owe me from that time I helped you last February?" or "I'll pay you back, with interest" or "I'll do your laundry for a month." Most of my students say they'll tell their friends the truth about what happened: would you? What else might you say to your own friend, particularly if he were giving you that skeptical look?

Suppose then that your friend is nearly as broke as you are, and you have to ask one of your parents or another family adult. Now what do you say to help loosen the parental purse strings? Do you tell the truth about what happens? (Does it matter which parent it is?) Do you say, "Hey, you *owe* me"? Some of my students have suggested choosing messages that foreground their impending starvation, their intense drive for a quality education, or their ability to learn a good lesson. Would your parent want you to offer to pay back the money? What else might you say?

Notice how easy it is for you to switch gears: nothing has changed but the audience, and yet you've quickly created a whole new message, changing both the content and the language you were using.

One more try: when your parent says there's just no extra cash to give you, you may end up at the local bank trying to take out a loan. What will you tell the bank? Should the loan officer hear how you lost your money, or how you promise you'll be more responsible in the future? Should you try looking hungry and wan? Probably not: by discussing collateral (your five-year-old Toyota) and repayment terms (supported by your fry-jockey job at McSkippy's), you're adjusting your message once again.

Sometimes writing teachers talk about a "primary" and "secondary" audience, as if *that* were really a complicated topic, but you know all about this idea, too. Take just a minute and think about writing a thank-you note. If it's a thank-you note to your grandmother, then your primary audience is your grandmother, so you write to her. But if your grandmother is like mine, she may show your note to someone else, and all those people become *secondary* audiences. Who might see, or hear about, your note to your grandmother? Neighbors, other relatives, her yoga group or church friends? If you know your note will be stuck up on the fridge, then you can't use it as a place to add snarky remarks about your younger brother: you write for a primary audience, but you also need to think for a minute to be sure your message is adjusted for the needs of your secondary audiences. (If you haven't written a thank-you note recently, try to remember the last time someone forwarded your email or text message to someone else, without asking you first.)

In a writing classroom, everyone knows that, in reality, your primary audience is the teacher—just as during rehearsal or team practice the primary audience is the director or coach who decides whether you'll be first clarinet or take your place in the starting line-up. Your classmates (or teammates) may be part of a secondary audience who also need considering. It can be tempting to take the middle-of-the-road route and forget about any other audiences. But in all these cases, you won't be practicing forever. It helps to imagine another primary audience—sometimes called a "target audience"—outside the classroom, in order to gain experience tailoring your performance to a "real" audience. It also helps to imagine a *very specific* primary audience (a person or small group or publication), so that instead of staring at the screen thinking vague "some people" thoughts, you can quickly come up with just the right words and information to match that audience's needs, and it helps to consider some exact secondary audiences so that you can include ideas that will appeal to those readers as well. (Who do you suppose are the specific primary and secondary audiences for this essay? How does the writing adapt to those audiences?)

5. PINK HOUSES & CHORUSES: KEEPING YOUR READER WITH YOU

Once you've identified a target audience, and put down all the detail you can think of to help show your ideas to those readers, you need to focus on not losing them somewhere along the way. Earlier in your writing career as you worked on writing cohesive essays, you may have watched writing teachers go totally ballistic over *thesis statements* and *topic sentences*—even though some teachers insisted that they weren't requiring any kind of set formula. How can this be? What's up with all this up-front information?

The concept is actually pretty simple, if we step out of the writing arena for a minute. Say you're driving down the interstate at sixty-five miles an hour with three friends from out of town, and you suddenly say to them, "Hey, there's that amazing Pink House!" What happens? Probably there's a lot of whiplash-inducing head swiveling, and someone's elbow ends up in someone else's ribs, and maybe one of your friends gets a glimpse, but probably nobody really gets a chance to see it (and somebody might not believe you if she didn't see it for herself!). What if you had said instead, "Hey, coming up on the right here in about two miles, there's an amazing huge neon Pink House: watch for it"? They'd be ready, they'd know where to look and what to look for, and they'd see what you wanted them to see.

Writers need to advise their readers in a similar way. That advice doesn't always need to be in a *thesis statement* or a *topic sentence,* but it does need to happen regularly so that readers don't miss something crucial.

"But," you say, "I'm not supposed to repeat things in my essay; it gets boring!" That's true, up to a point, but there are exceptions. Have you ever noticed how the very same company will run the exact same advertisement for light beer five or six times during one football game? It's not as if the message they are trying to get across is that complex: *Drink this beer and you will be noticed by this beautiful woman, or get to own this awesome sports car, or meet these wonderful friends who will never ever let you down.* The ad costs the company hundreds of thousands of dollars each time, but there it is again. Beer: sports car. Beer: sports car. Contemporary Americans have a very high tolerance for repeated messages; we even come to depend on them, like football fans relishing the instant replay. Beer: sports car.

If you'd rather think like an artist than an advertising executive, consider popular music. Pick a pop song, any song—"Jingle Bells," for instance, or whatever song everybody's listening to this month—and the next time you listen, count the number of times the chorus, or even the title phrase, comes up. Do we get bored by the repetition? Not usually. In fact, the chorus is crucial for audience awareness because it's often the first (or even the only) part of the song the listener learns and can sing along with. Repeating the chorus helps bring the audience along with you from verse to verse: the audience thinks, "Aha, I *know* this!"

Now, what you're trying to say in your essay is much more complex than *beer: sports car* or *I will always love you.* If you only say it once or twice—there, in the last paragraph, where you finally figured out the most important point, or maybe once at the start and once at the end—we might miss it, or only get a piece of it. Here you've spent hundreds of minutes working on this idea, and we zoom past it at sixty-five m.p.h. and miss it entirely! You have to bring it back to our attention throughout the essay. Of course, you don't want to repeat just anything. You certainly don't want to repeat the same examples or vague "some people" theories, stuffing baloney into the middle of the paper to fill it out. But the core idea—beer: sports car—needs to appear early and often, using the same key words, even, as an anchor for all the complex ideas and examples you're connecting to it, as a place for the audience to recognize the main idea and find a way to "sing along."

So as you're revising, add your chorus back into some key middle parts of your essay—the beginnings and endings of paragraphs, like commercial breaks, can be places that readers expect repetition—until you start to really feel uncomfortable about your repetition . . . and then add it one more time, and it might be enough, but it shouldn't be too much. (Since you read the essay dozens of times *and* you read your own mind, you'll get antsy about repetition long before your readers will in their one trip through your essay.) If you get a good balance, your reader—the same person who keeps laughing at the beer ad or mumbling the chorus to the pop song without knowing the rest of the lyrics—won't even notice that you're repeating. When I work with my students, I say: "I promise to tell you—no harm, no penalty—if you're ever *too clear* about your main point." I find that very few people make it that far, but they like having the encouragement to try. You and your peer readers can make the same agreement.

6. Fruit Jell-O: Balancing Arguments & Examples

"Great," you say, "so I'm supposed to have all these examples and to have all these Pink House reminders, but it's hard to keep it all straight."

That's a very smart observation—because one of the main challenges writers face, when we can't read someone's mind or get them to read ours, is learning how to balance the writing that states our *theories and arguments* with the writing that provides our *evidence and examples*. It turns out that it's easier to do just one of these things at a time when writing, but having theories and arguments without evidence and examples is a recipe for confusion and misunderstanding.

I find that it helps sometimes to think about fruit Jell-O™, the kind my mom used to take to family get-togethers: lime Jell-O with mandarin orange slices in it, or berry Jell-O with cherries in it. Fruit Jell-O is a pretty good *balance* of foods to take to an informal family gathering: it meets the needs of the audience.

You wouldn't want to take plain gelatin to show off to your family, after all. Think of the last time you ate plain old Jell-O, with no additional food (or beverage) added to it. Weren't you in a hospital, or a school cafeteria, or some other unhappy place? Hospitals serve plain gelatin because it *looks* and *behaves* like food, but it has so few ingredients that it won't irritate your mouth or upset your digestion. That same blandness means that not a lot of family members will choose it over the tortilla chips or the macaroons.

Writing just your opinions, theories, and arguments is a lot like serving plain Jell-O: it seems like you're doing something productive, but there's not much substance to it. Politicians often write plain Jell-O speeches with no details or examples, because that kind of talk motivates people but won't irritate voters with tiny details about time or money. Talent-show contestants sometimes choose to sing plain Jell-O songs for the same reason.

On the other hand, if you took a bowl of cherries with you, your family might perk up a bit, but cherries are kind of hard to serve. They roll out of the bowl and off of those flimsy paper plates and end up sliding into the cheese dip or being squished into the new carpet by your two-year-old cousin. People finger all the cherries but take just a few (using tongs on cherries just seems too formal!), and it's hard to know how to handle the pits, or to eat gooey already-pitted cherries with your hands.

Writing just your examples, reasons, and details is a lot like bringing cherries to the party: it's interesting and lively, but readers don't know what to make of it all. Some of your reasons or stories will roll out of readers' heads if they aren't firmly attached to an argument;

some readers will meander through all your details and just randomly remember one or two of them rather than building a whole picture.

Good writers blend argument and evidence as they write, so that readers get both elements together all the way through. Good revisers go back and adjust the recipe, seeking a workable combination. Sometimes as you're revising it can feel odd to be just adding cherries: it can seem like you're packing in too many extra details when there's already a perfectly good piece of fruit there. Other times it seems weird to be just adding Jell-O, because all those "chorus" sentences sound the same and have the same flavor, and you don't want to repeat yourself unnecessarily. It's hard to get the balance right, and you'll want to have your readers help you see where to adjust the ingredients. But if you remember that the fruit/evidence is the tastiest part (so you want the most vibrant examples), and the point of Jell-O/argumentation is to provide consistency to hold everything together (you want statements that sound alike), you may start to gain additional confidence in balancing your writing.

7. Wash-and-wear Paragraphs

If you're going to have Jell-O and cherries, a chorus and one-time-only examples, in every paragraph, that's going to take some managing—and you'll want to manage *rhetorically* rather than going by some rules you once heard about exactly how long a paragraph should be. What paragraph-length rules have you been taught? Should a paragraph be five to eight sentences? always more than two sentences? never longer than a page? Some of my students have learned rules that specify that all paragraphs have twelve sentences and each sentence has a specific job. That sounds complicated—and you know that a rule like that can't be universally true. What if you're writing for a newspaper? for a psychology journal? for a website? Paragraph length doesn't follow clear rules, but once again depends upon a rhetorical negotiation between the writer's needs and the reader's needs.

Switch gears for a minute and try out another metaphor: what do you know about how big a load of laundry should be? Right: it depends. What's wrong with a very small or a very large load? Paragraphs face the same kinds of boundaries: too small, and they can waste a reader's energy, always starting and stopping; too large, and they overload a reader and nothing gets clean. But there are no definite rules in laundry or in paragraphs. Is there ever reason to do one tiny laundry load, even if it might waste money or energy? Sure: maybe you've got an important event to attend Friday night and you just need to wash your best black shirt quickly, or maybe you have a small washing machine. Is there ever reason to do one slightly oversized load? Absolutely: perhaps you're low on quarters or there's only one machine open in the dormitory laundry room, and you need to get all those t-shirts clean. The same is true for paragraphs: sometimes, you have just one important thing to say, or your readers have a short attention span, so you want a short paragraph—even a one-sentence paragraph. On the other hand, sometimes you have a complex explanation that you want your reader to work through all at once, so you stretch your paragraph a little longer than usual, and hope your reader stays with you.

You want to write paragraphs that your target audience can handle without straining their brains or leaving suds all over the floor. I bet you're pretty good at sorting laundry into the basic loads: darks, colors, whites, like the three body paragraphs of a five-paragraph essay. But what if you're writing an eight-page paper using three basic points? What if you have an enormous pile of whites?

You sometimes have to split up even the loads that look alike. Would you split an all-whites pile into all the long-drying socks vs. all the quick-drying shirts? the dirty stuff vs. the really gross, stinky stuff? the underwear you need tomorrow vs. the towels you could wash later? You can find lots of ways to split a too-long paragraph based on how you want your reader to think about the issue: pros and cons, first steps and next steps, familiar information and more surprising information.

Writers need to remember that paragraphs help readers focus and manage their analytical energies. It's good to have some variance in size and shape but not to overtax your readers with too much variation; it's useful to write each paragraph with a clear beginning and ending to direct readers' attention; and it's helpful if paragraphs come with a blend of information and analysis to help readers "see what you mean" about your subpoints and see how they relate to the overall point of your essay. It's not true that paragraphs are "one size fits all," and it's not true that "anything goes": you need to adjust your paragraphs to connect your ideas to your readers' brains.

8. Hey Hey Hey and the Textbook Conspiracy: Annotating Your Reading

I know, you thought this was an essay about writing. But part of being a writer, and being a helpful companion to other writers, is being a careful reader, a reader who writes.

Besides, I want to be sure you get what you pay for: that kind of critical thinking helps all of us be better writers. Did you know that you pay for most textbooks in two ways, and most students never do the simplest thing to recoup their investment?

How do you pay? First, except for texts like the one you're reading right now, you've paid some exorbitant price for your books, even if you bought them used. Why would you do that, instead of checking them out of the library or sneaking a look from a friend? Right: you can read them whenever and wherever you get around to it. (No, I don't want to know where you read your class book!) But you may be overlooking one more benefit, which I'll get to in a minute.

Second, you pay for the book—even a free one like this one—with your time. You pore over page after page, the minutes ticking by, instead of building houses for orphans in Botswana or coming up with a cure for insomnia or even giving that double-crossing elf what he deserves in *World of Warcraft*. Did you ever finish all that poring (with a "p," not a "b," really) and realize you had tuned out and didn't remember a thing? Now you've paid dearly, and you may have to pay yet another time when you re-read it.

The simplest thing you can do to get your money's worth and your time's worth from your books and other reading material is this: you can *write* on them.

Whatever you pay for the book (minus whatever you might sell it back for), the only two benefits you get are convenient reading access, and the chance to *write in the book*. If you don't write in your book, or type notes into the document, you're being cheated, as if you'd paid for a Combo Meal but ate only the fries. (Do you think maybe you won't be able to re-sell your book if you write in it? Check with your friends: I bet someone's bought a used book that's been scribbled all over. So clearly someone will buy your book back even if you write in it. Don't let the textbook industry scare you out of getting what you pay for.)

Some of you may think you *are* writing on your text, but I wonder if that's true. Smearing it with hot pink highlighter pen doesn't count as *writing*. Why not? That takes another story and another metaphor. There's a classic *Far Side* cartoon from back in the twentieth century that reveals what dogs are *really* saying when they bark all day long. According to cartoonist Gary Larson, when we finally translate their secret language, we find that they say, "Hey! Hey! Hey!" (144). You can just see a dog thinking that way, everything new and surprising, but not much complexity of analysis. Hey!

When you read something and gloss it with your highlighter pen, that's what you're saying: Hey! Hey! Hey! You can come back six weeks later to write an essay or study for an exam, and you have an entire book filled with Hey! It's a good start, but as a smart writing student, you're ready to go further to get your money's worth.

Without having to expend much more energy, you can begin to add a wholly intelligent commentary, putting your own advanced brain down on the page, using an actual writing utensil such as a pen or pencil (or a comment function for an electronic document). For starters, let's just vary Hey:

Ha.
Heh.
Hee.
Hooboy!
Hmm.
Hmph.
Huh?
Whoa!

Each of those responses records some higher-brain *judgment:* if you go back later, you'll know whether you were saying "Hey, this is cool!" or "Hey, this is fishy." You can also use other abbreviations you know: LOL, OMG, WTH(eck), or ☺. You can underline short phrases with a solid or a squiggly underline, depending on your reaction. And of course, you can always go back to "Why? How so? *Show* me!" If you get really bold, you can ask questions ("will this take too much time?"), write quick summaries ("annotate so there's no hey") or note connections ("sounds like the mind-reading thing"). It doesn't take very long, and it keeps your brain involved as you read. What other short *annotations* could you write or type on this page right now?

Every time you write on the page and talk back to the text, you get your money's worth, because you make the text truly your own, and you get your time's worth, because you're staying awake and you're more likely to remember and learn what you read. If you don't remember, you still have an intelligent record of what you should've remembered, not just a pile of Hey! Bonus: being a writer when you're a reader helps you become a better reader *and* a better writer.

9. SHORT-TIME WRITING: USE YOUR HIGHER BRAIN

So far, we've been thinking about writing when you have plenty of time to consider your audience, play with your paragraphs, and re-calibrate your Jell-O/cherry balance. But you won't always have that much time: sometimes you'll get a late start or have an early deadline. In college, you might encounter essay questions on an exam. Learning how to be a good timed-exam writer can help you in lots of short-time writing situations.

What's hard about writing an essay exam? The stress, the pressure, the clock ticking, the things you don't know. It's like trying to think with a jet airplane taking off overhead, or a pride of hungry lions racing your way. But wait: the coolest thing about the essay exam is that, in contrast to a multiple choice exam that shows what you *don't* know, the essay exam allows you to focus on what you *do* know. The problem is that only your higher brain can show off that knowledge, and for most people in a stressful situation like an essay exam, the higher brain starts to lose out to the lower brain, the *fight-or-flight* brain, the brain that sees breathing in and breathing out as one of its most complicated tasks, and so the writing goes awry.

Essay exams—or those last-minute, started-at-1:22-A.M. essays that you may be tempted or forced to write this semester (but not for your writing teacher, of course!)—generally go wrong by failing to meet one of the three principles described at the beginning of this essay. Sometimes students fail to study well so that they can write from knowledge. (Unfortunately, I don't know if I can help you with your midnight cram sessions.) More often, though, some very smart, well-prepared students fail to adapt to their audience's needs, or fail to provide specific support. All that late-night study-session agony goes for nothing if your lower brain takes over while you're writing. Your lower brain can barely remember "I before E," and it knows nothing about complicated rhetorical strategies like ours: you have to make sure your higher brain sets the pace and marks the trail.

So the teacher hands out the questions, and the first thing you do is . . . panic? No. Start writing? Heavens, no. *Never* start an essay exam—or a truly last-minute essay—by starting to write the essay, even if (like me) you generally prefer to "just start writing" rather than doing a lot of restrictive planning. Freewriting is an excellent writing exercise, but only when you know you have plenty of time to revise. Instead, ignore all those keyboards clacking, all those pens scribbling: they are the signs of lower brains at work, racing off screeching wildly about lions without remembering the way writing happens. You're smarter than that. You're going to use your higher brain right at the start, before it gets distracted. Speed, right now, is your enemy, a trick of the lower brain.

The first thing you want to do is . . . *read the gosh darn question.* Really, really read it. Annotate the assignment sheet or exam prompt, or write the key question out on a separate piece of paper, so you know you're actually reading it, and not just pretending to. (If you're in a workplace setting, write down a list of the top things you know your audience—or your boss—wants to see.) In every essay exam I've ever given, *some*body has not answered the question. When I say this in a class, everyone frowns or laughs at me just the way you are now, thinking, "What kind of idiot wouldn't read the question? Certainly not me!" But someone always *thinks* she's read the whole question, and understood it, when she hasn't. Don't be that writer. Circle the verbs: *analyze, argue, describe, contrast.* Underline the key terms: *two causes, most important theme, main steps, post–Civil War.* Read it again, and read it a third time: this is your only official clue about what your audience—the teacher—wants. On a piece of scratch paper, write out an answer to the question, *in so many words:* if it asks, "What are two competing explanations for language acquisition?" write down, "Two competing explanations for language acquisition are ___ and ___ ." In an examination setting, this may even become your opening line, since readers of essay exams rarely reward frilly introductions or cute metaphors.

But don't start to write the whole answer yet, even though your lower brain is begging you, even though the sweat is breaking out on your brow and your muscles are tensing up with adrenaline because you know the lions and probably some rampaging T-Rexes are just around the corner. In real time, it has only taken you two minutes to read and annotate the question. Some students are still pulling out their pens, while across campus at least one student is just waking up in a panic because his alarm didn't go off. Meanwhile, far from being hopelessly behind, you're ahead of everyone who's writing already, because you're still working with your higher brain.

You have one more task, though. You know that *showing* takes longer, and is more complicated, than *telling*. Given the choice, your lower brain will tell, tell, and tell again, blathering on about Jell-O generalities that don't let readers see all the best thinking going on in your mind. Before your higher brain starts to abandon you, make it give you the cherries: write yourself a list of very specific examples that you can use in this essay, as many as you can think of. Do not just "think them over." That's a lower brain shortcut, a flight move, and it's a trick, because your lower brain will forget them as soon as the lions get a bit closer. Write them down. If you don't know all the possible transmission vectors for tuberculosis that were discussed, write down excellent examples of the ones you *do* know. If you can, number them in an order that makes sense, so that you leave a good breadcrumb trail for your lower brain to follow. Don't call it an "outline" if you don't want to; that can feel intimidating. Just call it a "trail guide."

Now you can start writing: take a deep, calming breath and begin with your *in so many words* sentence, then follow the trail your higher brain has planned. About every two or three sentences, you should start out with "For example, . . ." or "Another example of this is . . . ," to be sure that you're not forgetting your higher brain's advice or sliding into a vague "some people" sentence. About every three or four sentences, you should start out with "Therefore, . . ." or "In other words, . . ." and come back to a version of that very first, question-answering sentence you wrote on your paper. Bring the chorus back in; stay in tune and on the trail. Don't try for too much variation or beauty. Knowing that your higher brain has already solved the problem, all you have to do is set it down on paper, to *show what you know*. Writing is hard, especially under time pressure, but when you use higher brain strategies and don't get trapped in the rules or caught up in random flight, when you take control and anticipate your reader's needs, you can make writing work for you in very powerful ways even without a lot of time.

10. Rules vs. Rhetoric, or, The Five Paragraph Essay vs. "Try Something!"

We started out by thinking of all the rules—all those "Don'ts"—that writers can face. Each of the metaphors here replaces a *rule* with an *idea* that helps you consider how real people communicate with each other through writing, and how writers make judgments and choices in order to have the most powerful effect on their readers. That is, we've been thinking *rhetorically,* about the audience and purpose and context of a writing situation.

Interestingly, many of those rules are just short-cut versions of really good rhetorical principles. If you were a middle-school teacher faced with a room full of thirty squirrelly teenagers who all wanted to know *What's Due On Friday?* and who didn't have patience for one more part of their chaotic lives to be in the "it just depends" category, you might be tempted to make some rules, too. You might even come up with The Five Paragraph Essay.

That is, instead of saying, "Most readers in the U.S. prefer to know exactly what they're getting before they invest too much time," which is a thoughtful rhetorical analysis that can help writers make good choices, you might say, "Your thesis must come in the first paragraph." Instead of saying, "In Western cultures, many readers are comfortable with threes: three bears, three strikes, three wishes, even the Christian Trinity," you might make a rule and say, "You must write an essay with a beginning, an end, and three middle paragraphs." Instead of saying, "Your readers need to know how your examples connect to one another, and how each set of examples is related to your overall point," you might say, "Every paragraph needs to start with a transition and a topic sentence and finish with a concluding sentence." And instead of saying, "Writers in the U.S. face one of the most heterogeneous groups of readers in the world, so we need to be as careful as possible to make our meaning clear rather than assuming that all readers know what we're talking about," you might just say, "Each paragraph needs to include two concrete-detail sentences and two commentary sentences."

You would intend to be helping your students by saying these things, and for many young writers, having clear *rules* is more useful than being told, "It depends." But eventually the rules start to be more limiting than helpful, like a great pair of shoes that are now a size too small. Good writers need some space to grow.

As a writer in college now, and as a writer in the larger world full of real readers—whether they're reading your Facebook page, your letter to the editor, or your business plan—you need to free yourself from the rules and learn to make rhetorical decisions. From now on, when you hear someone tell you a rule for writing, try to figure out the rhetorical challenge that lies behind it, and consider the balancing acts you may need to undertake. What do you want to say, and what will help the readers in your primary audience "see what you mean" and follow your main points?

There aren't any easy answers: writing is still hard. But the good news is that you can use a few helpful "rules" as starting points when they seem appropriate, and set aside the rest. You can draw on some key principles or metaphors to help you imagine the needs of your readers, and when you come to an open space where there doesn't seem to be a perfect rule or strategy to use, you can *try something*. In the end, that's what writers are always doing as we write: trying this, trying that, trying something else, hoping that we'll make a breakthrough so that our readers will say "Aha, I see what you mean!"—and they really, truly will see it. You know James Bond 007 would *try something;* Jane Eyre would *try something;* those Olympic medalists and rock stars and pioneering cardiac surgeons and Silicon Valley whiz kids are always *trying something.* In the same way, being a good writer is always more about *trying something* than about following the rules, about adapting to a new situation rather than replicating last year's essay. So take a deep breath, push all those nay-saying rule-makers into the far corners of your brain, focus on your current audience and purpose, and write!

DISCUSSION

1. Which section of this essay do you remember most clearly? Write down what you remember about it, and explain how you might use an idea in that section to help with a writing task that you're doing this week. Why do you think this section stuck with you?

2. Without looking back at the essay, what would you say is the *chorus* of the essay, the "beer: sports car" message that keeps getting restated? Write it down: it may be a sentence, a phrase, and/or a few key words. Now go back to a section of the essay and underline or highlight sentences or phrases where Reid re-

peats this chorus or key words. Does she repeat them as much as you thought she did?

3. What other rules for writing have you been told to follow, either at school or outside of school in your workplace, community group, or online setting? List a couple of rules that weren't described in this essay, and note down whether you think they're most connected to the principle of writing from knowledge, showing enough detail, or adapting to readers' needs. Also, if there's another principle for writing that helps you a lot, something you always try to do, add a note about it so you can share it with your classroom peers.

4. Where in this essay does Reid practice what she preaches? Go back through the essay and label a few places where she seems to be doing what she says writers should do ("here she gives a Pink House heads-up sentence at the start of a section"), and note a few places where she doesn't. Even though Reid admits that writing is hard and depends on a specific context, her essay may make some of the strategies sound easier or more universal than they are. Which one of her suggestions seems like it would be the hardest for you to do, or seems like it would be the least effective in the kind of writing you do most often? Explain why this suggestion is trickier than it looks, and how you might cope with that challenge as a writer.

Works Cited

Blake, E. Michael. "Science Fiction for Telepaths." *100 Great Science Fiction Short Short Stories*. Ed. Isaac Asimov, Martin Greenberg, and Joseph D. Olander. New York: Avon, 1978. 235. Print.

Larson, Gary. *The Far Side Gallery 5*. Kansas City: Andrews and McMeel, 1995. Print.

Composition as a Write of Passage

Nathalie Singh-Corcoran

Welcome to English 101, a course that is designed to introduce you to college-level reading and writing. This intensive class emphasizes composing—the entire process—from invention to revising for focus, development, organization, active style, and voice.

Most colleges and universities require first year composition (hereafter FYC).*

The overarching goal of FYC is to familiarize you with academic discourse (i.e. college level reading and writing) so that you can apply what you learn in future writing situations. While the goal is sound, you might be feeling a disconnect between the writing you are doing in FYC and the writing you believe you will do in your major and career. I remember feeling that same disconnect when I was a freshman at the University of Arizona. In my first few weeks of English 101, I was ambivalent about what I was learning. I wasn't sure of the purpose of assignments like the personal narrative or the rhetorical analysis, because I believed I would never write those two papers again. If I were never going to have to write papers like that again, why did I have to do them in the first place?

Now, almost twenty years later, I teach FYC courses at West Virginia University, and I direct the writing center. In the first few weeks

---

of the semester, I see the same look of uncertainty on my students' faces, and I hear students in other FYC courses voicing their frustrations in the writing center. They know that the writing that they do in FYC is very different from the writing that they will do (or are already doing) in biology, forestry, marketing, finance, or even writing careers. Many also believe that writing will not be a part of their academic or professional lives. Recently, I heard a young man at the writing center say, "I'll be so glad when my [English 102] class is over because then, I won't have to write anymore." However, this person was mistaken; in reality, after he passes the FYC requirement, his writing life will not be over. Other courses will require written communication as will most professions.

Given that you will continue writing in your academic and professional lives, the questions that you have about the relevance of FYC are valid. There is even some debate among compositionists (those who study and teach composition courses) about the relevancy of FYC. However, given the research on FYC, the syllabi and assignment sheets that I've gathered, studies from other disciplines I have read, the anecdotal evidence from students that I have collected, and my own experience as a former FYC student and a current FYC teacher, I can tell you the positive effects of the university writing requirement are far reaching.

While the writing tasks in one's chosen major or even in the world of work may not resemble FYC assignments, a thoughtfully crafted FYC course does prepare you for *college level reading and writing* and for the critical reading and writing that you will do every day in your career after college. As I reflect on my FYC experience, I believe that the things I learned as a student laid the groundwork for my future writing life. The individual essays—the personal narrative, the rhetorical analysis, the argumentative research paper, etc.—helped me understand

- how I could use writing to think through my newly forming ideas;
- how a piece of writing always has an audience;
- how to locate, evaluate, and incorporate sources;
- and how important it is to get meaningful feedback so that I could produce better writing *and* become a better writer.

It did, however, take me a long time to come to the conclusion that FYC had value beyond filling needed college credit.

DOES KNOWLEDGE TRANSFER?

I used to be of the opinion that English 101 and 102 was a waste of time to students in the engineering discipline.

—Godwin Erekaife

Godwin Erekaife, a chemical engineering student who graduated in May 2010, is not alone in his early beliefs about FYC. His opinion about the requirement stemmed from his uncertainty about its practical application and his desire to reserve credit hours for his chosen field: engineering. Godwin's uncertainty is understandable. He wanted broad preparation for chemical engineering and to know how FYC would help him later on. His questions about FYC applicability speak to something called *knowledge transfer:* the degree to which we can use newly learned skills and abilities and apply them in other contexts. In short, Godwin didn't believe that what he learned in FYC would positively impact his engineering coursework.

Godwin's initial thoughts resonate with others. In her recent study—"Understanding Transfer From FYC: Preliminary Results from a Longitudinal Study"—Elizabeth Wardle discovered that after fulfilling their FYC requirements, her students didn't immediately see connections between FYC and other courses. Wardle also found that while they saw some value in what they learned—"new textual features (new ways of organizing material), how to manage large research projects (including use of peer review and planning, how to read and analyze research articles; and how to conduct serious, in-depth academic research" (72)—her students employed few of these new abilities in their first two years of college. In a similar study, "Disciplinarity and Transfer: Students' Perceptions of Learning to Write," Linda Bergmann and Janet Zepernick found that students at their schools saw FYC as a "distraction from the important work of professional socialization that occurs in the 'content area' courses" (138). In essence, their students, like Godwin (and maybe even like you), were eager to enter their fields of study and learn the discourses (ways of thinking, speaking, writing, interpreting, and generally making knowledge in a community) of those fields and would have preferred entering those discourse communities earlier rather than take FYC.

However, both studies also suggest that FYC can be a powerful tool in helping us all learn new discourses. Wardle found that people developed a "meta-awareness about writing, language, and rhetorical strategies" (82) when they took FYC. It helped them "think about writing in the university" (82), how it works, why it works differently in different contexts, and how to use it. Similarly, Bergmann and Zepernick's findings suggest that FYC is a requirement that can teach you "*how to learn to write*" (142). Bergmann and Zepernick provide a really useful metaphor to help you think through both the idea of *meta-awareness* and *learning how to learn to write*. They ask you to consider,

> [The] specific skills athletes learn in one sport (such as how to dribble a basketball) may not be directly transferable to another sport (such as soccer), but what athletes are able to transfer from one sport to another is what they know about how to learn a new sport. Everything about getting one's head into the game is transferable, as are training habits, on-field attitudes, and a generally competitive outlook on the whole procedure. 142

If you think about the FYC requirement in terms of the above sports metaphor, then each discreet writing assignment does not transfer to other courses (just as dribbling a basketball down the court will not help us learn how to dribble a soccer ball downfield). You may write a personal narrative in a FYC course, but you will probably never write another one in any other course. Because of this reality, you might be tempted to think that the FYC requirement is, a waste of time. However, if you think about the course as a whole or the totality of our FYC writing experiences, you can begin to see how FYC is designed to help writers develop critical tools that they can apply to any writing situation (just like learning one sport can help us understand how to learn other sports).

LEARNING HOW TO LEARN TO WRITE: THE PURPOSE AND GOALS OF FYC

As I began to write reports of a more technical nature, I realized the skills I acquired in my 101 and 102 classes could only serve to my advantage in areas of research, organization, and even citations.

—Godwin Erekaife

Godwin's perspective changed from 101 and 102 as a waste of time to an experience that gave him an advantage because he developed a meta-awareness of writing. This awareness could not have occurred if his FYC course did not have well articulated goals that were applicable to wider writing situations, that is, applicable to writing assignments or projects outside of FYC. At West Virginia University, all FYC share common goals. These goals come from the *Council of Writing Program Administrator's, Outcomes Statement for First Year Composition* (hereafter the "Outcomes Statement")–a document that paints writing in a broad context. The authors of the "Outcomes Statement" wanted to identify the "knowledge and common skills" that characterized FYC (1). In addition, the authors wanted the statement to emphasize that FYC was a jumping off point for college writing, and that "learning to write is a lifelong process" (1). Many FYC programs at colleges and universities across the country share these same goals. According to the "Outcomes Statement" by the end of FYC, writers should have an awareness of

- Rhetorical Knowledge
- Critical Thinking, Reading, and Writing
- Process
- Conventions
- Composing in Electronic Environments

Each assignment—be it a rhetorical analysis, an argumentative research paper, an interview essay, a personal narrative, etc—is designed to get at the above goals. Below, I include a fairly standard assignment that I've used in my English 101 class. We can use it to turn a critical eye toward the course and examine how such an assignment touches on the WPA goals.

Essay I: Analyzing Arguments

Overview of Essay

We have read and analyzed essays pertaining to the university community (e.g. articles about the value of a university education, students as consumers, and the effects of binge drinking). We have examined these written texts in terms of their purposes, their audiences, their persuasive strategies, and their effectiveness. Your task for this first major essay is to find an article that addresses the issue you have chosen to focus on this semester, and analyze the strategies the author uses in order to argue/persuade and appeal to her/his audience. You will also need to speak to the effectiveness of the article: In your opinion do you think the article is a successful piece of persuasion? You will need to guide your readers (your peers and your professor) through your analysis so that they too recognize the persuasive strategies the writer has used.

- As you brainstorm for this essay, look back at your notes. Recall the key questions from pp. 42–3 of *Everything's an Argument* like, Who is the audience for this argument? How does the audience connect with its audience? What shape does the argument take? How are the arguments presented or arranged? What media does the argument use? Take a look at the full list of questions, and answer as many as you can. I'm not expecting that your paper address all of them, but use questions that are generative—that is, the questions that inspire fruitful, interesting, and complex responses.
- Think about the conversations that we've had in class. We've identified arguments of the heart, arguments based on character, on value, and on logic. Where do you see these arguments in the text you've chosen? Consider how they work in the text to inform, to move the audience to action, to think differently, to consider other perspectives, etc.
- Remember, you are also creating an argument to persuade your reader to accept your point of view. Pay attention to your own persuasive strategies.

Assessment Criteria

I will be assessing your papers based on the following:

- How well you provide context for your readers (peers and professors). We will not have read the article you are analyzing, so you will need to provide a vivid and descriptive summary.
- How clearly and effectively you make your argument. Remember, you too are creating an argument to persuade your reader to accept your point of view. Pay attention to your own rhetorical choices.

- How thoughtfully you have analyzed the choices and strategies the author uses to argue/persuade her or his audience.
- How thoroughly you have provided your readers with relevant and specific examples/details.
- How cohesively and coherently your essay flows. Is it choppy or repetitive?
- How free your paper is of grammatical/punctuation/spelling errors.

Requirements and Due Dates

- Your paper should be between 5 and 6 pages (double-spaced and typed, 12 pt. font)
- You will need to include a works cited page using MLA format
- See syllabus for rough and final draft due dates

My "Analyzing Arguments Assignment" makes both explicit and implicit nods to the "Outcomes Statement." For example, the assignment asks writers to exercise their *rhetorical knowledge*. According to the "Outcomes Statement," rhetorical knowledge consists of an awareness of purpose, audience, rhetorical situation (a concept that refers to: the speaker/writer, audience, the necessity to speak/write, the occasion for speaking/writing, what has already been said on the subject, and the general context for speaking/writing), and an understanding of genre conventions (what kind of text—written, verbal, visual—is appropriate for a given rhetorical situation).

The underlined portion in the first paragraph identifies the purpose of the assignment and asks that writers be mindful of their own audiences (professor and peers) as they compose their essays:

> Your task for this first major essay is to find an article that addresses the issue you have chosen to focus on this semester, and **analyze the strategies the author uses in order to argue/persuade and appeal to her/his audience**. You will also need to speak to the effectiveness of the article: **In your opinion, do you think the article is a successful piece of persuasion?** You will need to guide your readers (your peers and your professor) through your analysis so that they too recognize the persuasive strategies the writer has used.

The assignment also asks writers to pay attention to an author's rhetorical situation: who he/she is writing to, the degree to which he/she is attentive to audience needs and concerns, what compelled him/her to write, why is there a need to write, and what has already been written on the subject.

Critical Thinking, Reading, and Writing is the degree to which we understand and use writing and reading as modes for thinking through ideas, for learning, for synthesizing material, and for conveying information. When writers respond to the prompt, they also exercise their *critical thinking, reading, and writing* skills. I ask my students to examine their chosen text and ask probing questions of them. I try prompting them to engage their critical thinking skills at several points:

> Think about the conversations that we've had in class. We've identified arguments of the heart, arguments based on character, on value, and on logic. Where do you see these arguments in the text you've chosen? Consider how they work in the text to inform, to move the audience to action, to think differently, to consider other perspectives, etc.

The above are examples of heuristics: questions posed to help writers think more deeply about the articles they are analyzing.

There are other goals that are more implicit in the assignment. For instance, I require at least two complete drafts of an essay (rough and final). The drafts are one way that I build writing as a *Process* into each assignment. The "Outcomes Statement" emphasizes that writing is recursive, that good writing requires multiple drafts, that we benefit from feedback, and that it is also useful to give feedback to others. I want my students to get feedback from each other and also other people such as the WVU Writing Center peer tutors, so that when they do hand in their final drafts, their papers represent their best effort. In the assignment, I also ask that writers follow a particular format (MLA) and that the paper be "error free," a nod to *Knowledge of Conventions.* The only goal that isn't immediately apparent is *Technology,* unless we can count that the paper be double-spaced and typed (12 pt font). While *Technology* isn't obvious in the assignment, in my classes we make ample use of message boards, email, and Google Docs as we compose. For example, students share and respond to drafts using

Microsoft Word's Track Changes feature, Blackboard and/or Google Docs.

Even though I've identified the goals for FYC and discussed those goals in relation to an assignment, it might not yet be clear how I can claim that the course teaches us how to learn to write. To further illustrate my point, it might be useful to return to Godwin and his experience. Above, he states that FYC *served to his advantage* later in his academic career. He went on to tell me that in a senior-level, chemical engineering courses, he and his classmates "were required to design an ethanol plant and write up a description of [their] model" (Erekiafe). When it came time to write up their plans and their research, they had to take into account their audience and the audience needs, concerns, and expectations. Godwin identified the professor as the primary audience because the prof was evaluating the collaborative project, but there was a secondary audience as well: chemical engineers. Because Godwin was writing a formal plan, his assignment had to conform to conventions specific to the chemical engineering profession. Godwin was also composing his ethanol plant plan with others. They composed their pieces separately but then had to find ways to bring their individual sections together. According to Godwin, this portion of the project required "drafting and redrafting on multiple occasions."

LEARNING HOW TO LEARN TO WRITE: OUTSIDE OF FYC

Because of his experience with assignments like the one I shared earlier, Godwin (and his co-authors) had the tools to identify how to write his ethanol plant plan. He understood the things he needed to pay attention to—purpose, audience, and process—in order to successfully write his plan. But Godwin's experience is not unique.

> In my Psychology 202 Research Methods class, our last major assignment for the semester was a research proposal. We were asked to pick a topic of interest, develop a research question, and create a hypothetical experience . . . Developing a research question and the experiment required a lot of critical thinking. We had to do research on a broad topic . . . and then think of an original experiment based on the research. This meant we had to have an understanding of the way a successful experiment was done and be creative enough to do something no one else had thought of.
>
> —Amanda King

Amanda, a Psychology major slated to graduate in May 2011, talks about an assignment that all Psych majors eventually complete. In her Psych 202 class, she had to identify an appropriate research question, seek out relevant research material, describe a feasible mock experiment, and present her information in a way that was appropriate in her discipline. She asserts that she employed her critical thinking skills—skills that are very discipline-specific. She was practicing discipline-specific problem solving. According to John Bean, a professor of English, Writing Program Administrator at Seattle University, and author of a resource book on the importance of writing across the disciplines, critical-thinking is "discipline-specific since each discipline poses its own kinds of problems and conducts inquiries, uses data, and makes arguments in its own characteristic fashion" (3). However, he goes on to say that critical thinking is "also generic across disciplines" (4) because all critical thinking involves identifying or exploring a problem, challenge, or question and formulating a response. That response might come in the form of concrete answers or even new questions that need to be asked.

Amanda obtained early experiences in critical thinking when she took FYC and composed essays like the "Argument Analysis." FYC at WVU also includes a persuasive research paper, an essay that required her to identify a research question on a topic of her choosing and to convince her audience to accept her answer/response to that question. Assignments like these are early training, designed to teach writers critical thinking, reading, and writing skills: an understanding of genre conventions and research skills.

LEARNING HOW TO LEARN TO WRITE:
THE WORLD OF WORK

When I first began my job, I had a hard time adapting the way I wrote to the tone of the business. I was used to writing 20 page papers for school.

—Lauren O'Connor

I make a claim very early in this essay that FYC's efficacy extends into the world of work. However, as Lauren O'Connor points out above, school writing is very different from workplace writing. After Lauren graduated from WVU in May 2008, she took a position as a Global Marketing Communications Manager for Hewlett-Packard (HP). Lauren's job required that she write all the time: emails to her co-workers, memos regarding deliverables, press-releases, and corporate announcements for new product launches. She didn't immediately know how to compose these documents, so she had to learn the way the HP community spoke and wrote. She "researched and read hundreds of marketing materials, white papers [reports that offer solutions to business problems], and web pages," before she could begin drafting any of these documents (O'Connor).

She also didn't have anyone guiding her as she was learning the discourse of HP. At the university, you are fortunate to have instructors, peers, and writing center tutors to coach you on how to compose FYC essays and discipline-specific texts. Lauren was on her own. However, because she had been in the habit of writing at the university, had so much experience learning how to write in school, and because of the coaches who modeled good writing for her, she knew what she needed to do when she got to HP—get her hands on as many texts as she could in order to learn the various genres—white papers, memos, web pages, press releases—that she would eventually have a hand in authoring.

Lauren also found that she never authored anything alone (aside from emails or memos). She collaborated on a team where each member would draft sections or portions of a text, circulate drafts among the other team members, comment on drafts, re-draft, and re-circulate. Depending on the size or impact of the project, the process could take weeks (O'Connor). While you might not yet enjoy or fully appreciate the writing process (brainstorming, drafting, receiving feedback, and re-drafting) in your FYC class, Lauren shows you that process extends beyond your college years.

CONCLUSION

So far, I have spent a lot of time talking about how FYC goals have wide applicability and how they are designed to get you to think about writing in a broader sense—what writing looks like across varying contexts. I have not, however, discussed, to any large extent, the impact of technology on writing in college or in the world of work. Perhaps that's because technology is so embedded in composing, it seems invisible. Few writers draft using anything but Microsoft Word anymore.

Writers also make a habit of emailing drafts to one another. I use the comment feature in Microsoft Word in order to give my student's feedback and I encourage them to do the same when they give feedback to each other. Writers in FYC also don't just draft traditional essays anymore—even though all of the examples that I include are more traditional. Your FYC courses might require that you compose blogs, audio essays, or digital stories in lieu of the more traditional texts. I believe the initial goals that I discuss still apply to these texts, but it will be interesting to see how they influence how you learn how to write.

Given what you have learned thus far from Lauren, Amanda, and Godwin—that you will indeed write beyond your FYC courses, that writing becomes increasingly specialized (within our majors and within our workplaces)—you should see how the fundamentals of FYC apply to most writing situations. The more you write and the more aware you are of how, why, when, and where you use writing, the better you will be at writing. It pays to be a good writer. The National Commission on Writing for America's Families, Schools, and Colleges (NCWAFSC) calls writing a "threshold skill [. . .] a ticket to professional opportunity" (qtd in National Writing Project Staff: Web). Their studies show that students who write well are more likely to be hired. This makes sense when you consider that employers get to know an applicant first through her employment documents (i.e. resumes and cover letters), in essence, the writing. By the time you put together resumes and cover letters, you will have consciously employed the multiple goals first established in FYC and then reaffirmed in other coursework. Again according to the NCWAFSC, "Writing is [. . .] a 'marker' of high-skill, high-wage, professional work" (qtd in National Writing Project Staff: Web).

When you are a new first-year student, a senior poised for the job market, or are in the world of work, writing will always be important. First year composition isn't just the beginning of a new writing awareness; *it's a write of passage.*

DISCUSSION

1. What kind of writing do you do on a day to day basis? Take a few minutes to jot down your list. Record everything you wrote today from morning until night (e.g., to do list, email, text message, Facebook status update, journal, etc.). How does

your purpose and audience inform how you compose each of these texts?

2. How do your school writing assignments compare to Godwin's Ethanol Plant Plan, Amanda's Research Proposal, or the assignment sheet (Analyzing Arguments)?

3. Can you think of any additional goals that your writing assignments touch on? What would you add to the WPA goals?

4. What kind of writing do you think you'll do in your future profession (e.g. business proposals, emails to colleagues, interoffice memos, patient plans of care, etc.)?

WORKS CITED

Bean, John C. *Engaging Ideas: The Professor's Guide to Integrating Writing, Critical Thinking, and Active Learning in the Classroom.* San Francisco: Josey Bass, 1996. Print.

Bergman, Linda S., and Janet Zepernick. "Disciplinarity and Transfer: Students' Perceptions of Learning to Write." *WPA: Writing Program Administration.* 31.1–2 (2007): 124–51. Print.

Council of Writing Program Administrators. "WPA Outcomes Statement for First-Year Composition." Council of Writing Program Administrators. Web 1 April 2010.

Erekaife, Godwin. Email Interview. 11 August 2009.

King, Amanda. Email Interview. 11 August 2009.

National Writing Project Staff. "Writing as a Ticket to Work . . . Or a Ticket Out." *National Writing Project.* Web. 10 September 2009.

O'Connor, Lauren. Email Interview. 11 August 2009.

Wardle, Elizabeth. "Understanding Transfer from FYC: Preliminary Results of a Longitudinal Study." *WPA: Writing Program Administration.* 31.1–2 (2007): 65–85. Print.

Critical Thinking in College Writing: From the Personal to the Academic

Gita DasBender

There is something about the term "critical thinking" that makes you draw a blank every time you think about what it means.* It seems so fuzzy and abstract that you end up feeling uncomfortable, as though the term is thrust upon you, demanding an intellectual effort that you may not yet have. But you know it requires you to enter a realm of smart, complex ideas that others have written about and that you have to navigate, understand, and interact with just as intelligently. It's a lot to ask for. It makes you feel like a stranger in a strange land.

As a writing teacher I am accustomed to reading and responding to difficult texts. In fact, I like grappling with texts that have interesting ideas no matter how complicated they are because I understand their value. I have learned through my years of education that what ultimately engages me, keeps me enthralled, is not just grammatically pristine, fluent writing, but writing that forces me to think beyond the page. It is writing where the writer has challenged herself and then offered up that challenge to the reader, like a baton in a relay race. The idea is to run with the baton.

You will often come across critical thinking and analysis as require-ments for assignments in writing and upper-level courses in a variety of disciplines. Instructors have varying explanations of what they actual-ly require of you, but, in general, they expect you to respond thought-fully to texts you have read. The first thing you should remember is not to be afraid of critical thinking. It does *not* mean that you have to criticize the text, disagree with its premise, or attack the writer simply because you feel you must. Criticism is the process of responding to and evaluating ideas, argument, and style so that readers understand how and why you value these items.

Critical thinking is also a process that is fundamental to all disci-plines. While in this essay I refer mainly to critical thinking in com-position, the general principles behind critical thinking are strikingly similar in other fields and disciplines. In history, for instance, it could mean examining and analyzing primary sources in order to under-stand the context in which they were written. In the hard sciences, it usually involves careful reasoning, making judgments and decisions, and problem solving. While critical thinking may be subject-specif-ic, that is to say, it can vary in method and technique depending on the discipline, most of its general principles such as rational thinking, making independent evaluations and judgments, and a healthy skepti-cism of what is being read, are common to all disciplines. No matter the area of study, the application of critical thinking skills leads to clear and flexible thinking and a better understanding of the subject at hand.

To be a critical thinker you not only have to have an informed opinion about the text but also a thoughtful response to it. There is no doubt that critical thinking is serious thinking, so here are some steps you can take to become a serious thinker and writer.

Attentive Reading: A Foundation for Critical Thinking

A critical thinker is always a good reader because to engage critically with a text you have to read attentively and with an open mind, ab-sorbing new ideas and forming your own as you go along. Let us imag-ine you are reading an essay by Annie Dillard, a famous essayist, called "Living like Weasels." Students are drawn to it because the idea of the essay appeals to something personally fundamental to all of us: how to live our lives. It is also a provocative essay that pulls the reader into the argument and forces a reaction, a good criterion for critical thinking.

So let's say that in reading the essay you encounter a quote that gives you pause. In describing her encounter with a weasel in Hollins Pond, Dillard says, "I would like to learn, or remember, how to live . . . I don't think I can learn from a wild animal how to live in particular . . . but I might learn something of mindlessness, something of the purity of living in the physical senses and the dignity of living without bias or motive" (220). You may not be familiar with language like this. It seems complicated, and you have to stop ever so often (perhaps after every phrase) to see if you understood what Dillard means. You may ask yourself these questions:

- What does "mindlessness" mean in this context?
- How can one "learn something of mindlessness?"
- What does Dillard mean by "purity of living in the physical senses?"
- How can one live "without bias or motive?"

These questions show that you are an attentive reader. Instead of simply glossing over this important passage, you have actually stopped to think about what the writer means and what she expects you to get from it. Here is how I read the quote and try to answer the questions above: Dillard proposes a simple and uncomplicated way of life as she looks to the animal world for inspiration. It is ironic that she admires the quality of "mindlessness" since it is our consciousness, our very capacity to think and reason, which makes us human, which makes us beings of a higher order. Yet, Dillard seems to imply that we need to live instinctually, to be guided by our senses rather than our intellect. Such a "thoughtless" approach to daily living, according to Dillard, would mean that our actions would not be tainted by our biases or motives, our prejudices. We would go back to a primal way of living, like the weasel she observes. It may take you some time to arrive at this understanding on your own, but it is important to stop, reflect, and ask questions of the text whenever you feel stumped by it. Often such questions will be helpful during class discussions and peer review sessions.

LISTING IMPORTANT IDEAS

When reading any essay, keep track of all the important points the writer makes by jotting down a list of ideas or quotations in a notebook. This list not only allows you to remember ideas that are central to the writer's argument, ideas that struck you in some way or the other, but it also you helps you to get a good sense of the whole reading assignment point by point. In reading Annie Dillard's essay, we come across several points that contribute toward her proposal for better living and that help us get a better understanding of her main argument. Here is a list of some of her ideas that struck me as important:

1. "The weasel lives in necessity and we live in choice, hating necessity and dying at the last ignobly in its talons" (220).
2. "And I suspect that for me the way is like the weasel's: open to time and death painlessly, noticing everything, remembering nothing, choosing the given with a fierce and pointed will" (221).
3. "We can live any way we want. People take vows of poverty, chastity, and obedience—even of silence—by choice. The thing is to stalk your calling in a certain skilled and supple way, to locate the most tender and live spot and plug into that pulse" (221).
4. "A weasel doesn't 'attack' anything; a weasel lives as he's meant to, yielding at every moment to the perfect freedom of single necessity" (221).
5. "I think it would be well, and proper, and obedient, and pure, to grasp your one necessity and not let it go, to dangle from it limp wherever it takes you" (221).

These quotations give you a cumulative sense of what Dillard is trying to get at in her essay, that is, they lay out the elements with which she builds her argument. She first explains how the weasel lives, what she learns from observing the weasel, and then prescribes a lifestyle she admires—the central concern of her essay.

Noticing Key Terms and Summarizing Important Quotes

Within the list of quotations above are key terms and phrases that are critical to your understanding of the ideal life as Dillard describes it. For instance, "mindlessness," "instinct," "perfect freedom of a single necessity," "stalk your calling," "choice," and "fierce and pointed will" are weighty terms and phrases, heavy with meaning, that you need to spend time understanding. You also need to understand the relationship between them and the quotations in which they appear. This is how you might work on each quotation to get a sense of its meaning and then come up with a statement that takes the key terms into account and expresses a general understanding of the text:

> **Quote 1**: Animals (like the weasel) live in "necessity," which means that their only goal in life is to survive. They don't think about how they should live or what choices they should make like humans do. According to Dillard, we like to have options and resist the idea of "necessity." We fight death—an inevitable force that we have no control over—and yet ultimately surrender to it as it is the necessary end of our lives.
>
> **Quote 2**: Dillard thinks the weasel's way of life is the best way to live. It implies a pure and simple approach to life where we do not worry about the passage of time or the approach of death. Like the weasel, we should live life in the moment, intensely experiencing everything but not dwelling on the past. We should accept our condition, what we are "given," with a "fierce and pointed will." Perhaps this means that we should pursue our one goal, our one passion in life, with the same single-minded determination and tenacity that we see in the weasel.
>
> **Quote 3**: As humans, we can choose any lifestyle we want. The trick, however, is to go after our one goal, one passion like a stalker would after a prey.
>
> **Quote 4**: While we may think that the weasel (or any animal) chooses to attack other animals, it is really only surrendering to the one thing it knows: its need to live. Dillard tells us there is "the perfect freedom" in this desire to survive because to

her, the lack of options (the animal has no other option than to fight to survive) is the most liberating of all.

Quote 5: Dillard urges us to latch on to our deepest passion in life (the "one necessity") with the tenacity of a weasel and not let go. Perhaps she's telling us how important it is to have an unwavering focus or goal in life.

WRITING A PERSONAL RESPONSE: LOOKING INWARD

Dillard's ideas will have certainly provoked a response in your mind, so if you have some clear thoughts about how you feel about the essay this is the time to write them down. As you look at the quotes you have selected and your explanation of their meaning, begin to create your personal response to the essay. You may begin by using some of these strategies:

1. Tell a story. Has Dillard's essay reminded you of an experience you have had? Write a story in which you illustrate a point that Dillard makes or hint at an idea that is connected to her essay.
2. Focus on an idea from Dillard's essay that is personally important to you. Write down your thoughts about this idea in a first person narrative and explain your perspective on the issue.
3. If you are uncomfortable writing a personal narrative or using "I" (you should not be), reflect on some of her ideas that seem important and meaningful in general. Why were you struck by these ideas?
4. Write a short letter to Dillard in which you speak to her about the essay. You may compliment her on some of her ideas by explaining why you like them, ask her a question related to her essay and explain why that question came to you, and genuinely start up a conversation with her.

This stage in critical thinking is important for establishing your relationship with a text. What do I mean by this "relationship," you may ask? Simply put, it has to do with how you feel about the text. Are you amazed by how true the ideas seem to be, how wise Dillard sounds? Or are you annoyed by Dillard's let-me-tell-you-how-to-live approach and disturbed by the impractical ideas she so easily prescribes? Do you find Dillard's voice and style thrilling and engaging or merely confusing? No matter which of the personal response options you select, your initial reaction to the text will help shape your views about it.

MAKING AN ACADEMIC CONNECTION: LOOKING OUTWARD

First year writing courses are designed to teach a range of writing—from the personal to the academic—so that you can learn to express advanced ideas, arguments, concepts, or theories in any discipline. While the example I have been discussing pertains mainly to college writing, the method of analysis and approach to critical thinking I have demonstrated here will serve you well in a variety of disciplines. Since critical thinking and analysis are key elements of the reading and writing you will do in college, it is important to understand how they form a part of academic writing. No matter how intimidating the term "academic writing" may seem (it is, after all, associated with advanced writing and becoming an expert in a field of study), embrace it not as a temporary college requirement but as a habit of mind.

To some, academic writing often implies *impersonal* writing, writing that is detached, distant, and lacking in personal meaning or relevance. However, this is often not true of the academic writing you will do in a composition class. Here your presence as a writer—your thoughts, experiences, ideas, and therefore who you are—is of much significance to the writing you produce. In fact, it would not be far-fetched to say that in a writing class academic writing often begins with personal writing. Let me explain. If critical thinking begins with a personal view of the text, academic writing helps you broaden that view by going beyond the personal to a more universal point of view. In other words, academic writing often has its roots in one's private opinion or perspective about another writer's ideas but ultimately goes beyond this opinion to the expression of larger, more abstract ideas. Your personal vision—your core beliefs and general approach to life—will help you arrive at these "larger ideas" or universal propositions that any reader can understand and be enlightened by, if not agree with. In short, academic writing is largely about taking a critical, ana-lytical stance toward a subject in order to arrive at some compelling conclusions.

Let us now think about how you might apply your critical think-ing skills to move from a personal reaction to a more formal academic response to Annie Dillard's essay. The second stage of critical thinking involves textual analysis and requires you to do the following:

- Summarize the writer's ideas the best you can in a brief paragraph. This provides the basis for extended analysis since it contains the central ideas of the piece, the building blocks, so to speak.

- Evaluate the most important ideas of the essay by considering their merits or flaws, their worthiness or lack of worthiness. Do not merely agree or disagree with the ideas but explore and explain why you believe they are socially, politically, philosophically, or historically important and relevant, or why you need to question, challenge, or reject them.

- Identify gaps or discrepancies in the writer's argument. Does she contradict herself? If so, explain how this contradiction forces you to think more deeply about her ideas. Or if you are confused, explain what is confusing and why.

- Examine the strategies the writer uses to express her ideas. Look particularly at her style, voice, use of figurative language, and the way she structures her essay and organizes her ideas. Do these strategies strengthen or weaken her argument? How?

- Include a second text—an essay, a poem, lyrics of a song— whose ideas enhance your reading and analysis of the primary text. This text may help provide evidence by supporting a point you're making, and further your argument.

- Extend the writer's ideas, develop your own perspective, and propose new ways of thinking about the subject at hand.

CRAFTING THE ESSAY

Once you have taken notes and developed a thorough understanding of the text, you are on your way to writing a good essay. If you were asked to write an exploratory essay, a personal response to Dillard's essay would probably suffice. However, an academic writing assignment requires you to be more critical. As counter-intuitive as it may sound, beginning your essay with a personal anecdote often helps to establish your relationship to the text and draw the reader into your writing. It also helps to ease you into the more complex task of textual analysis. Once you begin to analyze Dillard's ideas, go back to the list of important ideas and quotations you created as you read the essay. After a brief summary, engage with the quotations that are most important, that get to the heart of Dillard's ideas, and explore their meaning. Textual engagement, a seemingly slippery concept, simply means that you respond directly to some of Dillard's ideas, examine the value of Dillard's assertions, and explain why they are worthwhile or why they should be rejected. This should help you to transition into analysis and evaluation. Also, this part of your essay will most clearly reflect your critical thinking abilities as you are expected not only to represent Dillard's ideas but also to weigh their significance. Your observations about the various points she makes, analysis of conflicting viewpoints or contradictions, and your understanding of her general thesis should now be synthesized into a rich new idea about how we should live our lives. Conclude by explaining this fresh point of view in clear, compelling language and by rearticulating your main argument.

MODELING GOOD WRITING

When I teach a writing class, I often show students samples of really good writing that I've collected over the years. I do this for two reasons: first, to show students how another freshman writer understood and responded to an assignment that they are currently working on; and second, to encourage them to succeed as well. I explain that although they may be intimidated by strong, sophisticated writing and feel pressured to perform similarly, it is always helpful to see what it takes to get an A. It also helps to follow a writer's imagination, to learn how the mind works when confronted with a task involving critical thinking. The following sample is a response to the Annie Dillard essay. Figure 1 includes the entire student essay and my comments are inserted into the text to guide your reading.

Though this student has not included a personal narrative in his essay, his own world-vievvw is clear throughout. His personal point of view, while not expressed in first person statements, is evident from the very beginning. So we could say that a personal response to the text need not always be expressed in experiential or narrative form but may be present as reflection, as it is here. The point is that the writer has traveled through the rough terrain of critical thinking by starting out with his own ruminations on the subject, then by critically analyzing and responding to Dillard's text, and finally by developing a strong

Building our Lives: The Blueprint Lies Within

We all may ask ourselves many questions, some serious, some less important, in our lifetime. But at some point along the way, we all will take a step back and look at the way we are living our lives, and wonder if we are living them correctly. Unfortunately, there is no solid blueprint for the way to live our lives. Each person is different, feeling different emotions and reacting to different stimuli than the person next to them. Many people search for the true answer on how to live our lives, as if there are secret instructions out there waiting to be found. But the truth is we as a species are given a gift not many other creatures can claim to have: the ability to choose to live as we want, not as we were necessarily designed to. Even so, people look outside of themselves for the answers on how to live, which begs me to ask the question: what is wrong with just living as we are now, built from scratch through our choices and memories?

> **Comment:** Even as the writer starts with a general introduction, he makes a claim here that is related to Dillard's essay.

Annie Dillard's essay entitled "Living Like Weasels" is an exploration into the way human beings might live, clearly stating that "We could live any way we want" (Dillard 211). Dillard's encounter with an ordinary weasel helped her receive insight into the difference between the way human beings live their lives and the way wild animals go about theirs. As a nature writer, Dillard shows us that we can learn a lot about the true way to live by observing nature's other creations. While we think and debate and calculate each and every move, these creatures just simply act. The thing that keeps human beings from living the purest life possible, like an animal such as the weasel, is the same thing that separates us from all wild animals: our minds. Human beings are creatures of caution, creatures of undeniable fear, never fully living our lives because we are too caught up with avoiding risks. A weasel, on the

> **Comment:** The student asks what seems like a rhetorical question but it is one he will answer in the rest of his essay. It is also a question that forces the reader to think about a key term from the text—"choices."

> **Comment:** Student summarizes Dillard's essay by explaining the ideas of the essay in fresh words.

other hand, is a creature of action and instinct, a creature which lives its life the way it was created to, not questioning his motives, simply striking when the time to strike is right. As Dillard states, "the weasel lives in necessity and we live in choice, hating necessity and dying at the last ignobly in its talons" (Dillard 210).

It is important to note and appreciate the uniqueness of the ideas Dillard presents in this essay because in some ways they are very true. For instance, it is true that humans live lives of caution, with a certain fear that has been built up continually through the years. We are forced to agree with Dillard's idea that we as humans "might learn something of mindlessness, something of the purity of living in the physical senses and the dignity of living without bias or motive" (Dillard 210). To live freely we need to live our lives with less hesitation, instead of intentionally choosing to not live to the fullest in fear of the consequences of our actions. However, Dillard suggests that we should forsake our ability of thought and choice all together. The human mind is the tool that has allowed a creature with no natural weapons to become the unquestioned dominant species on this plant planet, and though it curbs the spontaneity of our lives, it is not something to be simply thrown away for a chance to live completely "free of bias or motive" (Dillard 210). We are a moral, conscious species, complete with emotions and a firm conscience, and it is the power of our minds that allows us to exist as we do now: with the ability to both think and feel at the same time. It grants us the ability to choose and have choice, to be guided not only by feelings and emotions but also by morals and an understanding of consequence. As such, a human being with the ability to live like a weasel has given up the very thing that makes him human.

Comment: Up until this point the student has introduced Dillard's essay and summarized some of its ideas. In the section that follows, he continues to think critically about Dillard's ideas and argument.

Comment: This is a strong statement that captures the student's appreciation of Dillard's suggestion to live freely but also the ability to recognize why most people cannot live this way. This is a good example of critical thinking.

Comment: Again, the student acknowledges the importance of conscious thought.

Comment: While the student does not include a personal experience in the essay, this section gives us a sense of his personal view of life. Also note how he introduces the term "morals" here to point out the significance of the consequences of our actions. The point is that not only do we need to act but we also need to be aware of the result of our actions.

Comment: Student rejects Dillard's ideas but only after explaining why it is important to reject them.

Here, the first true flaw of Dillard's essay comes to light. While it is possible to understand and even respect Dillard's observations, it should be noted that without thought and choice she would have never been able to construct these notions in the first place. Dillard protests, "I tell you I've been in that weasel's brain for sixty seconds, and he was in mine" (Dillard 210). One cannot cast oneself into the mind of another creature without the intricacy of human thought, and one would not be able to choose to live as said creature does without the power of human choice. In essence, Dillard would not have had the ability to judge the life of another creature if she were to live like a weasel. Weasels do not make judgments; they simply act and react on the basis of instinct. The "mindlessness" that Dillard speaks of would prevent her from having the option to choose her own reactions. Whereas the conscious- thinking Dillard has the ability to see this creature and take the time to stop and examine its life, the "mindless" Dillard would only have the limited options to attack or run away. This is the major fault in the logic of Dillard's essay, as it would be impossible for her to choose to examine and compare the lives of humans and weasels without the capacity for choice.

> Comment: Student dismantles Dillard's entire premise by telling us how the very act of writing the essay negates her argument. He has not only interpreted the essay but figured out how its premise is logically flawed.

Dillard also examines a weasel's short memory in a positive light and seems to believe that a happier life could be achieved if only we were simple-minded enough to live our lives with absolutely no regret. She claims, "I suspect that for me the way is like the weasel's: open to time and death painlessly, noticing everything, remembering nothing, choosing the given with a fierce and pointed will" (Dillard 210). In theory, this does sound like a positive value. To be able to live freely without a hint of remembrance as to the results of our choices would be an

> Comment: Once again the student demonstrates why the logic of Dillard's argument falls short when applied to her own writing.

interesting life, one may even say a care-free life. But at the same time, would we not be denying our responsibility as humans to learn from the mistakes of the past as to not replicate them in the future? Human beings' ability to remember is almost as important as our ability to choose, because remembering things from the past is the only way we can truly learn from them. History is taught throughout our educational system for a very good reason: so that the generations of the future do not make the mistakes of the past. A human being who chooses to live like a weasel gives up something that once made him very human: the ability to learn from his mistakes to further better himself.

> **Comment:** This question represents excellent critical thinking. The student acknowledges that theoretically "remembering nothing' may have some merits but then ponders on the larger socio-political problem it presents.

Ultimately, without the ability to choose or recall the past, mankind would be able to more readily take risks without regard for consequences. Dillard views the weasel's reaction to necessity as an unwavering willingness to take such carefree risks and chances. She states that "it would be well, and proper, and obedient, and pure, to grasp your one necessity and not let it go, to dangle from it limp wherever it takes you" (Dillard 211). Would it then be productive for us to make a wrong choice and be forced to live in it forever, when we as a people have the power to change, to remedy wrongs we've made in our lives? What Dillard appears to be recommending is that humans not take many risks, but who is to say that the ability to avoid or escape risks is necessarily a flaw with mankind?

> **Comment:** The student brings two ideas together very smoothly here.

> **Comment:** The writer sums up his argument while once again reminding us of the problem with Dillard's ideas.

If we had been like the weasel, never wanting, never needing, always "choosing the given with a fierce and pointed will" (Dillard 210), our world would be a completely different place. The United States of America might not exist at this very moment if we had just taken what was given to us, and unwaveringly accepted a life as a colony of Great Britain. But as Cole clearly puts it, "A risk that you assume by actually

> **Comment:** This is another thoughtful question that makes the reader think along with the writer.

doing something seems far more risky than a risk you take by not doing something, even though the risk of doing nothing may be greater" (Cole 145). As a unified body of people, we were able to go against that which was expected of us, evaluate the risk in doing so, and move forward with our revolution. The American people used the power of choice, and risk assessment, to make a permanent change in their lives; they used the remembrance of Britain's unjust deeds to fuel their passion for victory. We as a people chose. We remembered. We distinguished between right and wrong. These are things that a weasel can never do, because a weasel does not have a say in its own life, it only has its instincts and nothing more.

> **Comment:** The student makes a historical reference here that serves as strong evidence for his own argument.

Humans are so unique in the fact that they can dictate the course of their own lives, but many people still choose to search around for the true way to live. What they do not realize is that they have to look no further than themselves. Our power, our weapon, is our ability to have thought and choice, to remember, and to make our own decisions based on our concepts of right and wrong, good and bad. These are the only tools we will ever need to construct the perfect life for ourselves from the ground up. And though it may seem like a nice notion to live a life free of regret, it is our responsibility as creatures and the appointed caretakers of this planet to utilize what was given to us and live our lives as we were meant to, not the life of any other wild animal.

> **Comment:** This final paragraph sums up the writer's perspective in a thoughtful and mature way. It moves away from Dillard's argument and establishes the notion of human responsibility, an idea highly worth thinking about.

point of view of his own about our responsibility as human beings. As readers we are engaged by clear, compelling writing and riveted by critical thinking that produces a movement of ideas that give the essay depth and meaning. The challenge Dillard set forth in her essay has been met and the baton passed along to us.

DISCUSSION

1. Write about your experiences with critical thinking assignments. What seemed to be the most difficult? What approaches did you try to overcome the difficulty?
2. Respond to the list of strategies on how to conduct textual analysis. How well do these strategies work for you? Add your own tips to the list.
3. Evaluate the student essay by noting aspects of critical thinking that are evident to you. How would you grade this essay? What other qualities (or problems) do you notice?

WORKS CITED

Dillard, Annie. "Living like Weasels." *One Hundred Great Essays*. Ed. Robert DiYanni. New York: Longman, 2002. 217–221. Print.

Looking for Trouble: Finding Your Way into a Writing Assignment

Catherine Savini

The main character in the movie *Misery* is a writer named Paul Sheldon, who after a serious car accident is "rescued" by his self-proclaimed "number one fan," Annie Wilkes.* Annie holds him captive, withholding pain medications and torturing him mentally and physically while demanding that he write a novel that brings her favorite character, Misery Chastaine, back to life. The movie trailer for *Misery* reads, "Now Paul Sheldon must write as if his life depended on it . . . because it does." This is no one's ideal writing scenario, nor is it a common one, but the direct association of writing and suffering will not seem far-fetched to anyone who writes. Based on a Stephen King novella of the same name, *Misery* suggests that even a prolific writer like King, who has written screenplays, novels, short stories, and essays for the past thirty-five years, finds writing difficult, even painful.

Chances are, if you have ever written a paper, you've experienced the uneasiness caused by the combination of a blank page and a looming deadline. Though it may seem counterintuitive at the outset, one way to diminish the considerable difficulty of getting started on a new assignment is to look for something that troubles you, seek out difficulty, find problems. All academic disciplines seek to impart in their students the ability to identify, mull over, and sometimes solve chal-

---

* This work is licensed under the Creative Commons Attribution-Noncommercial-ShareAlike 3.0 United States License and is subject to the Writing Spaces' Terms of Use. To view a copy of this license, visit http://creativecommons.org/licenses/by-nc-sa/3.0/us/ or send a letter to Creative Commons, 171 Second Street, Suite 300, San Francisco, California, 94105, USA. To view the Writing Spaces' Terms of Use, visit http://writingspaces.org/terms-of-use.

lenging problems. Not surprisingly, the benefits of a willingness and mental acuity to greet complex problems extend well beyond the classroom.

We all deal with problems of varying complexity on a daily basis. If we are successful in dealing with life's challenges, it's likely that we follow a particular process for meeting these challenges, whether we are conscious of it or not. Here is an example of this process:

> **Problem:** My car broke down.
>
> **Questions that emerge from this problem:** Can I fix it myself? If not, where should I take it to get it fixed? Whom can I trust? Could I get a recommendation from someone? In light of the estimate is it worth getting it fixed or should I turn it in to cash for clunkers and buy a new car? How will I get around while my car is in the shop?
>
> **What is at stake?:** If you don't pursue these questions and you take your car to the first dealer you see, you might choose a mechanic who is notorious for overcharging or for sloppy work. Or you might be without wheels for awhile and unable to get to work. Precious time and your hard-earned cash are at stake here. In order to make an informed decision, we must sit with a problem and weigh our options.

Problems are an expected part of life, and our ability to deal with them can help determine our personal and professional success. In fact, recent studies suggest that the ability to wrestle with problems is what makes a successful leader. Successful leaders, according to Roger Martin, Dean of the Rotman School of Management at the University of Toronto, have one thing in common: the power of "integrative thinking." Martin borrows the words of F. Scott Fitzgerald, author of *The Great Gatsby,* to define integrative thinking as "the ability to hold two opposing ideas in mind at the same time and still retain the ability to function." According to Fitzgerald, integrative thinking is a sign of "first-rate intelligence"; according to Martin, who examined 50 successful managers for his book *The Opposable Mind: How Successful Leaders Win Through Integrative Thinking,* it is the sign of a successful leader. Integrative thinkers embrace complexity. They sit with problems eschewing the easy answers. They tap into the tension between two opposing ideas to produce a third idea. And, ultimately, they produce new insights and develop new alternatives. This habit of mind can and should be cultivated (Martin 62).

PROBLEMS AS PROCESS

You can cultivate and take advantage of this mode of thinking any time you have a paper to write. Let us return to the question of how one uses problems to begin a writing assignment. Despite the fact that writing assignments vary from class to class, discipline to discipline, and university to university, looking for trouble can be an effective approach regardless of the assignment. In fact, sometimes writing prompts or essay questions direct you toward trouble. Here is an example of one such prompt:

> Although Hegel differs from Rousseau in his hostility toward the notion of the noble savage and his rejection of origin stories, both Hegel and Rousseau are keen to understand contemporary civilization in light of historical processes. What is it, then, that allows them to come to such different conclusions about the present, with Hegel suggesting that freedom is on the march and Rousseau arguing that freedom is in retreat?[1]

This essay question does the work of problem finding for the students. The instructor highlights the problem in the question by juxtaposing Rousseau's and Hegel's ideas and theoretical approaches. Most of you are probably familiar with the compare and contrast paper; this assignment essentially asks students to compare and contrast Rousseau and Hegel. By identifying a specific problem and posing a question, this instructor helps students avoid a common pitfall of the unsuccessful compare and contrast essay. Unsuccessful compare and contrast essays simply catalogue similarities and differences without developing an argument. While it is possible that your high school teacher did not expect you to develop an argument in a compare and contrast essay, your college professor expects you to do so, whether or not the assignment explicitly says so.

Sometimes it will be your responsibility to locate a problem. Here is an example of an assignment that specifically asks students to find a problem:

> Identify and examine a human rights topic about which you
> would like to know more. You are welcome to consult with
> the instructors and TAs for ideas. You should use Internet,
> library, and other sources to gather information on this topic;
> this is not a full-scale research paper, so you need to find a
> small number of adequately comprehensive sources. Your
> essay should (1) identify the issue; (2) describe its scope and
> frequency in geographic, regime-type, temporal, socio-demo-
> graphic, or other terms, as appropriate; (3) identify the sense
> in which it is a human rights violation (of what article of what
> covenant, or with respect to what norm); (4) tell us what you
> have been able to learn about its causes, and (5) identify po-
> litical, social, cultural, economic or other factors that appear
> to contribute to its increase or decrease. You should critically
> assess biases or shortcomings in the information sources you
> used to research your topic.

While the prompt does not specifically use the term "problem," it is
clear that students are meant to focus on human rights "issues" or
"violations" rather than successes in the area of human rights. In other
words, these students have been sent out to look for trouble related to
human rights. Other writing assignments will not even hint at problems. For example:

> Food plays a significant role in Edith Wharton's *Age of In-
> nocence*. For this paper you should construct a persuasive ar-
> gument in which you consider how the depictions of food
> and the rituals surrounding it reflect and promote the larger
> themes of the novel. Consider the following questions: Who
> is depicted eating and why? What do they eat and how? What
> is Wharton doing with acts of eating in her text? How does
> she use depictions of food to create narrative effects? What are
> these effects? What narrative effects does she use depictions of
> food to create?

While there is no direct or indirect mention of problems in this particular assignment, your process and your product will benefit from a
focus on a specific problem.

  At this point, you may be wondering "What's all this about problems? What about thesis or argument?" Problems motivate good papers, and good problems will lead you to your thesis or argument.

Theses do not fall from the sky. Finding a rich problem can be a big step in the direction of developing a compelling thesis. But when you are left to find and articulate your own problem, how do you go about it?

Looking for Trouble in Four Steps

There are four steps toward finding problems and developing meaningful projects of your own:

1. Noticing;
2. Articulating a problem and its details;
3. Posing fruitful questions;
4. Identifying what is at stake.

Noticing

We all know that it is important to warm up before you exercise. Warming up decreases your chance of sustaining an injury and generally makes working out easier on your body. Noticing is the equivalent of warming up your mind. In your first encounter with a text, begin by noticing different aspects. In other words, look for anything that stands out to you as unique or odd, identify patterns, and consider how a text does or does not meet your expectations. For example,

- Identify a particular word, concept, idea, or image that strikes you as surprising or that is repeated several times;
- Notice something about the title;
- Focus in on something that perplexes you.

Keep in mind that there's no "right" or "wrong" when noticing. As you notice, take notes in the margins of the texts or on a separate sheet of paper. If you are like me, you might be in a hurry, and you might occasionally exercise without warming up. Similarly, you might feel compelled to skip "noticing." Here's a tip to keep in mind: the more complicated or unfamiliar the texts you are working with the more likely you'll want to spend some time noticing. You wouldn't dream of running a marathon without stretching, but you might bang out three miles without ever bending over to touch your toes (though I'm not recommending it!).

Articulating a Problem and its Details

After you've spent some time noticing, review what you've noticed and look specifically for tensions. Here are some approaches to finding problems worth pursuing:

1. Juxtapose texts from the same genre or on the same topic and identify tensions or contradictions in terms of their ideas and/ or definitions of key concepts.
2. Identify conflict between your own experiences and the theories or arguments offered by the text.
3. Identify troubling assumptions that underlie the central arguments/ideas of a text.
4. Note a gap or something relevant the text overlooks.

Posing Fruitful Questions

Problems naturally lead to questions. Once you've identified a problem or two that strikes you as worth considering, make a list of questions each problem raises for you. Good questions will lead you toward developing an argument of your own, but all questions are not good questions. You will need to assess your questions in a variety of contexts to determine whether or not they are worth pursuing.

First, consider your questions in the context of the academic discipline and genre for which you are writing. As a college student you are in the process of gaining access to a variety of new discourse communities. Anne Beaufort provides us with a succinct definition of a discourse community: "a social group that communicates at least in part via written texts and shares common goals, values, and writing standards, a specialized vocabulary and specialized genres" (179). Just as discourse communities have specialized vocabularies and standards, different discourse communities pursue different kinds of questions. Let's take a big problem like global warming and focus on Alaska. An environmental scientist, a pathologist, an economist, and an anthropologist would raise different kinds of questions about the same problem. The environmental scientist would ask questions like: how much has the water risen since we last checked? How have the increasing temperatures and rising water levels affected the vegetation and animal life? A pathologist would take a different approach: what new diseases have emerged in correlation with global warming? Economists would ask how global warming is affecting the economic situation in

Alaska. How has the lumber or the fishing industry been affected by global warming? How has global warming affected tourism? An anthropologist might ask how global warming is affecting the ways of life of certain indigenous groups. Because questions vary significantly from discipline to discipline, or field to field, it is important that you assess your questions according to the discourse community you are writing within.

While you are not typically expected to be an expert in any discipline or a full-fledged member of a discourse community as an undergraduate, your instructor will more than likely expect you to pursue questions that are relevant to his/her discipline whether or not he/she is consciously aware of this. Once you've selected a major, one way to develop a sense of the types of questions posed in your selected discipline is to read articles published in that field. For example, read a few of the articles assigned in class or published in the field and identify the questions these articles raise at the beginning of the texts. Of course, these questions are not always explicitly stated, so identifying an article's motivating questions might take some work. Write the questions out, make a list of defining characteristics, and assess your own questions next to this list. Also, pay attention to the types of questions your teacher poses either in assignments or in class. These are the kinds of questions you should be asking when you write for that course.

In addition to assessing whether or not you are asking the type of questions relevant to the discourse community or discipline you are participating in, it is also essential to consider the feasibility of your questions. Here are some questions you should ask yourself to consider feasibility: Do I have the expertise or experience to pursue this question? Do I need to conduct research to consider this question? Can I explore this question fully within the amount of time or space I am allotted? Often my students come up with *really* interesting questions that are impossible to tackle in a single paper within the confines of a semester.

Finally, know that some questions will lead you down dead ends and others will bear fruit. What makes a question fruitful? A question is fruitful if it leads you to discover new information or a new idea. Fruitful questions tend to begin with "why," "how," or "what" and can't be answered with a quick "yes" or "no." If you have come up with a yes/no question that strikes you as fruitful, try adding a "why" or "how" to it. For example, one might ask: "Are water levels rising in

Alaska?" The answer to this question is a quick yes. But asking how rising water levels are affecting Alaska transforms a dead-end question into a fruitful one.

What Is at Stake?

The next qualification of a fruitful question is that the question must be worth asking. It's likely you've heard a teacher ask "so what?" or "what is at stake?" or even, "why is this important?" It can be difficult to explain what is at stake, especially if your teacher has written the assignment. Not surprisingly, your initial response might be that what is at stake is a decent grade. This is true, but in order to motivate yourself and interest your reader, it is essential to identify why the question you or your teacher has posed is worth pursuing. Composition and rhetoric scholar Joseph Williams articulates this best when he asks: "What will you gain from answering your question or what will be lost if you do not answer your question?"

These steps, unfortunately, don't always lead directly to a worthwhile project; don't be surprised if every problem you isolate and every question you pose doesn't lead you down a well-paved path to a meaningful project and a complex argument. Also, you'll have more success if you're willing to cycle back in the process and refine your project and questions over the course of planning and drafting. Developing meaningful projects is hard work and takes practice. The more you practice, like most things, the more efficient you'll become.

LOOKING FOR TROUBLE: PRACTICE, PRACTICE, PRACTICE

Let's walk through the process using specific texts. A few years ago I was teaching an essay writing course at Columbia University, and I asked my students to read bell hooks's "In our Glory: Photography and Black Life."[2] In this essay, hooks describes the important role played by family photographs displayed on the walls of African American homes. When she was a child and media representation of black Americans was either negative or over-simplified, this semi-public display of personal photos served as a site of protest. In other words, on these walls her race was depicted in rich and complex ways unlike anything in the mainstream media. Here's how I went through the process of noticing, articulating problems, posing and assessing questions, and identifying what is at stake:

Noticing

What struck me the most, and even surprised me, was hooks' idea that what we hang on our walls—even the walls of our homes—could be so meaningful or powerful.

Articulating Problems

This naturally led me to consider what hangs on my walls. At the time, an image I took while on vacation in Nicaragua was hanging on my office wall. Here's the image:

Fig. 1. Nicaraguan woman on a side street in Granada.

Once hooks' ideas entered my office, trouble was not hard to find. I hung this picture on my wall because it appealed to me aesthetically: the vibrant pastel colors, the distinct patterns, the candid look on the woman's face. After reading hooks' essay, this 16" x 20" framed image hanging on my office wall became fraught with tension. I genuinely became troubled by it and worried I that I should take it down. Here are some problems, or germs of problems, that I brainstormed:

1. There is a tension inherent in the juxtaposition of the woman's context with the context of the image: the streets of Granada in the second poorest country in the west contrasts with the image's context, the walls of an Ivy League University in the richest country in the western hemisphere.

2. I do not know this woman, and she does not know me; yet, she hangs on my wall. Somehow the woman represented in this photo has come to represent something about me. When people come into my office and ask about the image, it leads into a discussion of my trip to Nicaragua. People tend to walk away with the impression that I'm somewhat adventurous.

3. hooks and her family represented themselves in images on the walls in their homes and in this way challenged the mainstream media's representation of black Americans. The tourist photos that I hang on the walls of my office (a semi-public space) have the power to influence people's perceptions of Nicaragua, a poor country that has a long history of civil unrest.

Posing Fruitful Questions

Questions I asked that emerged out of the above problems:

1. What is the story of this woman's life?
2. What percentage of Nicaraguan women are in the work force, and what kinds of work do they do?
3. Should I hang this photo on my wall?
4. What are ethical responsibilities of tourists when it comes to displaying and/or sharing pictures of their travels?

The first question regarding the woman's life story is impossible to answer without flying back to Nicaragua, tracking the woman down on the streets of Granada, and hiring a translator to interview her. While I think this has the potential to be interesting, it is not feasible for a one-semester course. If I were to fly back to interview her, my interview would likely be more productive if I had a specific purpose and genre in mind: would I write a piece for a newspaper? Would I write an academic article? Both genre and discipline shape the kinds of questions people ask and their approach to the same questions.

Question two is looking for a statistic; a statistic is a factual answer rather than an idea or an argument. In this case, either the answer is out there to be recovered and reported, or I would have to conduct a study and write a book about women in the Nicaraguan work force. Simply reporting this answer would not lead me to write an interesting paper unless I raised some new questions. If I were to conduct a study, I would probably need some disciplinary expertise in the field of economics. So either the question is a dead end (you uncover the answer and that is it), or it is not feasible (too big of a project requiring a tremendous amount of time and a certain level of expertise).

At this point, I hope you are getting a sense of what kinds of questions might not be appropriate for an undergraduate, academic paper. That is not to say that questions one and two are not worthwhile. It is simply that they do not work in the context of a one-semester course.

Questions three and four, on the other hand, are headed in the right direction. The third question is a yes/no question, which as I've said tends to lead toward a dead end, but I can reframe it as a why question: why should I or shouldn't I hang this photo on my wall? This question has potential for an academic paper provided that I consider the question's ramifications within a larger context that extends beyond my office. In other words, I'll need to explain the impact of the images we choose to hang in semi-public spaces like an office.

The final question emerges from hooks's ideas about the power of images and her claim that, "the field of representation (how we see ourselves, how others see us) is a site of ongoing struggle" (57). This last question is the most promising in the context of the assignment for this class, which is: "Use hooks's essay as a lens to analyze a personal experience and develop an argument of your own."

What Is at Stake Here?

Let's say that I decide to pursue the final question: What are the ethical responsibilities of tourists when it comes to displaying pictures of their travels? What do we gain by answering this question and/or what do we lose by not answering it? By answering this question, we can develop an ethical approach to taking tourist photos and displaying them. Developing an approach and a heightened awareness of how we represent other cultures seems particularly important when the received idea of these places is negative and overly-simplistic. The stereotype is that Nicaragua is a violent and dangerous country, and while there are unsafe pockets, this, of course, is not the whole picture. Additionally, tourism to Nicaragua has the potential to boost the economy; how I represent this country could influence people to either visit or to avoid the country. In fact, two separate friends of mine decided to visit after hearing about my trip. Considering what is at stake not only helps test the question's potential, it also leads in the direction of an argument. If I were to pursue this question with the help of hooks and my own experience, I might end up with an argument that goes something like this:

> Individuals who visit locales that are not your typical tourist destinations should be careful in how they represent these places to others particularly in the form of images. Tourists should seek to present the many dimensions of a place and its culture, in both their photos and their stories, and avoid reinforcing common misperceptions.

A common pitfall when attempting to answer the so-what question is to assume that your contribution has to solve major world problems, but the truth is that most published scholarly articles add a bit of information in a specific corner of knowledge, or they provide us with a new way of seeing or thinking about something.

PROBLEMS AS PRODUCT

So far we've been thinking about problems as central to the process of developing a complex argument. The good news is problems can do double duty for us: articulating complex problems and posing fruitful questions is not only part of the process, but it is also part of the product. That is to say that most nonfiction opens with a problem that leads to a question. Below are a few examples of introductions that present problems, raise fruitful questions, and identify what is at stake. Notice that in some cases, it takes more than one paragraph to accomplish these three steps.

What follows is an excerpt from the dust jacket for Michael Pollan's *The Omnivore's Dilemma*, which was named by *The New York Times* as one of the ten best books in 2006:

> What should we have for dinner? For omnivores like ourselves, this simple question has always posed a dilemma: When you can eat just about anything nature (or the supermarket) has to

offer deciding what you *should* eat will inevitably stir anxiety, especially when some of the foods on offer might shorten your life. Today, buffeted by one food fad after another, America is suffering from what can only be described as a national eating disorder. The omnivore's dilemma has returned with a vengeance, as the cornucopias of the modern American supermarket and fast-food outlet confronts us with a bewildering and treacherous food landscape. What's at stake in our eating choices is not only your own and our children's health, but the health of the environment that sustains life on earth.

This common and seemingly simple question—what should we have for dinner?—turns out to be not so simple at all. According to Pollan, behind this question is a national problem. This jacket blurb promises to present the complexity of the problem and pursue the question about what we should eat, and it also explicitly articulates the stakes of this question. The stakes in this case—the health of our children and the environment—are no small potatoes. Nonetheless, it is worth noting that Pollan is *not* asking the food question with the highest stakes: millions of people across the world do not have the luxury of deciding what to have for dinner because they do not know where their next meal will come from; how do we prevent the starvation of millions? There's a strong allure to ask the question with the highest stakes, and it is obviously important that people out there *are* asking these questions and working to solve these problems. It is also important to realize that smaller problems and questions are worth pursuing, and pursuit of these smaller questions in our everyday life can help us chip away at larger problems. Pollan's question ultimately suggests that individual actions can have large-scale implications.

The next excerpt comes from an article published in the *New England Journal of Medicine* entitled, "Should Physicians Prescribe Religious Activities?":

There is increasing interest among the general public and the medical community in the role of religion in medicine. Polls indicate that the U.S. population is highly religious; most people believe in heaven and hell, the healing power of prayer, and the capacity of faith to aid in the recovery from disease. The popular press has published many articles in which religious faith and practice have been said to promote comfort, healing, or both. A report that 77 percent of hospitalized patients wanted physicians to consider their spiritual needs is consistent with this trend.

Interest in the connection between religion and health has also emerged in the medical community. The National Institute for Healthcare Research, a privately funded, nonprofit advocacy organization, has published extensive literature reviews suggesting that religious faith and practice are positively associated with health status. The organization's World Wide Web site encourages physicians to pay more attention to religious matters and recommends that they take a spiritual history at the time of each complete physical examination, with any concerns raised by patients addressed during follow-up visits. In addition, the National Institute on Aging and Harvard Medical School sponsor meetings on the integration of spirituality and medical practice. A survey of family physicians found that they strongly support the notion that religious beliefs can promote healing. Some physicians believe that going to church promotes health, argue for spiritual and religious interventions in medical practice, hope that the wall between medicine and religion will be torn down, and assert that "the medicine of the future is going to be prayer and Prozac."

Nearly 30 U.S. medical schools now offer courses on religion, spirituality, and health. The American Association of Medical Colleges has cosponsored a conference entitled "Spirituality and Medicine: Curricular Development" for the past three years, and each year it has attracted more than 100 physicians, faculty members, and chaplains from hospitals and medical schools throughout the United States.

As chaplains in health care settings, representing a wide range of religious traditions, and as biomedical researchers, we are troubled by the uncritical embrace of this trend by the general public, individual physicians, and American medical schools. We are concerned that broad generalizations are being made on the basis of limited, narrowly focused, and methodologically flawed studies of the place of religion in medical practice. These generalizations fail to recognize the diversity among physicians, patients, and practice settings and fail to distinguish between superficial indexes of religiousness, such as self reports of church attendance, and personal religious motivation. Such generalizations will lead to considerable confusion until more and better research is done. (1913–14)

In "Should Physicians Prescribe Religious Activities?," Richard P. Sloan and Emilia Bagiella, et al. identify a significant problem in how medicine is practiced in America: the medical community has embraced the notion that religion plays a beneficial role in practicing medicine despite a lack of concrete evidence. The first three paragraphs pile up evidence of the medical community's uncritical acceptance of religion's curative powers. The question that emerges directly out of this problem is: "why should or shouldn't physicians prescribe religious activities?" You may have noticed that the title of the article simplifies this question into a snappy title by posing it as a yes/no question, but the essay pursues a fruitful "why" question. The article goes on to articulate several reasons why physicians should not prescribe religious activities. It urges physicians to stop recommending religious activity until more and better empirical studies are conducted. The stakes of their question are articulated in the final sentence of the introduction: confusion among the medical establishment and patients will spread if the question is not answered.

Here's one final example written by Johan, a student in my composition class at Columbia University. Johan happened upon this problem after reading an article by Steven Pinker published in the *New York Times Magazine* entitled "The Moral Instinct":

> You have two options: 1) wait in an endless queue for a kidney donation or 2) ask a friend or relative to donate a kidney. This was the dilemma Sally Satel, a 49 year old psychiatrist in Washington, was facing. She had been given a death sentence and the only possible appeal was to get a kidney transplant. This does not seem to be an insurmountable problem since "theoretically, kidneys should be in booming supply. Virtually everyone has two, and healthy individuals can give one away and still lead perfectly normal lives" (Satel 1). The National Organ Transplant Act of 1984, however, prohibits the sale of organs, leaving those in need of an organ to rely on altruistic donation. Sally found this very upsetting: "it was about the very fact that an organ had to be a gift" (Satel 4).

Sally's emotional reaction may be understood in light of the fact that her friends decided against donating a kidney to her and that "since 1999 more than 30,000 U.S. patients with kidney failure have died waiting for an organ that never arrived" (Hippen 2)—in short, altruism alone, as it now stands, is not enough to satisfy the demand of the many patients, like Sally, who urgently need an organ.

The majority of academic articles that discuss organ trading argue for legalizing a market in organs. Steven Pinker, a prominent experimental psychologist, asserts, however, that the general public considers organ trading taboo (38). This discrepancy in opinion between medical researchers and the public could be explained from the perspective that these researchers, unlike the public, have centered their arguments upon cost-effectiveness and number of lives saved rather than on morality per se. For example, Arthur J. Matas University of Minnesota, Minnesota, MN and Mark Schnitzler at the Washington and Minnesota Schools of Medicine respectively, found that organ trading could save "$94,579 (US dollars, 2002) [per kidney vended], and 3.5 quality-adjusted life years" (1). Benjamin E. Hippen, a transplant nephrologist in North Carolina, also argues for the cost and medical benefits of organ trading (1). However, scientific data by itself is not normative and cannot tell us what we should do—which is what Hippen is trying to do: "The National Organ Transplantation Act of 1984 which prohibits the sale of organs should be repealed" (1).

If these proponents wish to repeal the organ act, they will have to discuss the moral element of organ trading. They will have to discuss how this moral obstacle against organ trading can be overcome or appeased. After all "millions of people are suffering, not because the organs are not available, but because morality does not allow them to have access to the organs" (Kishore 362). What argument should the proponents construct to make organ trading compatible with morality? What argument will encourage the public, who consider organ trading taboo—that it is even too sinful to think about—accept it as morally defensible? An answer to this question will either bring an end to a "terrible policy failure" and of "human lives unnecessarily lost" (Hippen 1) or give us a more nuanced and rational rejection of the concept of organ trading—something that the many people dying from a lack of donor deserve.

The problem Johan has uncovered in his essay entitled "Organ Trading: Supply and Demand Meets Morality" is multi-layered. First, people in need of organ transplants are dying because there are not enough organs available. Second, despite the fact that donating an organ is a safe procedure, people are reluctant to donate even to close friends. Third, while the academic community is overwhelmingly in favor of organ sales, the general public on the whole rejects the practice. The third problem is the one that leads to his paper's fruitful questions: "What argument should the proponents construct to make organ trading compatible with morality? What argument will encourage the public, who consider organ trading taboo—that it is even too sinful to think about—accept it as morally defensible?" Johan articulates what is at stake explicitly at the end of his introduction by identifying what will be gained if this question is answered.

Each of these texts offers a useful model for how to present rich problems, pose fruitful questions, and articulate what is at stake in an inquiry. Reading texts this way not only provides you with approaches you can imitate, but it will also help you read more effectively. Studies suggest that reading texts on unfamiliar topics in unfamiliar fields can have a disorienting affect on a reader, making comprehension more difficult. Much of what you read as a college student is unfamiliar in content and form and requires a more attentive, deeper read. One way to get your bearings is to approach an unfamiliar text by identifying its purpose. Once you've identified an author's problem and question, you'll have a better handle on the rest of the text.

CONCLUSION: WHAT'S YOUR PROBLEM?

While it's unlikely that you'll ever have to write for your life as Paul Sheldon did in the movie *Misery*, when a grade hangs in the balance, it might feel like a life or death situation. In these high-pressure, high-stakes situations, it helps to have a specific approach and to know the expectations of academic writing. You might be thinking that the process I've outlined here is quite labor intensive. You are right. It is. Developing a complex idea of your own requires hard work.

On any given day, I can be heard asking students in the classroom or in my office, "What's your problem?" To a passerby it might seem like a rude question, perhaps the beginning of an argument. It is, in fact, the beginning of an argument but not the kind with raised voices. Academic arguments follow from problems. But obviously problems exist outside of the realm of academia, particularly problems that require quick solutions. The more you practice the process of articulating problems, posing questions, and identifying the stakes, and the more you cultivate your awareness of problems, the more successful you will be at writing academic papers and handling life's complexities.

DISCUSSION

1. What is your process for developing an argument or a thesis? How do you approach a writing assignment that does not provide you with a specific problem or question?

2. Examine the writing assignments you've received in your classes. Have your instructors provided you with problems and/or questions? How do the types of problems and questions provided differ form course to course? What types of problems and questions are characteristic of writing in your major?

3. Look at papers you've written over the course of your academic career. Do you tend to present problems, pose questions, and identify what is at stake? How do your introductions unfold?

4. Examine the introductions of several newspaper and scholarly articles and books. For each text, identify the problem, the question, and what is at stake.

NOTES

1. Prominent European philosophers, Jean-Jacques Rousseau (1712–1778) and Georg Wilhelm Friedrich Hegel (1770–1831) are credited with laying the groundwork for Marxism.

2. bell hooks is the pen name of feminist, author, and social critic, Gloria Jean Watkins. She intentionally does not use capital letters in her name.

WORKS CITED

Beaufort, Anne. *College Writing and Beyond: A New Framework for University Writing Instruction*. Logan, UT: Utah State UP, 2007. Print.

hooks, bell. "In Our Glory: Photography and Black Life." *Art on My Mind: Visual Politics*. New York: The New Press, 1995: 54–64. Print.

Martin, Roger. "How Successful Leaders Think." *Harvard Business Review* June 2007: 60–67. Print.

Misery. Dir. Rob Reiner. Perf. James Caan and Kathy Bates. Castle Rock Entertainment, 1990. DVD.

Pollan, Michael. *The Omnivore's Dilemma: A Natural History of Four Meals*. New York: Penguin, 2006. Print.

Savini, Catherine. *Nicaraguan Woman*. 2007. Photograph. Private collection.

Sloan, Richard P. and Emilia Bagiella, et al. "Should Physicians Prescribe Religious Activities?" *The New England Journal of Medicine* 342.25 (2000): 1913–1916. Print.

Williams, Joseph. "Avoiding 'So what?': Assignments that Help Students Find and Frame Problems Worth Solving." Columbia University, New York City. 25 Jan. 2008. Lecture.

How to Read Like a Writer

Mike Bunn

In 1997, I was a recent college graduate living in London for six months and working at the Palace Theatre owned by Andrew Lloyd Webber.[*] The Palace was a beautiful red brick, four-story theatre in the heart of London's famous West End, and eight times a week it housed a three-hour performance of the musical *Les Miserables*. Because of antiquated fire-safety laws, every theatre in the city was required to have a certain number of staff members inside watching the performance in case of an emergency.

My job (in addition to wearing a red tuxedo jacket) was to sit inside the dark theater with the patrons and make sure nothing went wrong. It didn't seem to matter to my supervisor that I had no training in security and no idea where we kept the fire extinguishers. I was pretty sure that if there *was* any trouble I'd be running down the back stairs, leaving the patrons to fend for themselves. I had no intention of dying in a bright red tuxedo.

There was a Red Coat stationed on each of the theater's four floors, and we all passed the time by sitting quietly in the back, reading books with tiny flashlights. It's not easy trying to read in the dim light of a theatre—flashlight or no flashlight—and it's even tougher with shrieks and shouts and gunshots coming from the stage. I had to focus intently on each and every word, often rereading a single sentence several times. Sometimes I got distracted and had to re-read entire para-

---

[*] This work is licensed under the Creative Commons Attribution-Noncommercial-ShareAlike 3.0 United States License and is subject to the Writing Spaces' Terms of Use. To view a copy of this license, visit http://creativecommons.org/licenses/by-nc-sa/3.0/us/ or send a letter to Creative Commons, 171 Second Street, Suite 300, San Francisco, California, 94105, USA. To view the Writing Spaces' Terms of Use, visit http://writingspaces.org/terms-of-use.

graphs. As I struggled to read in this environment, I began to realize that the way I was reading—one word at a time—was exactly the same way that the author had written the text. I realized writing is a word-by-word, sentence-by-sentence process. The intense concentration required to read in the theater helped me recognize some of the interesting ways that authors string words into phrases into paragraphs into entire books.

I came to realize that all writing consists of a series of choices.

I was an English major in college, but I don't think I ever thought much about reading. I read all the time. I read for my classes and on the computer and sometimes for fun, but I never really thought about the important connections between reading and writing, and how reading in a particular way could also make me a better writer.

WHAT DOES IT MEAN TO READ LIKE A WRITER?

When you Read Like a Writer (RLW) you work to identify some of the choices the author made so that you can better understand how such choices might arise in your own writing. The idea is to carefully examine the things you read, looking at the writerly techniques in the text in order to decide if you might want to adopt similar (or the same) techniques in your writing.

You are reading to learn about writing.

Instead of reading for content or to better understand the ideas in the writing (which you will automatically do to some degree anyway), you are trying to understand how the piece of writing was put together by the author and what you can learn about writing by reading a particular text. As you read in this way, you think about how the choices the author made and the techniques that he/she used are influencing your own responses as a reader. What is it about the way this text is written that makes you feel and respond the way you do?

The goal as you read like a writer is to locate what you believe are the most important writerly choices represented in the text—choices as large as the overall structure or as small as a single word used only once—to consider the effect of those choices on potential readers (including yourself). Then you can go one step further and imagine what *different* choices the author *might* have made instead, and what effect those different choices would have on readers.

Say you're reading an essay in class that begins with a short quote from President Barack Obama about the war in Iraq. As a writer, what do you think of this technique? Do you think it is effective to begin the essay with a quote? What if the essay began with a quote from someone else? What if it was a much *longer* quote from President Obama, or a quote from the President about something other than the war?

And here is where we get to the most important part: *Would you want to try this technique in your own writing?*

Would you want to start your own essay with a quote? Do you think it would be effective to begin your essay with a quote from President Obama? What about a quote from someone else?

You could make yourself a list. What are the advantages and disadvantages of starting with a quote? What about the advantages and disadvantages of starting with a quote from the President? How would other readers respond to this technique? Would certain readers (say Democrats or liberals) appreciate an essay that started with a quote from President Obama better than other readers (say Republicans or conservatives)? What would be the advantages and disadvantages of starting with a quote from a *less* divisive person? What about starting with a quote from someone *more* divisive?

The goal is to carefully consider the choices the author made and the techniques that he or she used, and then decide whether you want to make those same choices or use those same techniques in your own writing. Author and professor Wendy Bishop explains how her reading process changed when she began to read like a writer:

> It wasn't until I claimed the sentence as my area of desire, interest, and expertise—until I wanted to be a writer writing better—that I had to look underneath my initial readings . . . I started asking, *how—how* did the writer get me to feel, *how* did the writer say something so that it remains in my memory when many other things too easily fall out, *how* did the writer communicate his/her intentions about genre, about irony? (119–20)

Bishop moved from simply reporting her personal reactions to the things she read to attempting to uncover *how* the author led her (and other readers) to have those reactions. This effort to uncover how authors build texts is what makes Reading Like a Writer so useful for student writers.

How Is RLW Different from "Normal" Reading?

Most of the time we read for information. We read a recipe to learn how to bake lasagna. We read the sports page to see if our school won the game, Facebook to see who has commented on our status update, a history book to learn about the Vietnam War, and the syllabus to see when the next writing assignment is due. Reading Like a Writer asks for something very different.

In 1940, a famous poet and critic named Allen Tate discussed two different ways of reading:

> There are many ways to read, but generally speaking there are two ways. They correspond to the two ways in which we may be interested in a piece of architecture. If the building has Corinthian columns, we can trace the origin and development of Corinthian columns; we are interested as historians. But if we are interested as architects, we may or may not know about the history of the Corinthian style; we must, however, know all about the construction of the building, down to the last nail or peg in the beams. We have got to know this if we are going to put up buildings ourselves. (506)

While I don't know anything about Corinthian columns (and doubt that I will ever *want* to know anything about Corinthian columns), Allen Tate's metaphor of reading as if you were an architect is a great way to think about RLW. When you read like a writer, you are trying to figure out how the text you are reading was constructed so that you learn how to "build" one for yourself. Author David Jauss makes a similar comparison when he writes that "reading won't help you much unless you learn to read like a writer. You must look at a book the way a carpenter looks at a house someone else built, examining the details in order to see how it was made" (64).

Perhaps I should change the name and call this Reading Like an Architect, or Reading Like a Carpenter. In a way those names make perfect sense. You are reading to see how something was constructed so that you can construct something similar yourself.

WHY LEARN TO READ LIKE A WRITER?

For most college students RLW is a new way to read, and it can be difficult to learn at first. Making things even *more* difficult is that your college writing instructor may expect you to read this way for class but never actually teach you how to do it. He or she may not even tell you that you're supposed to read this way. This is because most writing instructors are so focused on teaching writing that they forget to show students how they want them to read.

That's what this essay is for.

In addition to the fact that your college writing instructor may expect you to read like a writer, this kind of reading is also one of the very best ways to learn how to write well. Reading like a writer can help you understand how the process of writing is a series of making choices, and in doing so, can help you recognize important decisions you might face and techniques you might want to use when working on your own writing. Reading this way becomes an opportunity to think and learn about writing.

Charles Moran, a professor of English at the University of Massachusetts, urges us to read like writers because:

> When we read like writers we understand and participate in the writing. We see the choices the writer has made, and we see how the writer has coped with the consequences of those choices . . . We "see" what the writer is doing because we read as writers; we see because we have written ourselves and know the territory, know the feel of it, know some of the moves ourselves. (61)

You are already an author, and that means you have a built-in advantage when reading like a writer. All of your previous writing experiences—inside the classroom and out—can contribute to your success with RLW. Because you "have written" things yourself, just as Moran suggests, you are better able to "see" the choices that the author is making in the texts that you read. This in turn helps you to think about whether you want to make some of those same choices in your own writing, and what the consequences might be for your readers if you do.

What Are Some Questions to Ask
Before You Start Reading?

As I sat down to work on this essay, I contacted a few of my former students to ask what advice they would give to college students regarding how to read effectively in the writing classroom and also to get their thoughts on RLW. Throughout the rest of the essay I'd like to share some of their insights and suggestions; after all, who is better qualified to help you learn what you need to know about reading in college writing courses than students who recently took those courses themselves?

One of the things that several students mentioned to do first, before you even start reading, is to consider the *context* surrounding both the assignment and the text you're reading. As one former student, Alison, states: "The reading I did in college asked me to go above and beyond, not only in breadth of subject matter, but in depth, with regards to informed analysis and background information on *context*." Alison was asked to think about some of the factors that went into the creation of the text, as well as some of the factors influencing her own experience of reading—taken together these constitute the *context* of reading. Another former student, Jamie, suggests that students "learn about the historical context of the writings" they will read for class. Writing professor Richard Straub puts it this way: "You're not going to just read a text. You're going to read a text within a certain context, a set of circumstances . . . It's one kind of writing or another, designed for one audience and purpose or another" (138).

Among the contextual factors you'll want to consider before you even start reading are:

- Do you know the author's purpose for this piece of writing?
- Do you know who the intended audience is for this piece of writing?

It may be that you need to start reading before you can answer these first two questions, but it's worth trying to answer them before you start. For example, if you know at the outset that the author is trying to reach a very specific group of readers, then his or her writerly techniques may seem more or less effective than if he/she was trying to reach a more general audience. Similarly—returning to our earlier example of beginning an essay with a quote from President Obama about the war in Iraq—if you know that the author's purpose is to address some of the dangers and drawbacks of warfare, this may be a very effective opening. If the purpose is to encourage Americans to wear sunscreen while at the beach this opening makes no sense at all. One former student, Lola, explained that most of her reading assignments in college writing classes were designed "to provoke analysis and criticisms into the style, structure, and *purpose* of the writing itself."

In What Genre Is This Written?

Another important thing to consider before reading is the genre of the text. Genre means a few different things in college English classes, but it's most often used to indicate the *type* of writing: a poem, a newspaper article, an essay, a short story, a novel, a legal brief, an instruction manual, etc. Because the conventions for each genre can be very different (who ever heard of a 900-page newspaper article?), techniques that are effective for one genre may not work well in another. Many readers expect poems and pop songs to rhyme, for example, but might react negatively to a legal brief or instruction manual that did so.

Another former student, Mike, comments on how important the genre of the text can be for reading:

> I think a lot of the way I read, of course, depends on the type of text I'm reading. If I'm reading philosophy, I always look for signaling words (however, therefore, furthermore, despite) indicating the direction of the argument . . . when I read fiction or creative nonfiction, I look for how the author inserts dialogue or character sketches within narration or environmental observation. After reading To the Lighthouse [sic] last semester, I have noticed how much more attentive I've become to the types of narration (omniscient, impersonal, psychological, realistic, etc.), and how these different approaches are utilized to achieve an author's overall effect.

Although Mike specifically mentions what he looked for while reading a published novel, one of the great things about RLW is that it can be used equally well with either published or student-produced writing.

Is This a Published or a Student-Produced Piece of Writing?

As you read both kinds of texts you can locate the choices the author made and imagine the different decisions that he/she might have made.

While it might seem a little weird at first to imagine how published texts could be written differently—after all, they were good enough to be published—remember that all writing can be improved. Scholar Nancy Walker believes that it's important for students to read published work using RLW because "the work ceases to be a mere artifact, a stone tablet, and becomes instead a living utterance with immediacy and texture. It could have been better or worse than it is had the author made different choices" (36). As Walker suggests, it's worth thinking about how the published text would be different—maybe even *better*—if the author had made different choices in the writing because you may be faced with similar choices in your own work.

Is This the Kind of Writing You Will Be Assigned to Write Yourself?

Knowing ahead of time what kind of writing assignments you will be asked to complete can really help you to read like a writer. It's probably impossible (and definitely too time consuming) to identify *all* of the choices the author made and *all* techniques an author used, so it's important to prioritize while reading. Knowing what you'll be writing yourself can help you prioritize. It may be the case that your instructor has assigned the text you're reading to serve as model for the kind of writing you'll be doing later. Jessie, a former student, writes, "In college writing classes, we knew we were reading for a purpose—to influence or inspire our own work. The reading that I have done in college writing courses has always been really specific to a certain type of writing, and it allows me to focus and experiment on that specific style in depth and without distraction."

If the text you're reading is a model of a particular style of writing—for example, highly-emotional or humorous—RLW is particularly helpful because you can look at a piece you're reading and think about whether you want to adopt a similar style in your own writing. You might realize that the author is trying to arouse sympathy in readers and examine what techniques he/she uses to do this; then you can decide whether these techniques might work well in your own writing. You might notice that the author keeps including jokes or funny stories and think about whether you want to include them in your writing—what would the impact be on your potential readers?

WHAT ARE QUESTIONS TO ASK AS YOU ARE READING?

It is helpful to continue to ask yourself questions *as* you read like a writer. As you're first learning to read in this new way, you may want to have a set of questions written or typed out in front of you that you can refer to while reading. Eventually—after plenty of practice—you will start to ask certain questions and locate certain things in the text almost automatically. Remember, for most students this is a new way of reading, and you'll have to train yourself to do it well. Also keep in mind that you're reading to understand how the text was *written*— how the house was built—more than you're trying to determine the meaning of the things you read or assess whether the texts are good or bad.

First, return to two of the same questions I suggested that you consider *before* reading:

- What is the author's purpose for this piece of writing?
- Who is the intended audience?

Think about these two questions again as you read. It may be that you couldn't really answer them before, or that your ideas will change while reading. Knowing *why* the piece was written and *who* it's for can help explain why the author might have made certain choices or used particular techniques in the writing, and you can assess those choices and techniques based in part on how effective they are in fulfilling that purpose and/or reaching the intended audience.

Beyond these initial two questions, there is an almost endless list of questions you might ask regarding writing choices and techniques. Here are some of the questions that one former student, Clare, asks herself:

> When reading I tend to be asking myself a million questions. If I were writing this, where would I go with the story? If the author goes in a different direction (as they so often do) from what I am thinking, I will ask myself, why did they do this? What are they telling me?

Clare tries to figure out why the author might have made a move in the writing that she hadn't anticipated, but even more importantly, she asks herself what *she* would do if she were the author. Reading the text becomes an opportunity for Clare to think about her own role as an author.

Here are some additional examples of the kinds of questions you might ask yourself as you read:

- How effective is the language the author uses? Is it too formal? Too informal? Perfectly appropriate?

Depending on the subject matter and the intended audience, it may make sense to be more or less formal in terms of language. As you begin reading, you can ask yourself whether the word choice and tone/language of the writing seem appropriate.

- What kinds of evidence does the author use to support his/her claims? Does he/she use statistics? Quotes from famous people? Personal anecdotes or personal stories? Does he/she cite books or articles?
- How appropriate or effective is this evidence? Would a different type of evidence, or some combination of evidence, be more effective?

To some extent the kinds of questions you ask should be determined by the genre of writing you are reading. For example, it's probably worth examining the evidence that the author uses to support his/her claims if you're reading an opinion column, but less important if you're reading a short story. An opinion column is often intended to convince readers of something, so the kinds of evidence used are often very important. A short story *may* be intended to convince readers of something, sometimes, but probably not in the same way. A short story rarely includes claims or evidence in the way that we usually think about them.

- Are there places in the writing that you find confusing? What about the writing in those places makes it unclear or confusing?

It's pretty normal to get confused in places while reading, especially while reading for class, so it can be helpful to look closely at the writing to try and get a sense of exactly what tripped you up. This way you can learn to avoid those same problems in your own writing.

- How does the author move from one idea to another in the writing? Are the transitions between the ideas effective? How else might he/she have transitioned between ideas instead?

Notice that in these questions I am encouraging you to question whether aspects of the writing are *appropriate* and *effective* in addition to deciding whether you liked or disliked them. You want to imagine how other readers might respond to the writing and the techniques you've identified. Deciding whether you liked or disliked something is only about you; considering whether a technique is appropriate or effective lets you contemplate what the author might have been trying to do and to decide whether a majority of readers would find the move successful. This is important because it's the same thing you should be thinking about while you are writing: how will readers respond to this technique I am using, to this sentence, to this word? As you read, ask yourself what the author is doing at each step of the way, and then consider whether the same choice or technique might work in your own writing.

WHAT SHOULD YOU BE WRITING AS YOU ARE READING?

The most common suggestion made by former students—mentioned by every single one of them—was to mark up the text, make comments in the margins, and write yourself notes and summaries both during and after reading. Often the notes students took while reading became ideas or material for the students to use in their own papers. It's important to read with a pen or highlighter in your hand so that you can mark—right on the text—all those spots where you identify an interesting choice the author has made or a writerly technique you might want to use. One thing that I like to do is to highlight and underline the passage in the text itself, and then try to answer the following three questions on my notepad:

- What is the technique the author is using here?
- Is this technique effective?
- What would be the advantages and disadvantages if I tried this same technique in my writing?

By utilizing this same process of highlighting and note taking, you'll end up with a useful list of specific techniques to have at your disposal when it comes time to begin your own writing.

WHAT DOES RLW LOOK LIKE IN ACTION?

Let's go back to the opening paragraph of *this* essay and spend some time reading like writers as a way to get more comfortable with the process:

> *In 1997, I was a recent college graduate living in London for six months and working at the Palace Theatre owned by Andrew Lloyd Webber. The Palace was a beautiful red brick, four-story theatre in the heart of London's famous West End, and eight times a week it housed a three-hour performance of the musical* Les Miserables. *Because of antiquated fire-safety laws, every theatre in the city was required to have a certain number of staff members inside watching the performance in case of an emergency.*

Let's begin with those questions I encouraged you to try to answer *before* you start reading. (I realize we're cheating a little bit in this case since you've already read most of this essay, but this is just practice. When doing this on your own, you should attempt to answer these questions before reading, and then return to them as you read to further develop your answers.)

- Do you know the author's purpose for this piece of writing? I hope the purpose is clear by now; if it isn't, I'm doing a pretty lousy job of explaining how and why you might read like a writer.
- Do you know who the intended audience is? Again, I hope that you know this one by now.
- What about the genre? Is this an essay? An article? What would *you* call it?
- You know that it's published and not student writing. How does this influence your expectations for what you will read?
- Are you going to be asked to write something like this yourself? Probably not in your college writing class, but you can still use RLW to learn about writerly techniques that you might want to use in whatever you do end up writing.

Now ask yourself questions *as* you read.

> *In 1997, I was a recent college graduate living in London for six months and working at the Palace Theatre owned by Andrew Lloyd Webber. The Palace was a beautiful red brick, four-story theatre in the heart of London's famous West End, and eight times a week it housed a three-hour performance of the musical* Les Miserables. *Because of antiquated fire-safety laws, every theatre in the city was required to have a certain number of staff members inside watching the performance in case of an emergency.*

Since this paragraph is the very first one, it makes sense to think about how it introduces readers to the essay. What technique(s) does the author use to begin the text? This is a personal story about his time working in London. What else do you notice as you read over this passage? Is the passage vague or specific about where he worked? You know that the author worked in a famous part of London in a beautiful theater owned by a well-known composer. Are these details important? How different would this opening be if instead I had written:

> *In 1997, I was living in London and working at a theatre that showed* Les Miserables.

This is certainly shorter, and some of you may prefer this version. It's quick. To the point. But what (if anything) is lost by eliminating so much of the detail? I *chose* to include each of the details that the revised sentence omits, so it's worth considering why. Why did I mention where the theater was located? Why did I explain that I was living in London right after finishing college? Does it matter that it was after college? What effect might I have hoped the inclusion of these details would have on readers? Is this reference to college an attempt to connect with my audience of college students? Am I trying to establish my credibility as an author by announcing that I went to college? Why might I want the readers to know that this was a theater owned by Andrew Lloyd Weber? Do you think I am just trying to mention a famous name that readers will recognize? Will Andrew Lloyd Weber figure prominently in the rest of the essay?

These are all reasonable questions to ask. They are not necessarily the *right* questions to ask because there are no right questions. They certainly aren't the only questions you could ask, either. The goal is to train yourself to formulate questions as you read based on whatever you notice in the text. Your own reactions to what you're reading will help determine the kinds of questions to ask.

Now take a broader perspective. I begin this essay—an essay about *reading*—by talking about my job in a theater in London. Why? Doesn't this seem like an odd way to begin an essay about reading? If you read on a little further (feel free to scan back up at the top of this essay) you learn in the third full paragraph what the connection is between working in the theater and reading like a writer, but why include this information at all? What does this story add to the essay? Is it worth the space it takes up?

Think about what effect presenting this personal information might have on readers. Does it make it feel like a real person, some "ordinary guy," is talking to you? Does it draw you into the essay and make you want to keep reading?

What about the language I use? Is it formal or more informal? This is a time when you can really narrow your focus and look at particular words:

> *Because of antiquated fire-safety laws, every theatre in the city was required to have a certain number of staff members inside watching the performance in case of an emergency.*

What is the effect of using the word "antiquated" to describe the fire-safety laws? It certainly projects a negative impression; if the laws are described as antiquated it means I view them as old-fashioned or obsolete. This is a fairly uncommon word, so it stands out, drawing attention to my choice in using it. The word also sounds quite formal. Am I formal in the rest of this sentence?

I use the word "performance" when I just as easily could have written "show." For that matter, I could have written "old" instead of "antiquated." You can proceed like this throughout the sentence, thinking about alternative choices I could have made and what the effect would be. Instead of "staff members" I could have written "employees" or just "workers." Notice the difference if the sentence had been written:

> *Because of old fire-safety laws, every theatre in the city was required to have a certain number of workers inside watching the show in case of an emergency.*

Which version is more likely to appeal to readers? You can try to answer this question by thinking about the advantages and disadvantages of using formal language. When would you want to use formal language in your writing and when would it make more sense to be more conversational?

As you can see from discussing just this one paragraph, you could ask questions about the text forever. Luckily, you don't have to. As you continue reading like a writer, you'll learn to notice techniques that seem new and pay less attention to the ones you've thought about before. The more you practice the quicker the process becomes until you're reading like a writer almost automatically.

I want to end this essay by sharing one more set of comments by my former student, Lola, this time about what it means to her to read like a writer:

> Reading as a writer would compel me to question what might have brought the author to make these decisions, and then decide what worked and what didn't. What could have made that chapter better or easier to understand? How can I make sure I include some of the good attributes of this writing style into my own? How can I take aspects that I feel the writer failed at and make sure not to make the same mistakes in my writing?

Questioning why the author made certain decisions. Considering what techniques could have made the text better. Deciding how to include the best attributes of what you read in your own writing. This is what Reading Like a Writer is all about.

Are you ready to start reading?

DISCUSSION

1. How is "Reading Like a Writer" similar to and/or different from the way(s) you read for other classes?
2. What kinds of choices do you make as a writer that readers might identify in your written work?
3. Is there anything you notice in *this* essay that you might like to try in your own writing? What is that technique or strategy? When do you plan to try using it?
4. What are some of the different ways that you can learn about the *context* of a text before you begin reading it?

WORKS CITED

Bishop, Wendy. "Reading, Stealing, and Writing Like a Writer." *Elements of Alternate Style: Essays on Writing and Revision.* Ed. Wendy Bishop. Portsmouth, NH: Boynton/Cook, 1997. Print.

Jauss, David. "Articles of Faith." *Creative Writing in America: Theory and Pedagogy.* Ed. Joseph Moxley. Urbana, IL: NCTE, 1989. Print.

Moran, Charles. "Reading Like a Writer." *Vital Signs 1.* Ed. James L. Collins. Portsmouth, NH: Boynton/Cook, 1990. Print.

Straub, Richard. "Responding—Really Responding—to Other Students' Writing." *The Subject is Reading.* Ed. Wendy Bishop. Portsmouth, NH: Boynton/Cook, 2000. Print.

Tate, Allen. "We Read as Writers." *Princeton Alumni Weekly* 40 (March 8, 1940): 505- 506. Print.

Walker, Nancy. "The Student Reader as Writer." *ADE Bulletin* 106 (1993) 35–37. Print.

Murder! (Rhetorically Speaking)

Janet Boyd

The college where I first started teaching writing called its freshman composition course "Logic and Rhetoric" after two of the three arts of discourse in the classical tradition (the third being grammar).* While the students could easily explain what logic is, they struggled with the definition of rhetoric; most of their responses were more or less a politer version of this succinct definition offered by one brave student: "bullshit." While I was surprised that he dared say such a word in class, and I am equally surprised that our publishers have so kindly agreed to print it, this offensive word so directly and memorably brings us to the crux of the matter: that choosing *how* to express your meaning is every bit as important as the message itself, which is really what rhetoric is. Every time you go to write anything (and every time you open your mouth), whether actively conscious of the purpose or not, you are making decisions about which words to use and what tone to establish as you order your thoughts based upon what is appropriate for your intended audience in that context.

Determined as I was to enlighten the class about the more positive and powerful aspects of rhetoric, we used no textbook in the program that could edify us. This turned out to be a good thing, for, out of necessity, I invented a simple, little exercise[1] for them that you will participate in here, now, and dazzle yourself with the rhetorical skills you *already* possess, skills that are crucial for your development as an academic writer. For purposes of comparison, I have also included responses from other student writers for you to consider—all of whom surprised themselves with their own rhetorical range and ability. First, I will give you five simple facts, nothing but the facts, as I did my students:

> Who: Mark Smith
> What: Murdered
> Where: Parking garage
> When: June 6, 2010; 10:37 p.m.
> How: Multiple stab wounds

You might read such straightforward facts in a short newspaper article or hear them in a brief news report on the radio; if the person was not famous, the narrative might sound like this: Mark Smith was found stabbed to death at 10:37 p.m. on June 6th, in the local parking garage. Next, imagine that you are the detective called out to investigate the crime scene, which will, of course, demand that you also write and file a report of your findings. (In fact, many people who go into law enforcement are shocked to discover how much writing such a job regularly entails.)

Take a moment to visualize the five facts, and then pick up a pen or turn to your keyboard and write for five or so minutes as if you were that detective. In writing up the case (whoops, I have given you a clue), you may add or invent as many details as you see fit, but you may not alter the given facts. Go ahead. Get started on writing your report of the murder scene. Then come back and read the next section.

GETTING IN TOUCH WITH YOUR INNER DETECTIVE

Welcome back. While it is usually the detective who asks all the questions, we will proceed first with me grilling you not about the murder but about your report:

- How does it begin? Where does it end?
- What types of details did you find yourself adding? Why? What details did you omit? Why?
- What kind of words did you choose?

- What tone did you take? (I will admit, *tone* can be a tricky thing to describe; it is best done by searching for a specific adjective that describes a feeling or an attitude such as "pretentious," "somber," "buoyant," "melancholic," "didactic," "humorous," etc.).
- How did you order your information?
- And, since I am working under the assumption that no undergraduates have yet had careers in law enforcement, how did you know how to write like a detective would in the first place?

The answer I get to my last question invariably is "from television, of course," nowadays particularly from shows such as the fictitious *CSI: Crime Scene Investigation* and reality-based *The First 48*. From such shows, and from detective movies or fiction, we get a glimpse not only into the work detectives are likely to do but also the language they choose. Gradually, and ever so subtly, we internalize this detective-speak, which is more than just the jargon they use. *Jargon* is the terminology used by those in a particular profession or group to facilitate clear and precise communication, but this rhetorical tool is not limited just to the professional world. For example, anyone who participates in a sport uses the lingo specific to that sport, which is learned by doing. Doctors use medical jargon and lawyers use legal jargon, and they go to school specifically to learn the terms and abbreviations of their professions; so do detectives. If you use any kind of *slang* words, you, too, use jargon, but if you studied these words in a book, they are probably not very hip or at least not very *au courant*. For slang is different in that it maintains a currency in a dual sense: it strives to be current, and it circulates among a select network of users. Jargon does not fall victim to fashion so easily as slang does, but it does have a similar effect in that they both exclude those outside of the community who do not understand the meanings of the words. And so purposefully in the case of slang and not necessarily purposefully in the case of jargon, the initiated constitute an "insiders club" for whom they themselves are their intended and best audience. When *you* write an academic paper, you are practicing how to use the jargon you have internalized through studying that discipline as you write for professors and students within that field.

Getting back to the detective writing . . . although you probably didn't think much about whom your *audience* would be, who would read such a report, when you got started you probably had no problem deciding how to begin your narrative: Am I right that it starts with you arriving at the crime scene, and that you wrote in first person? Every piece of writing needs a starting point and a perspective, it is true, and the demands of the genre—in this instance the reports of detectives—shaped the very first words of your response. This is why I say with confidence that you worked your magic with more than just detective jargon. As much as I am aware of my audience here—so much so that I am trying to engage in dialog with you through my casual tone, my informal language, and my addressing you directly by asking you questions and anticipating your responses—ultimately the format dictates that our "conversation" remain one-sided.

As much as I wish I could chat with you about the report you wrote, I cannot. Instead, I offer you here the "detective reports" of students much like you, students taking freshman composition classes who were given just the five facts about the murder, to present some rhetoric in action. "I arrived at the crime scene at roughly 22:45 (10:45) p.m.," writes Jeannette Olsavsky; "headquarters had received a phone call at 10:37 p.m. about a dead body lying stabbed in the parking garage on Franklin Ave." Ilya Imyanitov starts his report with: "My partner and I received a phone call at 11:02 p.m. from dispatch that a body was found in the parking garage on 34th and 5th. We were the first to arrive on the scene." Here's one more example: "On Saturday, June 6th, at 10:37 p.m., the Montclair Police Department received an anonymous call regarding a body found in the Hawk Parking Garage. Detectives Dan Barry, Randy Johnson, and I, Tamara Morales, were called to the scene. Upon arrival, we noted the cadaver was facing down and had multiple stab wounds."

Did you notice all of the things that these reports do similarly? Mere coincidence? I think not. They obey the conventions of the genre (which is a word we will gradually define). All of these opening sentences note some kind of phone call that gets them to the scene of the crime, all of them establish more specifically the location, all of them note precise times (which could be of significance), all of them are in first person, and two of our detectives work with partners. While the similarities continue to multiply as the three reports unfold, we can discern from these few sentences alone that writers attend to how they order their information and that writers can aspire towards objectivity even when writing in the first person.

Since detectives are trained observers who search for clues to aid in the investigation of a crime, they provide written, first-hand accounts of the tangible evidence they find. They also speculate as to what might have motivated the criminal to perpetrate the crime. In short, detectives have an *agenda:* in their reports, our three student-detectives try to identify the victim, establish injuries and cause of death, and look for signs of foul play. They also hope to interview witnesses to corroborate their findings, and one lucky detective does. Detective Imyanitov "took down a statement from the [garage] attendant, Michael Portnick." Portnick "states that he was making his rounds as usual," and "he remembers checking his phone" when "he discovered a body that appeared to be stabbed to death." Why such hesitation, Detective Imyanitov? You can tell from the verbs he uses (such as Portnick "states" and "remembers," and the body "appeared") that he is recording a version of the events he has not yet verified, and so he infuses his narrative with words that establish room for doubt. Through his *diction,* or choice of words, Imyanitov establishes a *tone* for his report that is formal, objective, inquisitive, and tentative all at the same time. Not surprisingly, Olsavsky's and Morales's reports adopt much the same tone, and all three also end the same way: with the call for a "full investigation" to ensue based on the preliminary findings.

These three detective reports, in fact all the detective reports I've ever collected from students, discuss to some degree the nature of the fatal wounds Mark Smith received. Now shift gears slightly to imagine that you are the coroner who is on duty in the city morgue when Mark's body arrives. The coroner must do a full examination of the corpse and, what else, write up a report (trust me, there are few jobs out there that do not require writing). Visualize yourself in your new occupation, recall the "five facts," and then take five minutes to write up your findings as a coroner might (remember, you may add or invent as many details as you like, but you may not alter the given facts). Really—go, write, and come back.

CULTIVATING YOUR INNER CORONER

Your first thoughts probably weren't so much about audience this time, either; you were probably thinking hard about jargon, though. You

know (from CSI or elsewhere) that coroners use very specific terminology that allows for precise and concise description, so to write a plau-
sible report you had to muster up as many factual and pseudo-medical
words as possible. In other words, your freedom to select words—to
choose your diction—was limited greatly by the jargon of this profession, which means that the tone was also mostly dictated. Because a
detective and a coroner have similar agendas in that they report causes,
effects, and facts, and because they often present to similar audiences,
their reports often assume a similar tone that is informative, authoritative, and forensic.[2] But the tone of the coroner's report is ultimately
much more technical and is prescribed by the medical community.
Every discipline has its own range of acceptable jargon, diction, and
tone to be learned and applied.

So how does your report read? If it is like that of my students, you
began it much like you did your detective report with the five, simple
facts relating to the crime. After that, however, it diverges. It becomes
focused on the body alone and for good reason—that's all you've got
to look at! Here I'd like to answer some relevant questions I asked but
never addressed with regard to your detective report: what details did
you include or omit and why? Of course the coroner cannot and does
not include details about the parking garage, but what would stop
him/her from recording whether Mark Smith was handsome or not, or
whether the tattoo on Smith's calf was cool or comical, or whether he
reminded the coroner of his/her brother-in-law? You think this a dumb
question, I know, because such subjectivity and personal observations
do not belong in an official, objective report. Perhaps the question is
dumb, but thinking about why it is dumb is not: even though you are
not a real coroner (you just play one here) you have an awareness not
only of what the genre demands but also what it rejects. You have a
sense of what is appropriate in this context, and in many, many other
rhetorical contexts, including when you assume the role of a student
writing an essay (we are getting closer to a definition of genre).

What surprises me most about all the times I've asked students
to write like coroners do is not that they can, even though this is the
most difficult exercise in the group, but that they do not include the
simplest information—a basic, physical description of Mark Smith.
They tend to jump right into gory descriptions of what got him to the
morgue but not anything like "The subject is a Caucasian male, is in
his early thirties, about five feet, ten inches tall and 175 pounds; he

has brown eyes and shoulder-length, dark brown hair. He has a birth-mark on his left forearm and a two-inch scar in the vicinity of where his appendix would be." Maybe students are just too eager to cover the "five facts" I have presented them; or maybe it is that they are not so eager to ponder Mark Smith as a real but dead person with personal features; or both.

After reporting the five facts in the first sentence of his coroner's report, and adding that Mark Smith was found by an off-duty police officer, Brett Magura writes:

> After post-mortem evaluation, it can be seen that only one of the six stab wounds was fatal. This stab came from behind, through the back and in between the ribs, puncturing the heart and causing internal bleeding. The fatal blow appeared to follow an effort to run away after the first five wounds occurred to the hands and arms. The wounds on the hands and arms are determined to be defensive wounds.

Magura concludes his report with the contents of Smith's stomach and a blood-alcohol level assessment. Like many students, Magura identifies the locations of the wounds and the exact cause of death, and like many students he admirably gropes for the words that coroners use. Instead of "back" or "behind," he might have substituted "posterior" and thrown in some words like "anterior" or "lateral" or "laceration," I would venture, but his report is on target even if his and my jargon would benefit from some medical schooling.

Lecille Desampardo is the only student I've known to give the report a case number, "Murder Case #123," which immediately suggests that her report is official and conforms to standards we would also find in Cases 1 through 122. Even better, one could easily keep track of and even reference such a report, which would be important if it should be needed as forensic evidence. Desampardo finds "remnants of some kind of black grease" in the stab wounds, and upon the miracles of further lab testing links it to the "Nissan Pathfinder owned by the victim." Coupled with the "irregular shape" of the stab wounds, the murder weapon was a "monkey wrench" she concludes. What kind of weapon did you deduce killed Mark Smith? Was it a hunting knife or a butcher's knife or scissors or something else? Does your report work to support that assumption? Chances are you found yourself knowing exactly what *content* to include but were frustrated at not having the exact words you desired at your disposal. In this rhetorical instance, you even know what it is you don't know (which, unfortunately, can also be the case when you are first learning academic writing).

On the other hand, perhaps these words came easy for Kristin Flynn who writes,

> Mark Smith was an amazing father, husband and good friend. His unfortunate murder and untimely demise come as a shock to all who knew him. Mark and I go way back [. . .]. His memory will be forever treasured, and it is truly a shame to have to say goodbye to him today.

Wait a minute? What happened to the knife, the parking garage, and the stab wounds? One would hope that such graphic details wouldn't make their way into a eulogy.

Yes, the next exercise I want you to write is a short eulogy for Mark Smith, which is a speech of remembrance delivered at a funeral. This exercise is perhaps one of the easier ones to write, but that is only if you liked Mark Smith and can write in honesty; imagine how difficult it would be if you didn't like him? So return now to the "five facts," invent the details that you need, and work for five minutes or so to fulfill the rhetorical demands of the genre of the eulogy (which I hope you'll never get much practice in).

Learning How to Say Goodbye

Many students get flustered with this exercise because they feel compelled to include all "five facts" while they intuitively know that an actual eulogy would not; the instructions I give require no such thing. I write "intuitively" here because, again, I cannot imagine that many of you are trained to write eulogies, and so you proceeded based on the knowledge you have internalized from your religion or culture. The example of the eulogy highlights very well the decisions all writers must make about what to include and what to omit based upon the expectations of the audience for whom they write (including an academic audience). You were probably rather surprised to read just on the heels of the coroners' reports an excerpt of the eulogy Flynn penned because you were expecting more blood and guts. It is a good time to admit that I did this on purpose, and that in my classes I aim for this element of surprise as well; my students don't know that they have been assigned different writing tasks relating to the facts of Mark Smith's murder, and when they read them aloud without identifying the piece the contrasts stand sharp. After only a few sentences, though, the students recognize what genre it is they hear because of the various rhetorical cues they so quickly discern.

So what did you include in your eulogy? Of the five facts, you probably mentioned Mark Smith by his whole name at first, and thereafter by his first name to foster a sense of familiarity, and then did your best to avoid the other four facts entirely, facts the detectives must write about so extensively. Flynn mentions the "unfortunate murder" in her eulogy, which could be considered daring, but she does so to commiserate with others in their sense of "shock." Notice, though, that she doesn't say that Mark Smith "died" or "croaked" or was "offed"; okay, clearly "croaked" and "offed" are too indelicate, but why not "died," which seems innocuous enough? She writes of Mark's "untimely demise," which is a *euphemism*. When people replace a word that can be considered offensive, discomforting, or controversial with another term to make it seem less so, they have chosen a *euphemism*. Death provides an excellent example of something that makes us uncomfortable, and so we have many euphemistic synonyms for dying such as "to pass on," "to leave this world," "to be with God," "to breathe one's last," and "to go to a better place." Interestingly enough, we have many irreverent synonyms for dying in addition to "croak," such as "to kick the bucket," "to bite the big one," "to push up the daisies," or "to buy the farm," which are *colloquial* and try to bring humor to this bother some subject. *Colloquial* refers to language that is informal and usually spoken but not written (such as "ain't" and "gonna"). These particular death *colloquialisms* can also be considered *dysphemisms* in that they exaggerate rather than soften what could be offensive. While colloquialisms and dysphemisms usually do not belong in academic writing, euphemism can serve its purpose depending on your tone.

But enough talk about talk. Let's get back to the writing. Adi Baruch wrote her eulogy in the form of letter (also known as an *epistle*) to Mark Smith, which is a bit of a departure from the genre in its strictest sense, but she nevertheless avoids mentioning anything about the murder while still conveying that he has, well, left us: "Whoever knew quite how cruel life could be? Surely, neither you nor I. We've known each other for the past ten years, always growing closer. Unfortunately enough, for me and many others,[3] your life has come to an end. We can no longer continue to make great memories together. . . . Your memory will live on with every life you've ever touched." Does your eulogy sound like this? Is it written in first-person, is it evasive of specifics but generally positive, is the diction a bit stilted and the tone sentimental, wistful, and poignant? Does yours, like hers, eventually end with saying good-bye to the deceased (aka the dead person)?

Or does your eulogy sound more like this one from Micheal Lynch:

> For those of you who knew Mark Smith as I did, I am sure you are not the least bit surprised to hear that he was murdered and quite violently with multiple stab wounds. Mark was our friend and our benefactor, but of course we all know he was a low-life criminal. With the number of enemies Mark made, I'm sure that the only surprise is that it took them until 10:37 p.m. on Saturday, June 6th to catch up with his sorry butt. It is ironic, you must agree, that he "bought it" in a parking garage since the only thing he ever did in a parking garage is rip off the things that everybody who parked there had brought! Yes, we'll miss you Mark and those little surprises he used to bring to each of us. Rest in peace, buddy!

When we read this one aloud in class, much laughter broke out. Why is it funny? Because it runs contrary to our established expectations, and incongruity is often a source of humor. The students recognized that while Lynch conforms to the rhetorical conventions of eulogy— he writes in first-person, remembers the deceased fondly, and says goodbye—he also works against the conventions of the genre in terms of content, diction, and tone. In short, this incongruity makes the piece ironic, which Lynch might be trying to flag when he points to the situational irony of the location of the murder.

I imagine that Lynch, like many students, assumed he had to work in all "five-facts" and saw his way to a very creative solution; knowing that such facts don't belong in a eulogy and wanting to respond to the assignment as he interpreted it, Lynch turned the genre on its head. He showed savvy in writing it and his classmates in laughing at it, for they all recognized how much one can push or play with a given genre and still maintain its identifiable qualities. The content is graphic, the diction is crass, and the tone is irreverent. Nonetheless, it remains a eulogy, one that would likely get recited among friends (but not family) with shots of whiskey in hand. Herein we might find our definition of *genre,* which by necessity remains perpetually loose: when the traits or attributes considered normal to or typical of a particular kind of creative piece, such as in literature, film, or music, make it that kind and not another. For example, we know horror films when we see them and we recognize classical music when we hear it because we can classify these things according to the conventions of their genres. And we can identify the genre of the piece I am writing for you as an expository essay with its thesis, its body paragraphs of support and detail, and, as you will see, its conclusion, even if my tone is playful.

Whether or not Mark Smith was a low-life, petty thief as Lynch makes him out to be, the person who murdered him is most definitely a criminal, which brings us to our last rhetorical scenario. Your final task is to write a closing argument as if you were the prosecutor addressing the jury who will find the accused murderer guilty or not. Go ahead. Put on a suit and become a lawyer (in this profession, if you are not off researching you are usually writing), and then come back to see how your closing argument compares with the others.

LEARNING TO LOVE YOUR INNER LAWYER

Notice how I kindly provided a big clue to get you started, since you've had so much to think about already. When you wrote the eulogy I did not call attention to the fact that your audience was friends and family, for whom you wrote nonetheless, but here I do remind you that you were to address the jury. This is your signal not to soften the blow of the loss of Mark Smith for your audience, as you did in the eulogy, but to write it big, to write it bold . . . perhaps to the point where you could be accused of exaggeration (in writing aka *hyperbole*). You must play upon your audience's heartstrings here, too, of course, but you must balance it with cold, hard, irrefutable facts as per the genre's demands. How did you begin?

Despite my clue, only some of your peers start their closing arguments as Christopher Traina and Ricardo Ataide did with the requisite and respectful "ladies and gentlemen of the jury" (Traina did admit that both of his parents are attorneys, but it is unlikely he attends any of the closing arguments they might make!). What effect does this address have? It alerts the members of the jury that what follows is directed specifically to them, reminds them of their important role, and helps to establish a rapport between them and the attorney. The closing argument is a good example of how the different rhetorical tools available carry different weight given the rhetorical situation. Although awareness of audience is always hugely important when one goes to write anything, a direct address is not, which we see with the lack thereof in the detective's and coroner's reports. They write for an *implied audience* (as you do in your academic writing), which is more often than not comprised of attorneys and, funnily enough, eventually of judges and juries (which is why their work is ultimately forensic). Furthermore, when it comes time to communicate to the jury how Mark Smith was murdered, the attorney would do best to translate the medical jargon of the coroner's report into *layperson's terms,* or language for people who are not experts; plain, simple diction would prevail over sophisticated jargon in this context. And while the detective's and the coroner's reports should be devoid of emotion, just as the eulogy should be saturated with it, the attorney aims to persuade the jury with both objective facts, what Aristotle calls *logos,* and simmering emotion, what he calls *pathos;* and lastly, depending on the lawyer, the jury will also likely be persuaded by his/her *ethos,* or credible character.

Appealing to his jury in first person, Traina states for "what reasons" the "accused" committed the "heinous murder . . . you and I will never know. But I do ask you to do what is right. That is when you go to deliberate, you remember the grieving family. Remember the horrendous photos. Remember the lack of emotion on the accused's face. You must remember all of these facts, find the defendant guilty, and put him in jail where he will not be a danger to society. I thank you for your time and hope for your diligence in [reaching] your verdict." Traina charges the jury with the moral duty to do what is right based on the evidence provided while he also beseeches them—in short sentences of parallel form that one can imagine him articulating very slowly and deliberately—to dwell not only on the family's agony but on the defendant's lack of remorse. This *appeal to emotion* (aka *pathos*) doesn't alter the facts per se, but it provides a less than neutral lens, a *bias,* through which the attorney hopes the jury will view them (although in academic writing one is often encouraged to avoid such bias). The tone Traina establishes is one full of urgency and gravity for the case and also of reverence for the jury, whom he thanks at the end and so maintains the rapport he initially established.

You might find that your closing argument reads so much like Traina's that they can be considered "generic" closing arguments. Or maybe you went the route that Ataide did, which is to highlight the significant points of the investigation as you constructed a summary— a conclusion. Ataide looked a bit at the criminal mind of the defendant who "harbored feelings of despair and hatred for quite some time" before murdering his former professor, all of which are documented "in his emails and Twitter updates." Ataide concludes his argument by directly reminding the jury that while the professor "will never again teach a class, you have the opportunity to teach the accused, Lucas Brown, a lesson here today. A conviction should be your only choice." This clever twist on teaching a lesson provides eloquent *closure* to his argument.

Or perhaps you, like Chelsea Vick, felt mounting drama to be the most persuasive approach. She tells the jury that "the defendant has not only physically stabbed my client Mark Smith; he has stabbed the judicial system. Every entrance wound on my victim's body is another blow to the system our government runs on." She, like Traina, conjures up fear with the prospect of returning such a person to the streets, and she, too, "leaves you [the jury] to deliberate whether to send a murderer to jail or to another parking garage." By making reference to the "system our government runs on," Vick plays with the sometimes subtle line between the *connotation* and *denotation* of words. What a word *denotes* is its literal definition or what you would find should you look it up in the dictionary, but words have *connotations,* too, which are the emotional associations, positive or negative, we bring to them. While an apple pie denotes a dessert made of sliced apples and sugar baked in a single or double flour crust, in the United States it can also conjure up positive emotions about home and/or patriotism about country. We imagine apple pies to be lovingly-baked by apron-clad moms who raise citizens who are, well, as the saying goes, "as American as apple pie." Vick's comment that the defendant has metaphorically "stabbed the judicial system" in addition to Mark Smith is meant to produce negative connotations beyond the actual murder; she conjures up the looming threat that our entire way of life would be at stake should the jury do anything other than convict the defendant.

If we envision in our minds the passionate delivery of these closing arguments, we might imagine that we have finally come close to the first definition of "rhetoric" that the *American Heritage Dictionary* online offers us, which is "the art or study of using language effectively and persuasively," rather than that one-word definition my brave student once proffered. Yes, our attorneys all did perform admirably in their endeavors to persuade the jury with their words, but we find examples of effective rhetoric in all of the writing scenarios we have considered.

Here I offer my definition: *rhetoric* is what allows you to write (and speak) appropriately for a given situation, one that is determined by the expectations of your *audience,* implied or acknowledged, whether you are texting, writing a love letter, or bleeding a term paper. When you go to write, you might not always be actively aware of your audience *as* an audience. You may not even consciously realize that you are enacting certain rhetorical strategies while rejecting others. But each time you write you will find yourself in a *rhetorical situation,* in other words within a *context* or *genre,* that nudges you to choose the right *diction* or even *jargon* and to strike the right *tone.* In this essay, I put you in three rhetorical situations for which you have no formal training—writing hypothetically as if you were a detective, a coroner, and a lawyer—and you knew what to do, as you did with the eulogy. This shows the extent to which we absorb and internalize our rhetorical tools by watching media, reading books, and participating in our culture. More importantly, you can now see that when I told you at the beginning that you are already in possession of the rhetorical skills necessary for mastering the genre of academic writing and that you need only apply them, I wasn't just feeding you a bunch of bull.

DISCUSSION

1. Which of the exercises did you find easiest to write? Why?
2. Which of the exercises did you find hardest to write? Why?
3. What does the rhetorical situation of academic writing demand? Who is the audience? What tone is appropriate? What jargon might be needed? What information might be included and/or rejected in an academic paper?

NOTES

1. Oddly enough, my moment of inspiration came when I got on a bus to commute to New York City and found myself sitting next to the famous author and columnist Anna Quindlen. Thanks, Anna!

2. While coroners are forensic scientists, the terms are not exactly synonymous, for forensic actually means "legal," and a forensic scientist can be anyone in the discipline who gathers evidence of interest in legal matters.

3. And I would add, unfortunately for Mark, too!

WORK CITED

"Rhetoric." *The American Heritage Dictionary of the English Language, Fourth Edition*. 2003. Houghton Mifflin Company, n.d. Web. 24 July 2009.

The Complexity of Simplicity: Invention Potentials for Writing Students

Colin Charlton

[T]he "format" of this piece—it goes against what I've been taught: to keep things orderly and clump ideas together. This piece is my way of taking everything that has been fumbling around in my mind and putting it on paper. Essentially, this is my brain splattered in ink and words on the paper before you. This is my baby-step attempt at experimentation. I am "painting a picture with words,"... as cliché as that may sound.

—*Brittany Ramirez, "My Written Mess," Reflective Portfolio Cover Letter, English 1301-Rhetoric & Composition I*

This is a chapter for you if you're in a first year writing class right now and this thought has recently crossed your mind: *What am I going to write?*[*] I hope it helps you do two things: (1) realize everyday potentials you have to write something unexpected, and (2) realize that, rather than one strategy, you can and should develop many writing strategies that work during the course of a writing class. When we face a new writing situation, regardless of its origin, we want direction. We crave instruction. "Just tell me what you want!" is not a cry owned solely by

One part of the brain attacks another,
seven parts attack nine parts,
then the war begins to subside
from lack of ammunition,
but out there I know the mules are bringing
fresh supplies from over the mountain.
--Jim Harrison,
Poem 8 from the *After Ikkyū* cycle

light cyan

7/8 qt vodka
1 T glycerin
1 T propylene glycol
powdered pigment,
a blender, and aseptic training

--ingredients, tools, and
suggestions by
Anne Marie Helmenstine,
"mix Your Own Tattoo Ink,"
About.com: Chemistry

freshmen writers, but one felt and repeated by anyone who struggles with a fresh scene. In the unfamiliar territory of a research project that begins with a question instead of an already known answer, we still hope for a light at the end of the research and writing tunnel. The trick is to find ways to keep the struggle going, to make manageable the hard work of writing, reading, and re-seeing what we've created in light of new questions we cannot foresee.

I'm talking about invention, or how we bring a variety of ideas and/or objects together to make a meaning that is more than the sum of its parts. If you find a confident writer in a room full of doubt, chances are you've found someone who has figured out through trial and error how to invent as a writer. In the following pages, then, you will find a variety of strategies for coming up with ideas based on real students and their writing. These won't be plug-and-play strategies. Instead, they enact philosophies for invention that you can adapt to your writing situations. You will also find a critical look at the writing classroom and how you can bring ideas of invention into it. This blend of reflection and action, of theory and practice, of thinking and doing, is the *praxis,* or practice, of writing. This essay is, simply put, a demonstration and an invitation to transform the uncertainty of *What am I going to write?* into an opportunity to make new connections between texts, people, and ideas. Throughout the essay and the visual essay that is embedded in the following pages, you'll get to hear from students who experimented with invention, both in terms of their major writing projects and their reflections on our work together. Erika, Adbe, Ozzy, and Brittany's work and ideas, I think, illustrate the challenge and the reward of a writing class that emphasizes potentials over outcomes.

. . . College

The first year of college is about making stuff up.

Maybe that's a brash way to describe a time that is hyped by universities, held sacred by the extended families of first-generation college students, and analyzed by faculty whose bread and butter is in teaching *required* classes. Still, I'm willing to bet that it's part of a larger truth about how new college students learn to survive higher education initiations. I remember doing it myself in the early '90s, and I see my students doing it every year. You develop new ways to resist what you don't like or don't think you can handle. You find quasi-ritualistic ways to handle too much studying mixed with too little sleep. If you're ever in the market for memory aids and survival advice, don't consult the teachers you see a few times a week—they haven't been in the college trenches for a while. Go visit a dorm hall full of new engineering students, and you'll soon be exposed to a hotbed of coping and studying strategies that will leave you dizzy.

Gerald Graff, a well known English professor and author, borrowed a concept from social psychology, cognitive dissonance, to describe what new students experience at a university as they move from class to class, teacher to teacher, worldview to worldview, and theory to theory, with no one doing a very good job helping them see any connective tissue among the competing ideas. Such a dissonant environment breeds a divide-and-conquer strategy—find out what one teacher wants, deliver the goods, move on to the next teacher. To be fair, there is an intelligent type of adaptation that emerges from doing this, but also a practical one that works at keeping ideas segregated by class and subject area. Even in that setting, students are constantly "making stuff up," socially as well as intellectually. You have found, or will find, supportive peer groups; you'll create reasons to keep reading an article or book when you're struggling to see its personal relevance; you'll mark out favorite places on campus for study, for talk, for pause. Perhaps the one universalizing constant at every college campus I've seen is that students inject their identity into the surroundings—in the tinny music we catch from passing headphones, on organizational flyers, through fashion, in questions, even during the occasional foray into the teacher-space of a classroom or office. These moves—*your* moves—like any moves in an unfamiliar place, are full of stutters, dodges, successes, and hopeful repetitions; but through them, critical social and intellectual patterns emerge. And if invention happens everywhere at college, why not make it work for us in the writing classroom?

One way of engaging your inventiveness rather than choosing to sit back, modeling passivity by invoking that tried and tired excuse of apathy is to consciously imagine a different kind of writing class, one we can better understand if we think of it in terms of three questions being negotiated from the point of view of the teacher, the project, and you, the student. At minimum, you have a teacher who is trying to strike an odd balance between guiding you and prescribing to you.

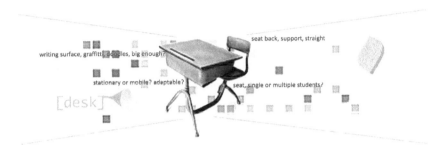

TEACHER: How can I best help students without doing the work for them?

You have a project your teacher has assigned, full of potential, that exists between the teacher and you. Even though its voice is a quiet one, it is still asking a question of both teacher and student.

PROJECT: How do I reflect what the teacher values and make a space where students, as writers, can creatively resist, enact, adapt, and experiment with those values?

And there's you, the student, who needs to figure out the answer to the following question before you can take on any project with confidence and creativity.

STUDENT: How do I make this writing matter for me?

. . . College → First Year Writing

These three questions mark the productive dissonance of the first year writing class you're in right now. It is a complicated, transitional space for you as you experiment with new networks of places, people, and identity. If you surveyed your class about their attitudes towards reading and writing—and I do every semester, every class—I bet the majority would describe in great detail how they aren't good writers, how they're easily bored by readings they don't choose, and how they struggle with writing intensive classes because of the pressure *and* the lack of control they promise. Do you see yourself in one or more of those answers? We all know this writing and reading stuff is important, but it's rare to find many students who can articulate that importance in their own terms, in the contexts of their lives. My guess is that, over the years, you've heard more people preaching the abstract importance of writing in your life than fostering invention.

Perfect example: you're in a class and find out over half the class hasn't read an assigned reading or prepared a complete draft of a writing project. Does your teacher get mad and reprimand your class, and make a case for why the work should've been done? Do disengaged students hide while prepared students silently seethe? I don't find these situations, and the assumptions about student intent that underly them, very helpful. Instead, imagine if the students and teacher could figure out how to make the situation work, how to invent a moment for learning with what is readily available, how to bang two rocks together and try to make a spark.

Invention Potential 1: Less Can Be More

Let's try that, banging two rocks together, first with reading. You didn't read and prepare for class today. Whether it was too many hours at work or too many other things due in your other classes, something just had to give, and you let the reading go for your writing class. But you have a few minutes before class to pull something together. You have the reading, you have some paper and a pen or a laptop, and you have the course syllabus. Take five minutes, and make them count. Quickly answer these questions.

- What is the title of the reading? In general, what is the abstract (the summary paragraph that may precede the article) or the first paragraph talking about?
- What is the title and subtitle of your class? What goals has the teacher identified for you and the class (now often found in lists called Goals for Instruction or Student Learning Outcomes)?

- What is one idea or question you can think of that connects the assigned reading to at least one of the goals you found in the syllabus?

Even if you don't feel like sharing your idea or posing your question in class, it's an opening connection that you've made in your own words. It's a start at writing your way into the class as opposed to letting the class always be written for you. This is writing and invention potentials helping you make sense of a class meeting, and we haven't even begun to work with a formal writing assignment.

Let's consider a situation where you were thinking about writing—there will be a day when something is due and either you're not happy with what you've brought to class, or your teacher sees your work as incomplete, or both. But since writing is a process filled with successes and failures, those days when drafts are due or some kind of writing deadline has arrived, I try to make space for a workshop that can help everyone in the room, from those with nothing to show to those with too much. We circle up, one circle inside another, a set of ten to fifteen workshop partners. You get five minutes to explain what you wrote, what you were trying to do, and how this meets the demands of the assignment. And you need to prompt some feedback from your partner—*What do you think? Does it make sense? What's your favorite part of my writing? What would you like to see developed in my next revision? What question do I make you think of with my writing?* Ten minutes and an exchange later, we switch partners and repeat until class time is over. Very simple setup, and it doesn't matter if you have confusion, an unwritten idea, or something of a draft. After one of these speedback sessions (where feedback meets speed-dating), and regardless of whether you started with less or more, you will have likely clarified your goals and learned about how your peers are trying to meet theirs.

I make room for these sessions on a regular basis, but you can do the same outside of class. Speedbacking requires a place, a timer, any

brick flyers

work/ideas you have prepared for class, and some time set aside before a class when a piece of writing is due. You can organize this type of feedback in small groups of students, meet in a comfortable environment, and push each other to listen and respond to each other's writing quickly. It will be less stressful than sitting blank in front of a monitor for hours.

Feedback activities depend on your desire to connect—ideas, people, pieces of writing. They do not depend on imposed trips to writing centers, complicated workshop setups, reading quizzes, or any number of things writers find themselves doing to make sure work is getting done. And when you can find feedback strategies you enjoy, you will find ways to make invention part of the real writing you experience every day instead of relegating it to solitary places outside of class where we often think preliminary and catch-up work has to be done.

The trick here is that in college, especially in writing- and reading-intensive classes, you can take control of getting started and getting feedback by creating a student network willing to talk to each other about their ideas, their potentials, for a writing assignment. You may feel blocked, but maybe you just need several other perspectives on what you're thinking. And if you can create a speedback situation, or some other feedback stratgey that happens while you're writing and not just after a deadline, you're more likely to feel like you're responding to real questions and not just an assignment.

. . . College → First Year Writing → Objects of Study

Increasing opportunities for feedback helps you tap into your emerging networks and invent compelling writing projects—ones that blend your interests with what your teacher wants from you according to your assignment, ones that create intriguing experiences and arguments for public audiences, and often look like. . . . Well, over the years, I've seen T-shirts, board games, bracelets, student-designed care packages, photo essays, house blueprints, even a letter to college students, divided into seven paragraphs and hung from trees all over campus. All very original, these student projects were created in first semester college writing classes, their authors' ages ranging from sixteen to fifty-six, with experiences from Central Mexico to Northern Indiana. With that in mind, I want to turn to some course documents, while bringing in some student voices, and a couple of extended examples so that, with this rich context, you can see the potential for re-thinking how you can generate ideas in a first year writing class.

Invention Potential 2: Displacing Focus with Rhetorical Drift

As I think through the types of projects I've made room for over the years, it strikes me that even if we just think about the ones I listed above, they seem to be a pretty loose group. Not much holding them together. So far this essay of philosophizing mixed with examples might make you think that I let my students write anything they want and that I'm encouraging you, as well, to write anything you want; in other words, trading rules for freedom. I don't think writers have to choose one over the other. I don't think you can. If I try to convince you to write whatever you want, I'm using a traditional strategy for engaging students: your choice, your interests, your whatever. But any writing choice is a *choice*. At the end of a semester, Adbe Guerrero, a former student, taught me about the positions that expertise and choice occupied in relation to his experiences, my teaching, and one of our later readings:

> I have begun to notice that all of my [question and response papers] are negative. Ha, well, I don't plan on stopping. Throughout our last reading, the authors talk about "nurturing creativity" and I suppose this isn't something I'm used to since most of my teachers didn't give a rat's ass about what the students had to say. It was always what they wanted. . . . In your class I had so much more freedom to write the way I wanted and made my voice be heard the way I wanted it to be (rude and realistic). Personally, I can't stand being polite in my papers because, if there is something that irritates me, I want to be able to express it the way I would when I'm speaking to an individual in person. But in high school they wouldn't allow anything close to that.

In class, I do talk about and privilege rhetorical choices rather than impose top-down requirements. Adbe frames our class in terms of voice and choice (and he's quite aware of the choices he's making for his preferred written voice and the limits they have in other situations), but his comments and the range of work students might complete in first year writing courses is a challenge to that most misunderstood of misunderstood writing-teacher-terms: focus. You can't easily find the focus of what my students are writing while I'm busy pushing invention.

That's by design.

Regardless of how traditional your experience with writing instruction has been, the idea of focus is inescapable. Even though I shy away from talk of focus at the beginning of a project, it's natural to crave it. We often see the amount of focus as a corollary to the quality of the writing. Both students and teachers want goals, and we should have them. They inspire, direct, and demarcate. But when our goals be-

come expressed by questions like *How many words? How many pages? How many sources?*, we've let the goals displace writing as learning and invention. We have to balance our need to know with our desire to understand. Then we can offset the obstacle of focus and try to generate cohesion in writing through experimentation and drift. So why not ask: *How many new ideas should we come up with for this writing project?*

I'm introducing words here like *experiment, invention,* and *drift,* so I should explain what they mean in this context. I want writers who leave me behind early in their college careers to be able to analyze and adapt to the writing situations they will face after my class. If we believe that there is one type of academic discourse that college authorities value and that we should try to use as a model, you end up learning a long list of rhetorical moves, sentence types, written tones, etc. It may be quite a long list, but it's still defined by an ideal type of writing. There are a lot of reasons not to believe in an ideal type of writing. We're not sure if, and to what extent, writing skills transfer from one class to another. You may have teachers from multiple generations who may have very different ideas about how people should write at a university. And your ideas about good writing need an invitation to the party because, otherwise, teachers risk stagnation in their own ideas as writing experts and writing teachers.

Faced with these realities, you can make room to test the effects of different ways of writing (experiment), combine seemingly disconnected forms of writing (invention), and even try to be open to that which you can't predict or control as writers (drift). In the context of the project sequence I use, I want to share an example from Brittany Ramirez, the student quoted in the epigraph for this chapter, as she works with what Adbe calls *freedom* of my projects, what I think of as *inventive potential*. While Erika, Adbe, and Ozzy will chime in about the class and their work in the images I bring in throughout the essay, I want to discuss a sequence of three projects by Brittany to highlight how you can work with experimentation and drift as alternatives to a more focused writing sequence. I think Brittany's work is a compelling example of how subtle and measured the shifts can be as a writing project develops. And you'll see how what begins for her as a default essay becomes a mock-up of an ACT exam reading passage with questions.

Invention Potential 3: If You Can Ask WHY?, You're a Theorist

The first part of a writing sequence that revolves around invention begins with one of three projects. In Project 1-Breaking Ice, I explain our goals this way:

> To start a conversation with each of you about this project, I would start with some questions: *How did you get here? What do you want? How do you think you're going to get it?* Then, after we talked for a long time, I would say, *So what does all that have do with writing and/or learning?*
>
> See, I'm not sure how you think writing happens or how learning works, and I want to know about your theories even while we are reading other people's ideas. I also don't think that "writing" and "learning" are easily defined, or that they

happen only in classrooms, or that we always have control over what we write and what we learn. . . . **For this project, then, I want you to create a *text* in which you explain a theory you have about writing and learning.** You'll have to come up with (1) a real question you have about your experiences with writing and learning, (2) an idea of what a project about that question could look like, and (3) a way to answer (1) and create (2). To begin the project and get the gears turning, I already asked everyone to write in class about the strangest piece of writing they ever did (see the blog notes on day one). After you write about and we discuss your ideas for Project 1 as a whole class, we'll also discuss potential audiences and purposes based on who you think is invested in the question driving your project.

Beginning with Project 1, I ask students to explain the forms they chose for their theory of how writing and learning work. A student could, for instance, write a manifesto to their high school writing teachers calling for an end to test-teaching. We can imagine a letter to parents about how they taught you to learn and how you're working with strategies at college. Maybe we can even imagine writing a profile to a teacher explaining how a particular type of student works best. I don't get much of that, regardless of how many examples I throw out. I get "essays" and student explanations that the essays do what essays do. Totally normal, especially when I get a summary of the essay rather than an explanation of how a student crafted it and wanted it to work. Here are excerpts from an early draft of Brittany's Project 1 that emerged from her response writing. She decided to test the connections between her experiences in high school and in our class. Worth noting is that, without my direct prompting, she and several students began to blend characteristics from their question and response papers into their longer projects, a good sign that they were testing how the familiar meshed with the strange.

Brittany Ramirez
English 1301.02s1–09
6.14.09
Project 1

Q: If you can comprehend difficult material (i.e. Downs & Wardle Article), does that affect your writing capability?

Merely a Misconception

From the elementary level to secondary schooling, educators are consistent upon the insistence that their students read more because it will help improve their vocabulary, writing, etc. School districts have even gone as far as instituting incentive programs in order to encourage reading (i.e. Accelerated Reader or A.R.) or otherwise force it on students. However, the question here is, does reading more really help; and if so, does reading more difficult material play a role in one's writing level?

. . . I believe that one's writing can be improved through reading and that in some part, your reading level does affect your writing capability, but it is not always the case. Different people learn differently. Writing requires practice all on its own in order to better oneself at it and requires the reading of not just more difficult pieces but a multitude of pieces. In order to improve one's writing one needs to be exposed to different varieties of writing in order to hone the ability of comprehension. Everyone has their own method and style of writing, however no one style of writing is original. It is just like art, an artist can no longer claim their work to be original because everything has been done before. What can be done is to take what others have given us and use it to our advantage; learn from it.

As Brittany tries to work out the relationship between reading and writing, the tension that strikes me is between her idea of how art blends original work with old work and how that might contribute to "universal characteristics." She talked in her blog and in-group workshops about how reading about writing studies challenged her to think more about what happened to us in class on a daily basis. She was hyper-reflective, and as a result, she turned to look more closely at pre-college testing, the place where reading and writing ability get measured without an explanation for how they link or work together.

What she's concerned with are values. She's asking *Why?* I would argue that this is a writer's job, this is your job as a first year writing student, almost in any context. Whether you come out and try to answer that question in a piece of writing, or deep down it's the reason you started a writing project at all, a writer who has a question tugging away at the gray areas, memories, and experiences is a writer who is inventing possible solutions. What makes Brittany a good example here is that she doesn't stop from expressing her belief. She's not backing away from engaging me and her peers with her value system, even though it will certainly mean more discussion, negotiation, and revision.

Invention Potential 4: Finding a Question before an Answer

For Project 2-Questioning Writing (Studies), I asked students to build out of their Project 1:

> Think about how your interests connect to the field of writing studies we've been reading, blogging, talking, and thinking about. What I want you to do for Project 2 is to develop a question you have related to writing studies as we are coming to understand it through our work so far in English 1301. Once we've discussed that question in several ways—class discussion, peer review, blog postings and comments—you'll investigate that question, and then write a report of your investigation in which you will:
>
> - Explain how you came to the question, why it is important, and what it involves;
> - Describe how you investigated it, both in terms of the strengths of your design and its limitations;
> - Discuss your findings and their significance for one or more invested stakeholders, and brainstorm about possible

> ways to adapt what you've learned by investigating Project
> 2 to a public Project 3 that puts your findings and your
> theories about reading, writing, and/or learning to work.

Brittany looked at a specific test she had experience with so that: 1) she
could draw from her experience; 2) she could quickly work through
relevant testing information and materials; 3) and she could manage
a small amount of materials while trying to explore her questions further. At this point in her process, I even suggested she focus on one
type of testing question rather than risk generalizing about all tests
and measurements of student ability. At this point, I felt comfortable
that she had roamed widely in our class readings and her own research
to understand how deep the rabbit hole of writing studies went. Her
title: "Extreme Makeover: ACT Edition." Here is a taste of her essay's
introduction and conclusion:

> In the educational universe there is a perpetual cycle: High
> school, the dawn of junior/senior year, then the counselors and
> their persistent hounding "Have you signed up for your ACT/
> SAT . . . make sure to sign up!" College Entrance Exams:
> what exactly do these three words entail? To some, they are
> the factor that will basically determine the rest of their lives.
> The question I pose, however, is: Does the ACT accurately
> determine (i.e. my) readiness for college level courses, in this
> case, in terms of English?
> . . . These tests assume "writing is writing," as stated in the
> Downs and Wardle article "Teaching about Writing, Righting
> Misconceptions: (Re)Envisioning 'First Year Composition' as
> 'Introduction to Writing Studies.'" Downs and Wardle point
> out that "The content-versus-form misconception—as old as
> FYC itself—appears in standardized testing, with the SAT
> 'writing' test giving better scores to longer essays and com-
> pletely discounting factual errors" (555). This serves as further
> testament to my belief that these tests are inadequate in deter-
> mining one's readiness for college. In college, it is not about
> length, it is about content. While some instances may require
> you to write an essay of a limited word count, it is still what
> you are writing about that is the most important factor. . . .
> It's time for a full-scale renovation.

Brittany is doing a lot of what I want to see in this early draft—making connections between the position in a text and her experiences, tweaking a found challenge to suit her own beliefs, values, and interests, and explaining evidence. She's doing all this as a concurrently enrolled student living in both worlds of "readiness," but she was not an exception in her class. In a mixed class of high school and college students, one thing they learned immediately from the required blog interactions was that their assumed likenesses—as students, as people from the same geographic area, as a class made entirely of students with Hispanic backgrounds—were much less interesting than the differences in how they had experienced public education, writing, and learning.

Reading about Brittany's writing, I don't know how connected you feel to your first year writing class and your writing in it. I do know that you are an expert in experiencing and surviving pre-college education, that you are a reader, that you are a writer, even if you don't like how academics describe those identities. And I know you have questions about your learning, about writing, about reading, and about why you think the way you do about all three. When you find a way to articulate those questions, to make them bridges to how you write or what you have to write about, you are no longer writing and reading because you have to. I think you start writing and reading because you need to.

Invention Potential 5: Adapting Forms as Public Invention

Because the blog helped us re-invent their diversity, Brittany was able to springboard from her Project 2 argument to an application of it in Project 3. In Project 3-Going Public, I asked that students take their ideas from Project 2 and adapt them to a new format that requires them to consider a public audience's desires, needs, limitations, expectations, etc., while experimenting with new forms for their ideas in a public context.

I have to stress here that Brittany was not a closet document designer, a trained graphic artist, or an expert in testing beyond her role as testing subject before our class. For Project 3, she produced a mockup of an ACT exam reading and question set (which I've abbreviated).

DIRECTIONS: The passage in this test is followed by several questions. After reading the passage, choose the best answer to each question and fill in the corresponding oval on your answer document. You may refer to the passage as often as necessary.

Rhetoric & Composition: This passage is adapted from the article "Teaching about Writing, Righting Misconceptions: (Re)Envisioning 'First-Year Composition' as 'Introduction to Writing Studies' by Douglas Downs & Elizabeth Wardle (©2007 by Douglas Downs & Elizabeth Wardle). *This article was part of the required reading curriculum in a first-semester university class (1301: Rhetoric & Composition).

SYSTEMATIC MISCONCEPTION AND MISDIRECTION OF MAINSTREAM FYC

A number of assumptions inform the premise that academic writing is somehow universal: writing can be considered independent of content; writing consists primarily of syntactic and mechanical concerns; and academic writing skills can be taught in a one or two introductory general writing skills courses and transferred easily to other courses. . . . Despite research demonstrating the complexity of writing, misconceptions persist and inform FYC courses around the country that attempt to teach "academic discourse."

1. What "assumptions," as stated by Downs & Wardle have become common misconceptions of writing?
    a. That writing mainly deals with grammatical concerns and has nothing to do with content.
    b. Writing is merely to do with content.
    c. Writing varies between focusing on content and syntactics.
    d. That writing is both content and mechanics.
. . .
2. Write a short explanation (about 4–5 sentences) in which you discuss the significance of Downs & Wardle's argument to a first-year college student.

Study Guide

Students will be given a passage with a set of questions in which they will decipher the answer. The main difference in this adaptation is the alteration in passage material being tested on. The testing procedures are the same, but the questions being asked are ones that will test on whether or not the test-taker comprehends the material.

In #5 for example, the reader is asked to put pen to paper and answer the question that will be graded on a scale of 1–4 purely on content. The resulting score will determine if the student fully comprehends this piece and can incorporate it into a situation that they will possibly face going into first-year English in college.

If students are tested over material that they will witness in an actual college class, such as the Downs & Wardle article, not only are they exposed to it, but it gives them a view into what an actual college course and its professor is going to want to see from them as students.

The exam allows students to "get their feet wet" in writing, well, about *writing*. In FYC, the focus is mainly that, so this gives them an idea as to what to expect and what will be expected of them in terms of writing. This being a writing exam, having actual questions that require written responses makes more sense. Scores will more accurately reflect the college-capability of the test-taker.

Brittany questioned the form and function of a test, so it made sense for her to try and create one that met her goals. In the end, she created what we might now call an example of high school and college alignment—an exam in high school that might have prepared her for our college writing class. It is wishful thinking, but classmates were prompted to talk about how to approach tests that they needed to take but didn't agree with, and my colleagues and I learned that alignment discussions can be had among all stakeholders, rather than among teachers and administrators alone.

Looking back at where Brittany started, I hope you can see that what matters here is not *only* having a defined audience as a writer. Depending on your project, your audience may occur to you or develop at any time of your writing process. What matters here is that

Ⴘ *antimony*

I never really paid much attention to the education system, which I'm part of, until now. I would go to school and was a good student overall because I had the grades to prove it. It didn't cross my mind that education could be flawed. Currently, I'm more aware about the subject and can easily say that the education system is poorly structured. If only I knew what I know now back then I would have been different today. I would be the boy in class who always had something to say about everything, eventually getting on the teacher's last nerve.

—Ozzy Ozuna, Project 3 Reflection

Sir,
The following content is a fair warning of what is to come. While you are sitting in the calm of high school or summer vacation, the storm of college is brewing, moving towards you at great speed. Some will be prepared and some... won't be prepared. For the few that are ready, I commend you on your hard work in your AP classes and other college preparation courses. Those who will face it unprepared, don't be discouraged. With determination you will face this storm head on and overcome its towering power. For those who struggled through their previous education and felt incompetent compared to other students—do not feel alone because I was once in your shoes. *There will be many changes.*
—Adbe Guerrero, "The Silence Dogood Letter for College Freshmen"

Brittany went through real re-vision in terms of her audience. Writing about her ideas several times, in a variety of situations, and with a lot of feedback, she found a form that made sense for what she had to say. And she thought about saying it to different people along the way. If you want to create a document that can engage people who care about your issue/idea/question, you should experiment writing for different audiences so that you develop a sense of adaptation.

. . . College → First Year Writing → Objects of Study → Reflection

Is Brittany's version of an ACT passage and questions "college writing?" Did she invent something useful, creative, and challenging? I would suggest here that the thinking and experimentation that go into adapting an argumentative essay to a mock ACT test require not that you think outside the box. Rather, you will need to re-draw the lines of the box itself by recognizing a potential for writing and then negotiating that potential with your writing teachers. There are still issues Brittany can address in her reasoning, in surface choices, in organization, changes that matter to her because she is trying to make an unforeseen form work for a variety of interested parties—herself as writer, me as her writing teacher, her peers in high school and college who face testing situations that seriously affect their lives and outlooks. The unforeseen form in this example makes those issues negotiable for both of us. We are able to write ourselves and our values into the project, and I think we are both better off for the experience.

I hope that Erika, Adbe, Ozzy, Brittany, and I have helped you see that you have something insightful to say, that you can now find interesting ways to share these insights quickly and meaningfully in university settings, and that first year writing is a rich beginning and not a mysterious necessity. And these insights depend on considering a variety of forms during all stages of a project rather than letting one formula or a desire for focus overcome the openness of an initiating question.

The ease of familiarity and the intrinsic value of focus, in the end, may be two of the most damaging myths we need to re-invent in a writing classroom. As my students, my colleagues, and I continue to think about and create new types of hybrid texts, we invite you to see where our curiosity leads us. Coming in Spring 2011, you can find more projects and contexts online at http://redrawingthelines.blogspot.com/.

DISCUSSION

1. What are the three questions the author says are negotiated that you need to be aware of when engaging in invention activities? How do these questions move you to consider unusual perspectives? Do theses questions work for you? Could you rewrite them so they work more efficiently for your circumstances, for a particular assignment?

2. What are the six potentials the author talks about in the title? How would you define these potentials in terms practical to your own writing? Which of these would you be moved to try/ consider first?

3. The author uses sequence connectors throughout, such as this final one: . . . College → First Year Writing → Objects of Study → Reflection. What does this mean to you in the context of this essay? How would you juxtapose these sequences to the rest of the sections of the essay (the potentials for invention)? How could you use this sequence to inform how you approach writing in courses other than first year writing or freshman English?

4. Which of the student authors do you most relate to? Why? What, if anything, specifically moved you to inspiration, perhaps to try a similar process or seek a similar epiphany?

5. Does the author talk about college writing that you know— something that is familiar to you? Are you uncomfortable with the methods the author talks about? Why? Are you intrigued by the author's ideas about invention? What do you want to try first in your own project—which invention strategy do you

think will move you forward toward creativity and perhaps, eventually, focus?

NOTE

1. I created the images for *inSights,* the visual essay throughout the essay, but I have to give special thanks to Jacqueline Casas, a student in the same English 1301 as Brittany and Adbe, who made sure we had readable images of all our whiteboard work. Her skills with a cell phone camera at the end of several classes meant that we could spend class time making connections rather than taking notes.

WORKS CITED

Downs, Douglas, and Elizabeth Wardle. "Teaching about Writing, Righting Misconceptions: (Re)Envisioning 'First Year Composition' as 'Introduction to Writing Studies.'" *CCC* 58.4 (2007): 552–85. Print.

Graff, Gerald. *Beyond the Culture Wars: How Teaching the Conflicts Can Revitalize American Education.* New York: Norton, 1992. Print.

Harrison, Jim. *After Ikkyū and Other Poems.* Boston: Shambhala, 1996. Print.

Helmenstine, Ann Marie. "Mix Your own Tattoo Ink." *About.com.* 22 Sept. 2009. Web. <http://chemistry.about.com/cs/howtos/ht/tattooink.htm>.

Hutchison, Grant, Scott Hutchison, Bill Kennedy, and Andy Monaghan (Frightened Rabbit). "A Modern Leper." *Midnight Organ Fight.* Fat Cat Records, 2008.

Writing "Eyeball To Eyeball": Building A Successful Collaboration

Rebecca Ingalls

INTRODUCTION

"Yesterday, all my troubles seemed so far away."[*] The speaker in the song, "Yesterday," laments his loneliness, but the mastermind behind one of the most successful and most covered songs in music history was actually a team of two individuals: Beatles members John Lennon and Paul McCartney. While they might have made it look easy, and while the rewards were huge, these collaborators worked diligently and systematically to create, share, and merge their ideas into what we know today as "Hey Jude" and "Eleanor Rigby." In one of the later interviews that Lennon did with the mainstream press, he was asked to describe his collaborations with McCartney: "[McCartney] provided a lightness, an optimism, while I would always go for the sadness, the discords, the bluesy notes" (Sheff 136–37). Lennon referred to this process as writing "eyeball to eyeball":

> Like in "I Want to Hold Your Hand," I remember when we
> got the chord that made that song. We were in Jane Asher's
> house, downstairs in the cellar playing on the piano at the
> same time. And we had, "Oh you-uu . . . got that something .
> . ." And Paul hits this chord and I turn to him and say, "That's
> *it!*" I said, "Do that again!" In those days, we really used to
> absolutely write like that—both playing into each other's
> nose. We spent hours and hours and hours . . . We wrote in
> the back of vans together. . . . The cooperation was functional
> as well as musical. (Sheff 137)

In this merging of minds between artists and friends, one would
write a verse, and the other would finish the song; one would start
the "story" of a song, and the other would see the plot through (Sheff
139–40). Ultimately, this collaboration would form the core of a band
that would produce countless number one hits, sell over one billion
records, and reinvent rock and roll ("The Beatles")

For Lennon and McCartney, the writing stakes were high: deadlines, fans, their integrity as musicians, a potentially galactic payout of
profits and stardom. So, it wasn't just casual loafing around and making up songs; it was inspiration and creativity that *had* to happen, or
they wouldn't achieve and sustain the success they hoped for. In order
to create together, they had to establish and rely on some important
elements: an openness to one another's independent interests and experiences, an ability to communicate productive feedback, a trust in
their shared goals. With these components of collaboration working
for them, they were able to establish a process of tuning in to one another's skills and creativity that was so powerful, Lennon could still
remember the moments of inspiration, the words they exchanged, and
the obscure locations where it all happened. Together, in their collaborative song writing, they were an even greater musical force than they
were as solo writers.

In addition to this famous duo, there are many other famous writing collaborations that have produced some celebrated work in popular media: Matt Damon and Ben Affleck (*Good Will Hunting*), Google
co-founders Larry Page and Sergey Brin, Simon and Garfunkel, the
Indigo Girls, Dr. Dre and Snoop Dog, Tina Fey and Amy Poehler,
the Farrelly brothers (*There's Something About Mary*), Larry David and
Jerry Seinfeld. On a global scale, writing teams have produced memorable Presidential speeches, garnered funding to fight worldwide dis-

eases like AIDS, laid down the philosophical foundations of entire nations, and, yes, made hilarious comedy that has resonated across cultures. They have demonstrated over and over again the tremendous advantages of composing together, and the fruits of their collaborative labors are still growing today.

Your writing classroom can be a laboratory for collaborative work. Though you may be most accustomed to writing on your own, the high-impact, innovative possibilities of collaborative writing can spotlight and enhance who you are as an individual, and how creative and original you can be, when you allow your ideas to mix and develop with others' ideas. This chapter aims to encourage and support your collaborations from beginning to end by offering insight and tools that you can use to engage work that is challenging, productive, and even enjoyable. You'll learn about some mindful, structured strategies that focus on planning, communicating, and working with a diversity of perspectives in a group of equal members. You'll also hear from students who—like you—have experienced the ups and downs of composing with others, and who have found something unique in the spirit of working together.

Why collaborate? you might ask. What's in it for me? The collaborative work that you take on now in college prepares you for the challenges of higher stakes teamwork that you will encounter in your professional life. The realms of publishing, medicine, law, scientific research, marketing, sales, education, architecture, engineering, and most others show us that collaborative work, and very often collaborative writing, is key to expressing the voices of employees to one another, creating productive change, following legal protocols, communicating with clients, and producing cutting-edge products. Whether it's the composition of a patient's medical history, a legal brief, a plan for a company's expansion, a proposal for a city playground, an application for federal research funds, the instruction manual for repairing a submarine's navigation system, or a marketing campaign for a new computer, the requirements of many professional writing tasks necessarily call upon a group of people to create, revise, and polish that writing together. The combined efforts of individuals with specific expertise and common goals help to produce the highest quality writing for audiences that expect nothing less.

And, for those of you who have the kind of Lennon-McCartney hopes of making a giant impact on your world, you never know where the ideas of a few smart students working together may lead . . .

GETTING STARTED

As you read, you may be tapping into your memories of group work—some of these memories may be positive, and some may be less so. Some of you may have some memories of collaboration that leave you wondering if it can really work at all; what if a group just can't seem to get it together? How is it possible to make sure each group member carries an equal load? Others may have hopeful memories of a project or two that went well . . . maybe even *really* well. There was a motivation, a synergy, a collective feeling of pride among you. What we remember about our collaborative experiences can shape how we see collaboration now, so it's useful to dig into those memories and reflect on them before you get started. Once we know why we see collaboration in certain ways, and once we share some of those stories, we can begin to create the kind of common ground that collaboration asks for.

Your Experiences Matter

Take some time to think through some of the collaborative work you've done in the past. Without worrying about mechanics or organization—spend fifteen minutes just writing about one or two experiences you've had. After you've spent some time writing, go back and re-read your freewrite, paying careful attention to the emotions you read in your words. Do you see inspiration? Anxiety? Pride? Frustration? Confidence? Confusion? What were the sources of these emotions in your experience? How do they shape the ways in which you view collaboration today?

Now, spend some time thinking about how those collaborations were set up. Specifically,

- What was the purpose of the collaboration?
- How was the group selected?
- How did you make creative and strategic decisions?
- How did you divide labor?
- If there were tensions, how did you resolve them?
- How did you maintain quality and integrity?

- In what ways did you offer praise to one another?
- How did you decide when the project was complete?

In my classroom, I often ask students at the beginning of a collaborative project to write about their experiences, and I have found that many of them measure the effectiveness of collaborative work according to those experiences. And why wouldn't they? Experiences are powerful lenses, and they can help us to stay positive, as the one student who recalled, "Working in groups has worked well for me most of the time." They can also make us more skeptical or even fearful of future collaborative experiences, as was the case with another student, who reflected, "I did my best to get out of them, and find a way to work alone. . . . Many times, it was one person pulling the weight of a whole group, and many times that was me."

Rather than just labeling a collaborative experience "good" or "bad," however, we can study the answers to these questions above and think more critically about how and why collaboration succeeds or fails. We can also take a more specific look at our *own* actions and tendencies for working in a group. Go back to that memorable collaboration, or even to other forms of group work that you've experienced, and ask yourself:

- What role did I play in that collaboration?
- More broadly, what role(s) do I tend to take in collaborative work? Why?
- How do I measure motivation and expectations of my group members?
- How do I measure fairness in dividing tasks?
- How do I measure success?
- How do I find the words to speak up when I want to challenge the group?

By looking at how a collaborative project was structured, and by examining our personal behavior in a collaborative situation, we can think more critically about how we might keep or change our approaches in future contexts.

Structuring the Path Ahead: Setting Up Your Project

Remember that Lennon and McCartney depended on their mutual respect, communication skills, and shared goals in their collaborative compositions. So, too, can you focus on these elements in your own collaborative work—the key is to build a structure that supports those components. Before you begin to research, design, and write your composition, prepare yourself and your group for the work ahead by considering three important steps to setting up your project: opening your mind, selecting group members, and articulating goals in a group contract.

Keep an Open Mind

Go back to the freewrite you composed about your experiences with collaboration, and re-acquaint yourself with the mindset you had about those experiences. Then look carefully once again at the ways in which that collaboration was structured. What would you change? What would you keep the same? Perhaps one of the most important approaches you can take to collaborative work is to keep an open mind; draw from your experiences, and be willing to learn something entirely new. Do not only assume that because a certain approach did or did not work in the past it will or will not work in the future. For example, though your group's biology lab in your junior year of high school seemed to write itself, you may encounter new writing challenges now that you're working with a brand new group of students. Likewise, though the senior year capstone collaborative project seemed dominated by the one student who struggled to incorporate others' ideas, you may find that your group members in college are less willing to be silenced. A brand new collaborative situation offers you the opportunity to see yourself and your peers as credible sources of information. Each of you has something to offer, and whether your offerings coincide or clash, the valuable chance to learn from one another is there. If each group member pledges to allow for the thoughts and ideas of other members, you've gotten off to a promising start.

Selecting Group Members

A teacher will often invite students to decide how they want to be grouped in collaborative work. If this is the case, think carefully about this critical part of the project. Want to work with your friends? Sometimes this is a great plan; after all, we often choose our friends based on common interests and views on the world. But consider the insight of teacher and scholar Rebecca Moore Howard. In her work on collaboration, Howard describes one collaborative assignment in which she explained to her students

> that choosing their own groups would allow them maximum comfort but would leave some students feeling unloved, and . . . that the comfort of self-chosen groups could sometimes result in poor decision-making, with too much consideration for established relations and not enough for the collaborative project. (64–65)

If you decide to work with your friends, it could be the best collaboration ever. But it could also put additional pressures on the friendships, which may detract from the tasks at hand. And what about those students who don't have any close friends in the class? With these cautionary notes in mind, Howard's students decided to be randomly grouped together. However you decide to group your project, go back to that "Keep an Open Mind" idea and consider how you might populate your group most effectively for the benefit of the class, the project, and your own development as a writer and student.

Establishing a Group Contract

Once you've established your group, there is an important step to take before you dive into the work, and in many ways it acts as your first collaborative writing activity: the group contract. This contract serves as a kind of group constitution: it lays out the collective goals and ground rules that will adhere group members to a core ethos for productive, healthy, creative work. It also gives you a map of where to begin and how to proceed as you divide the labor of the project. In composing your contract, consider the following issues.

- **Understanding the project at hand.** From the get-go, group members should have a clear, shared understanding of what is expected from your teacher. Engage in a discussion in which you articulate to one another the goals of the project: what is the composition supposed to accomplish? What should it teach you as the authors? Discuss the parameters of the project: form, length, design, voice, research expectations, creative possibilities.

- **Communication practices.** Spend a few minutes discussing together what "good communication" looks like. This conversation may offer you a valuable opportunity to share some experiences and get to know one another better. Once you have outlined your standards for communication, establish ground rules for communication so that your group fosters sharp listening and makes space for a diversity of ideas and perspectives. Will you meet regularly in person, or will you rely on electronic means like email, chatting, a wiki, online collaborative software like Google Docs, or Facebook? If you use email, will you regularly include all group members on all emails to keep everyone in the loop? How will you vote on an idea? What if everyone agrees on a concept except one person? What if tensions arise? Will you deal with them one-on-one? In front of the whole group? Will you involve your teacher? When and why?

- **Meeting deadlines.** Discuss your group members' various schedules, and establish a deadline for each component of the project. Decide together how you will ensure that group members adhere to deadlines, and how you will communicate with and support one another in achieving these deadlines.

- **Ethics.** Discuss academic integrity and be sure that each group member commits to ethical research and the critical evaluation of sources. Each member should commit to checking over the final product to be sure that sources are appropriately documented. Rely on open, clear communication throughout the process of research and documentation so that you achieve accuracy and a shared understanding of how the text was composed, fact-checked, and edited.

- **Standards.** Discuss together what "quality" and "success" mean to each of you: is it an A? Is it a project that takes risks? Is it consensus? Is it a collaborative process that is enjoyable? Is it the making of friends in a working group? How will you know when your product has reached your desired quality and is ready to be submitted?

As you can see, this contract is not to be taken lightly: time and effort spent on a reliable contract are likely to save time and energy later. The contract acts as the spine of a group that is sensitive to differences of experience and opinion, and that aims to contribute to the intellectual growth of each of its members. While the contract should be unified by the time you're done with it, allow space for group members to disagree about what is important—working with this disagreement will be good practice for you when it comes to composing the project itself. When it's completed, be sure that each group member receives a copy of the contract. You should also give a copy to your teacher so that he/she has access in the event that you want your teacher to be involved in conflict resolution. Keep in mind, too, that the best contracts are used to define your responsibilities and enhance communication, not to hold over one another—your contract is a thoughtfully composed articulation of your goals, not a policing tool.

WORKING TOGETHER: INVENTING, PLANNING, GETTING UNSTUCK, AND CHECKING IN

Now, with your contract signed, sealed, and e-delivered to one another, you're ready to launch into developing your project. In this section, we'll explore some activities that will help you to make decisions about topics, carry out the specifics of project administration, resolve conflict, and re-calibrate your contract.

Choosing a Worthy Topic

In many cases your teacher may assign you the specific topic for your collaborative project; in other cases, you may actually be grouped together according to your common interests or fields of study. In still other cases, you may find yourself in a situation in which your group is composed of a diversity of interests, and where there are fewer constraints on the assignment. For example, maybe you've been assigned to write a proposal that offers a solution to a citywide problem, maybe you've been asked to work together to research and compose an analytical report on a debate in the latest Presidential election, or maybe you've just been asked to get together to defend one side of an issue that is important to you. In any of these cases, you're likely to face one big question: what should your topic be?

It can be tempting to hurry past this important point in the process so that you can get down to business with the project itself. Often, students toss some ideas around and use a "majority rules" method of choosing a topic, or they might look for a topic based on how "easy" it seems rather than on how compelling it might be to research. But think about the journey you're about to undertake, do yourselves a favor, and commit to choosing a *worthy* topic that is likely to keep you focused and interested for the duration of the project. Use the opportunity of many brains working together to pick a unique, fascinating topic that will stretch those brains in new ways. After all, what's college for if not to challenge you?

One technique that can be helpful in an open-topic situation actually comes from the world of business: it is called an "affinity diagram," and it can be useful in mapping group members' individual interests and sketching out how those interests may be combined into categories. In their research on engineering students in first year composition, Meredith Green and Sarah Duerden found affinity diagrams to be particularly useful not just for deciding on topics, but also for resolving conflict later in the process of collaboration ("Collaboration, English Composition"). You'll find that the affinity diagram helps you to delve deeper into the advantages and disadvantages of choosing certain topics, and helps you to imagine what it would be like to see a topic through from beginning to end. Later, too, you may find that creating this kind of diagram helps you to "see" a disagreement, as it arises in your group, in a way that talking around it, or even directly about it, doesn't seem to capture.

How do you begin? Let's say your group has been asked to select a campus-wide problem and write a proposal for its solution, and you've got to decide together on a problem that you each agree is worth investigating. Start with a brainstorm. Each member of the group writes down on separate small pieces of paper two or more major individual concerns for your campus. Lay out all of the pieces of paper before you, and see whether you have common concerns, or whether some concerns might be related to one another. Once you've narrowed the list of concerns, begin to create sub-categories for each concern: effects of the problem on campus, resources for researching the problem (including primary and scholarly research), hypothetical solutions, and potential challenges in taking on the topic. Your affinity diagram might look a little something like Figure 1.

Much more than a pro-con list, the affinity diagram puts some multi-faceted wisdom into the decision-making by showing you the magnitude of your campus concerns (who is affected by the problem), the availability of sources to support your research, and the feasibility

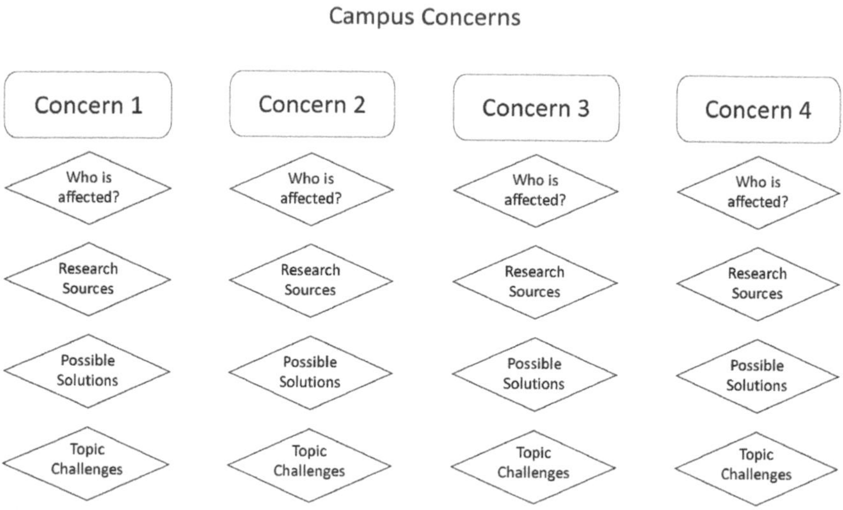

Campus Concerns

Concern 1	Concern 2	Concern 3	Concern 4
Who is affected?	Who is affected?	Who is affected?	Who is affected?
Research Sources	Research Sources	Research Sources	Research Sources
Possible Solutions	Possible Solutions	Possible Solutions	Possible Solutions
Topic Challenges	Topic Challenges	Topic Challenges	Topic Challenges

Fig. 1. Affinity diagram for deciding on a topic.

of what needs to be done to remedy the problem. Filling in these categories above may help you to see more clearly what challenges may lie ahead for you if you decide to take on any one of these campus concerns. Thus, once you've enriched your diagram, you can begin to see together which topics have the most promise in terms of enjoyment, challenge, and sustainability. Moreover, as Green and Duerden found to be true for their students, don't hesitate to give the diagram some time to "incubate" (4). That is, if class time is only an hour or so, get the diagram started, but check back in with group members later in the day, or even the next day. Talk to others, do some initial online research, let the ideas marinate so that you can best represent them in the diagram before you make a decision together about which topic you want to tackle.

Project Management

Now that you've selected a topic you can all invest in, you're ready to lay out work for the next few weeks. Together, divide the project into logical stages of development, taking into consideration what the composition will need in terms of its research, analysis, organizational sections, graphics, fact-checking, editing, and drafting. Also consider the responsibilities necessary for each of these stages. Again, you may find that the affinity diagram is helpful here to illustrate the major steps toward completion, the sub-steps of each, and the places where steps in the process may be combined. The diagram can be a tangible way to see or imagine the process of the project when you don't yet have the final product in hand.

Next, divide the labor mindfully and fairly by discussing who will take on each responsibility. Think back on your experience and tendencies with collaboration. Is there an opportunity to do more listening, leading, negotiating, or questioning than you have in the past? Are there unique talents that individuals can bring to the project's various elements? Is one of you interested in design or illustration, for instance? Is another interested in multimedia approaches to presentation? You may elect a "divide and conquer" approach, but consider, too, that some sections of the project may require a sub-set of group members, and that other sections will need everyone's input (like research, editing, checking for documentation accuracy, decisions on design). In combining your individual skills with common goals, you're likely to find that the work you're doing is much greater than the sum of its parts. While individual group members' specific skills will be spotlighted in their own ways, this plan for the management of the project should also reveal that every stage of the process gets input from each member.

When Conflict Gets You Stuck: Writing Your Way Out

Though your group contract is meant to help you to avoid or foresee conflict before it arises, you still may encounter some unexpected patches of conflict along the way that you didn't see coming. Maybe it's late and the group is hungry, tired, and grumpy. Maybe one group member brought some of his personal struggles with him to the scheduled meeting. Maybe another group member suddenly decides that she doesn't like an idea you all agreed upon last week. Either way, the conflict that sneaks up on you can be challenging to work through, and it can make you all feel a little stuck.

One cause of conflict is what philosopher Richard Rorty called "abnormal discourse," or, as Kenneth Bruffee explains, the "kooky" or "revolutionary" comments or gestures that someone might make in a group (qtd. in Bruffee 648). What does abnormal discourse look like? Well, let's say that as a group you're working on a proposal to improve the computer labs on campus, and you're talking about which images to include in your composition. Someone pulls up a photograph

of a group of students all sitting around a monitor, their faces lit by
the screen, and most members of the group chime in excitedly that
the photo does a nice job of showing how an improved computer lab
might help to enhance student community. In the middle of your conversation, however, one of your group members dismissively remarks,
"That's a terrible photo. I can't believe you all want to use it," and then
leaves the room. How rude, right? Maybe not.

You may be taken aback by what seemed like an outburst from
your fellow group member. You might think that a group agreeing
animatedly on a photo is yet another positive step toward the completion of your project, and you may even be annoyed and think that
the naysayer is a buzz kill and will stall the project. But consider this:
abnormal discourse can actually be a *good* thing, an opportunity for
positive growth or change inside the group. In the situation described
above, the student may have a very good reason for rejecting the photo,
but perhaps did not want or know how to communicate disagreement
in any other way. For example, maybe all of the students in the photo
are Caucasian, and the student of color who rejected it is offended because he feels excluded by it. Maybe the photo is all male students, and
a female group member is disappointed that her other female group
members would support it. The point is, the tension that arises around
abnormal discourse can be alarming and can make you feel stuck for
a bit, but it may prove to be enlightening, and as a group you owe it to
yourselves to get to the bottom of it. So, take a deep breath and make
space for the conversation to happen. While the student's behavior
seemed to come out of left field, you may find that his resistance is actually really important to understand.

So, what do you do? Dive into the argument? Maybe. In the middle
of the conflict, launching into conversation about the issue at hand
may seem like steps ahead of the tense moment, so you might find
some relief in writing first, then turning to one another with your
concerns. You might be thinking, how in the world will we as a group
have the presence of mind to stop and write about our conflict before
we begin to discuss it? After all, this write-before-you-speak approach
is itself a form of abnormal discourse—we're not used to doing it in
our everyday interactions, right? But you may find that writing first
helps you to process your thoughts, gather your questions, calm your
mind a bit before you get to the heart of the matter. You might even
write this method into your group contract so that you remember that,

at one point in the planning of this complex project, you promised one another that you would use this technique if you ever encountered tension.

Revisiting Your Contract

While you've worked hard to compose your group contract, it can be difficult to keep the elements of the contract in the forefront of your mind when you and your group members immerse yourselves in the project. Instead of moving the contract to the back burner, be sure to return to it once or twice throughout the project. In reflecting on collaborative work, one student in my class remarked, "People's roles in the project, responsibilities, work done, that can all be adjusted, but when it is time to submit it you have no room to improvise." The "adjustments" that this student refers to can happen when you and your group touch base with the goals you set from the beginning. You might also find that it's useful to meet briefly as a group in a more informal setting, like a coffee shop, so that you can take a refreshing look at the status of the project so far. Specifically, you might examine the following aspects of your collaboration:

- Revisit your goals. Is your composition heading in the right direction?
- Rate the overall effectiveness of communication. Call attention to any points of conflict and how you managed them.
- Discuss the workload of tasks completed thus far. Has it been fair?
- Measure the quality of the work you think the group is doing thus far.
- Remind yourselves of past and future deadlines. Do they need to be revised?
- Raise any individual concerns you may have.

If this extra step seems like more work, consider the possibility that as you push forward with the project, your goals may change and you may need to revise your contract. This step acts as a process of checks and balances that helps you to confirm your larger goal of creating a healthy, productive, enjoyable collaboration.

Concluding Your Project: Looking Back, Looking Ahead

Collaborative Review

Before you turn that project in, remember: even if you divided it up, the completed product belongs to all of you and should get each group member's final review and approval before you submit it. This final review includes editing for mechanics, style, and surface issues (including proper documentation, fact checking, and document layout). It can be especially helpful to go over the entire final composition together, *as a group.* Each person takes a turn reading aloud, while other members of the group follow along and check for errors. This shared editing session can also be an opportunity to pat one another on the back.

The Post-Mortem

That's it, right? On to the next thing? Not yet. Too often, we progress from project to project, from class to class without pausing to think back on what we have accomplished. We often miss out on reflection of the goals we had for ourselves, neglecting to ask critical analytical questions: what did I hope to accomplish? In what ways did I grow as a person? As a student or scholar? What evidence do I have for that growth? How does this growth prepare me for what is next? When it comes to the high-impact learning potential involved in collaborative work, it can be an invaluable exercise to take stock by reflecting on the stages of the process and making sense of what you experienced. Someday, in the not-too-distant future, a prospective employer or graduate school is going to want to know, "How did you get to where you are today?" This final step in the process—called a "post-mortem"—will give you some practice at formulating an answer to this complex question.

Less morbid than it sounds, the "post-mortem" is an activity that you are likely to see in the professional world, and it involves looking back on the processes used to design/write/build the project, and reflecting on your successes, failures, and personal perspectives on the process in general. For many professionals, it is an invaluable component in understanding what does and does not work as they think about future endeavors. With truly complicated endeavors like collaboration, a post-mortem can help to give you insight that you can only get once you're on the other side of your project. Here are some guiding questions:

- Was your project a success? If so, why? If not, why?
- What were some of the most poignant lessons you learned about yourself?
- What surprised you about this collaboration?
- What might you have done differently?
- In what ways did this collaboration change or maintain your perceptions of collaborative work?
- How would you instruct someone else in the process of collaboration?

Once you've done your own reflecting, take your observations back to your group, and discuss together what you've concluded about the process. Not only does this final step bring some healthy closure to the project, but it also opens up opportunities for resolution of lingering conflict, mutual recognition of your accomplishments, and, for those of you who've got an especially good thing going with your work, a conversation about possibly taking your project beyond the classroom.

What Difference Does a Mindful Collaboration Make?

Does it really make a difference to do all of this prep-work and strategizing and management and reflection? I wanted to find out. Several months after my students completed a collaborative project, I did a kind of post-mortem by anonymously surveying them to get their views on collaboration. I was curious: most of them had never before taken these structured steps toward the preparation, management, and reflection on their group work. I learned from their pre-project reflections that most had worked in groups without talking about goals or communication strategies, making assumptions that their group members knew what they had to do and why. They had only known how to "launch in" and (gulp) hope for the best. And for many of these students, tensions loomed from the start. Would these new strategies change their views?

In my survey, I asked them,

- How would you rate the importance of collaboration in the university classroom?

- What do you think are the most important ingredients for successful collaboration?
- Did this collaborative project change the way you viewed collaboration before?
- How will you approach collaborative work in future academic and professional endeavors?
- How would you advise entering college students to approach collaborative work?

Despite even the most negative of experiences some students described before they began their group work, a majority of those who completed the survey rated collaboration as either "very important" or "extremely important." What's more, several of the students' responses emphasized the goals behind collaboration, and many who were initially concerned about group work came to see collaboration more positively than they had before. Take a look at what some of my students wrote:

> At first I felt like learning to work with someone really didn't matter. I was fine doing the work on my own. I learned in my project that it is indeed very important.

> I believe the collaborating in a university classroom is important because it prepares you for the difficulties that you will have to face with collaboration in the work field in the future. Having experienced many obstacles and difficulties while working with assigned partners and group members I know that learning to resolve these issues is a social skill that will be extremely helpful in the future.

> Integral to the collaboration process is being able to understand one another, and have the patience to see what others are saying.

> I feel that the most important ingredients for successful collaboration are communication, as well as compensation. Group members must be sure to communicate amongst themselves—relay problems, conflicts, concerns, and comments amongst each other. Moreover, if a given group member is having trouble completing his/her part, then the remaining members must at least make an effort to help the troubled group member.

> *I thought that the most important parts were an ability to listen to your peers and to also find a way to organize the group such that each person contributed to the discussion.*

> *One aspect that can make everything a lot easier is organization. When you are organized, you save time, and everyone is able to be on the same page. The [project] gave the opportunity for students to get organized and figure how the group is going to function.*

> *I think when you collaborate on a project it is not always going to work perfectly with people who have the same ideas as you. In order to be successful you all need to be able to negotiate and work together for a common goal.*

Communication, structure, negotiation, organization, deadlines. These aspects stand out for these students as some of the most important elements of successful collaboration. While they may seem like common sense, you probably know by now how challenging it can be try to juggle all of these conceptual balls in the air when you don't have a mindful structure to guide you. The invention, management, and reflection tools we've talked about in this chapter can help to form the backbone of a creative, communicative, and rewarding collaboration.

Though flying solo can produce some extraordinary individual work, we might again heed the words of Lennon, who describes his first meeting with McCartney: "I thought, half to myself, 'He's as good as me.' I'd been kingpin up to then. Now I thought 'If I take him on, what will happen?' . . . The decision was whether to keep me strong or make the group stronger. . . . But he was good, so he was worth having. He also looked like Elvis. I dug him" (Norman 109). Lennon asked himself: what will happen? Ask yourself the same thing when you begin a group project. It could be something pretty good. It might also be something great.

DISCUSSION

1. Does the collaborative experience described in this essay at all resemble any joint activity you have engaged in? A team, a club, a group? Being in a family, working with a best friend to create a project, a world, a fort, or planning an event? Write about any part of this process that you have experienced. What appeals most to you about this structured approach—something that you are fa-

miliar with? What about the parts you are unfamiliar with—what would you like to try and why?

2. The essay uses a powerfully successful partnership to describe the possibilities of group work. How can you apply what you know of great partnerships to the process of group work modeled here? Would you want to try working with a partner within a group? How could you apply this same process for working with one other person?

3. As a class, create a survey of previous collaborative experiences based on the questions the essay asked you to write about in the section, "Your Experiences Matter." Take the survey, tally the results, and discuss as a class what you have found. How can your understanding of your own past inform your construction of the future? What did you notice when you started to talk about your past experiences together?

4. The section, "When Conflict Gets You Stuck," invites you to see conflict as an opportunity in collaboration. Where do you see this approach to conflict happening in the public sphere? What are some of the challenges and benefits of taking this perspective?

5. What's your "post-mortem" for this chapter? How can you apply the ideas in this chapter to your own reading/learning experience?

WORKS CITED

"The Beatles Biography." *Rolling Stone Music*. 28 March 2008. Web. 18 Sept. 2010.

Bruffee, Kenneth. "Collaborative Learning and the 'Conversation of Mankind.'" *College English* 46.7 (1984): 635–52. Print.

Green, Meredith, and Sarah Duerden. "Collaboration, English Composition, and the Engineering Student: Constructing Knowledge in the Integrated Engineering Program." *Proceedings of the 26th Annual Frontiers in Education* 1 (1996): 3–6. Web. 15 Sept. 2010.

Howard, Rebecca Moore. "Collaborative Pedagogy." *A Guide to Composition Pedagogies*. Ed. Gary Tate, Amy Rupiper, and Kurt Schick. New York: Oxford UP, 2001. Print.

Ingalls, Rebecca. "Collaborative Work in the Composition Classroom." Survey. 10 Aug. 2009. 31 Aug. 2009.

Norman, Philip. *John Lennon: The Life*. New York: Harper Collins, 2008. Print.

Sheff, David. *All We Are Saying: The Last Major Interview with John Lennon and Yoko Ono*. New York: St. Martin's Press, 2000. Print.

On the Other Hand: The Role of Antithetical Writing in First Year Composition Courses

Steven D. Krause

Besides my own experiences as a student many years ago in courses similar to the ones you and your classmates are in now, I think the most important influence on how I have approached research and argumentative writing came from academic debate.* Debate taught me at least two ways to approach an argument that were not part of my formal schooling. First, academic policy debate[1] taught me that argumentation is a contest—a sport, not at all different from tennis or basketball or figure skating or gymnastics, an activity where you have to work with a team, you have to practice, and the goal is to "win." And winning in academic debate happens: while it is a sport that is judged, it is an activity, like gymnastics or figure skating, where the rules for judging are surprisingly well codified. I will admit that seeing a debate or argument as something "to be won" has not always served me well in life, for there are any number of situations in which the framework for an argument is perhaps better perceived as an opportunity to listen and to compromise than to score points.

Second, because of the way that academic debate is structured, I learned quickly the importance of being able to perceive and argue multiple and opposing views on the same issue. Not unlike other sports where players play both offense and defense—baseball and basketball immediately come to mind—debaters have to argue both for and against the year's resolution, which was the broad proposition that framed all of the particular cases debate teams put forward for the entire season. In fact, it was not at all uncommon for a team to strenuously advocate for a controversial position one round—"the U.S. should engage in one-on-one talks with North Korea"—only to strenuously argue the opposite position—"the U.S. should *not* engage in one-on-one talks with North Korea"—the very next round. Seeing "multiple positions" was not simply a good idea; it was one of the rules of the game.

I've brought these past experiences into my current teaching in a number of ways, including one of the exercises I am discussing here, what my students and I call antithesis writing. These exercises will help you gain a better understanding of how to shape an argument, how to more fully explore a topic, and how to think more carefully about your different audiences.

In this essay, I borrow heavily from my own online textbook, *The Process of Research Writing,* which is available for free at http://stevendkrause.com/tprw. You might want to visit that site for additional information about this exercise and other exercises I've put together for teaching the research writing process.

Thesis ~~Is Not~~ Doesn't Have to Be a Bad Thing (Or Why Write Antithesis Essays in the First Place)

Somewhere along the way, "thesis" became a dirty word in a lot of writing courses, inherently bound up and attached to all that is wrong with what composition historians and the writing scholars call the "Current-Traditional" paradigm of writing instruction. Essentially, this approach emphasizes the product and forms of writing (in most nineteenth century American rhetoric textbooks, these forms were Exposition, Description, Narration, and Argument), issues of syntax and grammar, correctness, and so forth. It didn't matter so much what position a writer took; what mattered most was that the writer got the form correct.

"Thesis" is often caught in/lumped into this current-traditional paradigm, I think mainly because of the rigid role and placement of a thesis in the classic form of the five-paragraph essay. Most of you and your classmates already know about this: in the five-paragraph formula, the thesis is the last sentence of the introduction, is divided into three parts, and it rigidly controls the structure of the following four paragraphs. Certainly this overly prescriptive and narrow definition of thesis is not useful. Jasper Neel describes this sort of formula in his book *Plato, Derrida, and Writing* as "anti-writing," and I think that Sharon Crowley is correct in arguing that the kind of teaching exemplified by the five-paragraph essay is more akin to filling out a form than it is to actual "writing."

But when I discuss "thesis" here, I mean something much more broad and organic. I mean an initial direction that every research-writing project must take. A thesis advocates a specific and debatable position, is not a statement of fact nor a summary of events, and it answers the questions "what's your point?" and "why should I care?" You should begin with a working thesis that attempts to answer these questions simply as a way of getting your research process started. True, these initial working theses are usually broad and unwieldy, but the emphasis here is on *working*, because as you research and think more carefully, you will inevitably change your thesis. *And this is good*—change is the by-product of learning, and seeing a working thesis differently is both the purpose and the opportunity of the antithesis exercise.

So, I think the first and probably most important reason to consider antithesis writing is to test and strengthen the validity of the working thesis. After all, there isn't much "debatable" about a working thesis like "crime is bad" or "cleaning up the environment is good," which suggests that there probably isn't a viable answer to the questions "what's your point?" and "why should I care?" Considering opposing and differing views can help you find the path to make a vague generalization like "crime is bad" into a more pointed, researchable, and interesting observation.

The second general value for antithesis exercises is to raise more awareness of your audience—the potential readers who would disagree with your working thesis, along with readers who are more favorable to your point. Sometimes, readers won't be convinced no matter what evidence or logic a writer presents; but it seems to me that writers have an obligation to at least try.

Generating Antithetical Points in Five Easy Steps

I've already discussed this step in some detail:

Step 1: Have a Working Thesis and Make Sure You Have Begun the Research Process.

Developing a good antithetical argument is not something you can do as a "first step" in the research process. Generally, you need to have already developed a basic point and need some evidence and research to develop that point. In other words, the process of developing an antithetical position has to come *after* you develop an initial position in the first place.

Step 2: Consider the Direct Opposite of Your Working Thesis.

This is an especially easy step if your working thesis is about a controversial topic:

> *Working thesis:*
>
> To prevent violence on campus, students, staff, and faculty should not be allowed to carry concealed weapons.

> *Antithesis:*
>
> To prevent violence on campus, students, staff, and faculty should be allowed to carry concealed weapons.

> *Working thesis:*
>
> Drug companies should be allowed to advertise prescription drugs on television.

> *Antithesis:*
>
> Drug companies should not be allowed to advertise prescription drugs on television.

This sort of simple change of qualifiers also exposes weak theses, because, generally speaking, the opposite position of a proposition that everyone accepts as true is one that everyone easily accepts as false. For example, if you begin with a working thesis like "Drunk driving is bad" or "Teen violence is bad" to their logical opposites, you end up with an opposite that is ridiculous—"Drunk driving is good" or "Teen violence is good." What that signals is that it is probably time to revisit your original working thesis.

Usually though, considering the opposite of a working thesis is a little more complicated. For example:

> *Working Thesis:*
>
> Many computer hackers commit serious crimes and represent a major expense for internet-based businesses.
>
> *Antitheses:*
>
> Computer hackers do not commit serious crimes.
> Computer hacking is not a major expense for internet-based businesses.

Both of the antithetical examples are the opposite of the original working theses, but each focuses on different aspects of the working thesis.

Step 3: Ask "Why" about Possible Antithetical Arguments.

Creating antitheses by simply changing the working thesis to its opposite typically demands more explanation. The best place to develop more details with your antithesis is to ask "why." For example:

> **Why** should drug companies not be allowed to advertise prescription drugs? Because . . .
>
> • The high cost of television advertising needlessly drives up the costs of prescriptions.
> • Advertisements too often confuse patients and offer advice that contradicts the advice of doctors.
>
> **Why** are the crimes committed by computer hackers not serious? Because . . .
>
> • They are usually pranks or acts of mischief.
> • Computer hackers often expose problems for Internet businesses before serious crimes result.

The point here is to dig a little further into your antithetical argument. Asking "why" is a good place to begin that process.

Step 4: Examine Alternatives to Your Working Thesis.

Often, the best antithetical arguments aren't about "the opposite" so much as they are about alternatives. For example, the working thesis "To prevent violence on campus, students, staff, and faculty should not be allowed to carry concealed weapons" presumes that a serious potential cause for violence on campuses is the presence of guns. However, someone could logically argue that the more important cause of violence on college campuses is alcohol and drug abuse. Certainly the number of incidents involving underage drinking and substance abuse outnumber those involving firearms on college campuses, and it is also probably true that many incidents of violence on college campuses involve drinking or drugs.

Now, unlike the direct opposite of your working thesis, the alternatives do not necessarily negate your working thesis. There is no reason why a reader couldn't believe that *both* concealed weapons *and* alcohol and substance abuse contribute to violence on campuses. But in considering alternatives to your working thesis, the goal is to "weigh" the positions against each other. I'll return to this matter of "weighing your position" later.

Step 5: Imagine Hostile Audiences.

Whenever you are trying to develop a clearer understanding of the antithesis of your working thesis, you need to think about the kinds of audiences who would disagree with you. By thinking about the opposites and alternatives to your working thesis, you are already starting to do this because the opposites and the alternatives are what a hostile audience might think.

Sometimes, potential readers are hostile to a particular working thesis because of ideals, values, or affiliations they hold that are at odds with the point being advocated by the working thesis. For example, people who identify themselves as being "pro-choice" on the issue of abortion would certainly be hostile to an argument for laws that restrict access to abortion; people who identify themselves as being "pro-life" on the issue of abortion would certainly be hostile to an argument for laws that provide access to abortion.

At other times, audiences are hostile to the arguments of a working thesis because of more crass and transparent reasons. For example, the pharmaceutical industry disagrees with the premise of the working thesis "Drug companies should not be allowed to advertise prescription drugs on TV" because they stand to lose billions of dollars in lost sales. Advertising companies and television broadcasters would also be against this working thesis because they too would lose money. You can probably easily imagine some potential hostile audience members who have similarly selfish reasons to oppose your point of view.

Of course, some audiences will oppose your working thesis based on a different interpretation of the evidence and research. This sort of difference of opinion is probably most common with research projects that are focused on more abstract and less definitive subjects. But there are also different opinions about evidence for topics that you might think would have potentially more concrete "right" and "wrong" interpretations. Different researchers and scholars can look at the same evidence about a subject like gun control and arrive at very different conclusions.

Regardless of the reasons why your audience might be hostile to the argument you are making with your working thesis, it is helpful to try to imagine your audience as clearly as you can. What sort of people are they? What other interests or biases might they have? Are there other political or social factors that you think are influencing their point of view? If you want to persuade at least some members of this hostile au dience that your point of view and your interpretation of the research is correct, you need to know as much about your hostile audience as you possibly can.

STRATEGIES FOR ANSWERING ANTITHETICAL ARGUMENTS

It might not seem logical, but directly acknowledging and address-ing positions that are different from the one you are holding in your research can actually make your position stronger. When you take on the antithesis in your research project, it shows you have thought carefully about the issue at hand and you acknowledge that there is no clear and easy "right" answer. There are many different ways you might incorporate the antithesis into your research to make your own thesis stronger and to address the concerns of those readers who might oppose your point of view. For now, focus on three basic strategies: directly refuting your opposition, weighing your position against the opposition, and making concessions.

Directly Refuting Your Opposition

Perhaps the most obvious approach, one way to address those potential readers who might raise objections to your arguments, is to simply refute their objections with better evidence and reasoning. Of course, this is an example of yet another reason why it is so important to have good research that supports your position: when the body of evidence and research is on your side, it is usually a lot easier to make a strong point.

Answering antithetical arguments with research that supports your point of view is also an example of where you as a researcher might need to provide a more detailed evaluation of your evidence. The sort of questions you should answer about your own research—who wrote it, where was it published, when was it published, etc.—are important to raise in countering antithetical arguments that you think come from suspicious sources.

Weighing Your Position Against the Opposition

Readers who oppose the argument you are trying to support with your research might do so because they value or "weigh" the implications of your working thesis differently than you do. For example, those opposed to a working thesis like "Drug companies should not be allowed to advertise prescription drugs on TV" might think this because they think the advantages of advertising drugs on television—increased sales for pharmaceutical companies, revenue for advertising agencies and television stations, and so forth—are more significant than the disadvantages of advertising drugs on television.

Besides recognizing and acknowledging the different ways of comparing the advantages and disadvantages suggested by your working thesis, the best way of answering these antithetical arguments in your own writing is to clearly explain how you weigh and compare the evidence. This can be a challenging writing experience because it requires a subtle hand and a broad understanding of multiple sides of your topic. But if in acknowledging to your readers that you have carefully considered the reasons against your working thesis and you can demonstrate your position to be more persuasive, then this process of weighing positions can be very effective.

Making Concessions

In the course of researching and thinking about the antithesis to your working thesis and its potentially hostile audiences, it may become clear to you that these opposing views have a point. When this is the case, you may want to consider revising your working thesis or your approach to your research to make some concessions to these antithetical arguments.

Sometimes, my students working on this exercise "make concessions" to the point of changing sides on their working thesis—that is, in the process of researching, writing, and thinking about their topic, a researcher moves from arguing for their working thesis to arguing for their antithesis. This might seem surprising, but it makes perfect sense when you remember the purpose of research in the first place. When we study the evidence on a particular issue, we often realize that our initial and uninformed impression or feelings on an issue were simply wrong. That's why we research: we put more trust in opinions based on research than in things based on gut instinct or feelings.

But usually, most concessions to antithetical perspectives are less dramatic and can be accomplished in a variety of ways. You might want to employ some qualifying terms to hedge a bit. For example, the working thesis "Drug companies should not be allowed to advertise prescription drugs on TV" might be qualified to "Drug companies *should be closely regulated* about what they are allowed to advertise in TV." I think this is still a strong working thesis, but the revised working thesis acknowledges the objections some might have to the original working thesis.

Of course, you should use these sorts of concessions carefully. An over-qualified working thesis can be just as bad as a working thesis about something that everyone accepts as true: it can become so watered-down as to not have any real significance anymore. A working thesis like "Drug company television advertising is sometimes bad and sometimes good for patients" is over-qualified to the point of taking no real position at all.

BUT YOU STILL CAN'T CONVINCE EVERYONE ...

I'd like to close by turning away a bit from where I started this essay, the influence of competitive debate on my early education about argument. In debate, an argument is part of the game, the catalyst for the beginning of a competition. The same is often true within college classrooms. Academic arguments are defined in terms of their hypothetical nature; they aren't actually real but rather merely an intellectual exercise.

But people in the real world do hold more than hypothetical positions, and you can't always convince everyone that you're right, no matter what evidence or logic you might have on your side. You probably already know this. We have all been in conversations with friends or family members where, as certain as we were that we were right about something and as hard as we tried to prove we were right, our friends or family were simply unwilling to budge from their positions. When we find ourselves in these sorts of deadlocks, we often try to smooth over the dispute with phrases like "You're entitled to your opinion" or "We will have to agree to disagree," and then we change the subject. In polite conversation, this is a good strategy to avoid a fight. But in academic contexts, these deadlocks can be frustrating and difficult to negotiate.

A couple of thousand years ago, the Greek philosopher and rhetorician Aristotle said that all of us respond to arguments based on three basic characteristics or appeals: logos or logic, pathos or emotional character, and ethos, the writer's or speaker's perceived character. Academic writing tends to rely most heavily on logos and ethos because academics tend to highly value arguments based on logical research and arguments that come from writers with strong character-building qualifications—things like education, experience, previous publications, and the like. But it's important to remember that pathos is always there, and particularly strong emotions or feelings on a subject can obscure the best research.

Most academic readers have respect for writers when they successfully argue for positions that they might not necessarily agree with. Along these lines, most college writing instructors can certainly respect and give a positive evaluation to a piece of writing they don't completely agree with as long as it uses sound logic and evidence to support its points. However, all readers—students, instructors, and everyone else—come to your research project with various preconceptions about the point you are trying to make. Some of them will already agree with you and won't need much convincing. Some of them will never completely agree with you, but will be open to your argument to a point. And some of your readers, because of the nature of the point you are trying to make and their own feelings and thoughts on the matter, will never agree with you, no matter what research evidence you present or what arguments you make. So, while you need to consider the antithetical arguments to your thesis in your research project to convince as many members of your audience as possible that the point you are trying to make is correct, you should remember that you will likely not convince all of your readers all of the time.

Discussion

1. When was the last time you had to argue for a specific position on an issue? What was the issue? Were you alone or did you have friends to back you up? How did you find evidence to support your position? Did you "win" the argument by getting your way or by convincing the opponents of you were right? Why did you win or not win?

2. What are some issues have you recently talked about in courses (other than writing)? What were some theses offered by students in those classes (or by the professor)? Pick one or two of the theses you found most intriguing (or that elicited the most conversation) and see if you can write the antithesis. Is this impossible without doing some research? Why or why not? What would you do next, if you needed to follow up on this thinking exercise as a writing project?

3. Because of research on a particular issue, have you ever changed your mind about what you believed was right? What was the issue? Why did you change your mind? Or why not?

4. When you've been in classes and not agreed with other students or the professor, did you offer your differing opinion? Was that based on research or your gut instinct or your own experience? What was the most effective process you've used for participating in debate in classes? Or has this been something you're unwilling to be involved in? Why has that been the case?

Note

1. Explaining "academic policy debate" is not my goal in this essay. But I will say that academic debate bears almost no resemblance to "debates"

between political candidates or to the stereotypical way debate tends to be depicted on television shows or in movies. Certainly debate involves a certain intellectual prowess; but I think it's fair to say that debate is a lot closer to a competitive sport than a classroom exercise. Two excellent introductions to the world of academic debate are the Wikipedia entry for "Policy Debate" (http://en.wikipedia.org/wiki/Policy_debate) and the 2007 documentary movie *Resolved*.

WORKS CITED

Crowley, Sharon. *The Methodical Memory: Invention in Current-Traditional Rhetoric.* Carbondale: Southern Illinois UP, 1990. Print.

Neel, Jasper. *Plato, Derrida, and Writing.* Carbondale: Southern Illinois UP, 1988. Print.

Introduction to Primary Research: Observations, Surveys, and Interviews

Dana Lynn Driscoll

PRIMARY RESEARCH: DEFINITIONS AND OVERVIEW

How research is defined varies widely from field to field, and as you progress through your college career, your coursework will teach you much more about what it means to be a researcher within your field.[*] For example, engineers, who focus on applying scientific knowledge to develop designs, processes, and objects, conduct research using simulations, mathematical models, and a variety of tests to see how well their designs work. Sociologists conduct research using surveys, interviews, observations, and statistical analysis to better understand people, societies, and cultures. Graphic designers conduct research through locating images for reference for their artwork and engaging in background research on clients and companies to best serve their needs. Historians conduct research by examining archival materials—newspapers, journals, letters, and other surviving texts—and through conducting oral history interviews. Research is not limited to what has already been written or found at the library, also known as secondary

---

research. Rather, individuals conducting research are *producing* the articles and reports found in a library database or in a book. Primary research, the focus of this essay, is research that is collected firsthand rather than found in a book, database, or journal.

Primary research is often based on principles of the scientific method, a theory of investigation first developed by John Stuart Mill in the nineteenth century in his book *Philosophy of the Scientific Method*. Although the application of the scientific method varies from field to field, the general principles of the scientific method allow researchers to learn more about the world and observable phenomena. Using the scientific method, researchers develop research questions or hypotheses and collect data on events, objects, or people that is measurable, observable, and replicable. The ultimate goal in conducting primary research is to learn about something new that can be confirmed by others and to eliminate our own biases in the process.

Essay Overview and Student Examples

The essay begins by providing an overview of ethical considerations when conducting primary research, and then covers the stages that you will go through in your primary research: planning, collecting, analyzing, and writing. After the four stages comes an introduction to three common ways of conducting primary research in first year writing classes:

- *Observations.* Observing and measuring the world around you, including observations of people and other measurable events.
- *Interviews.* Asking participants questions in a one-on-one or small group setting.
- *Surveys.* Asking participants about their opinions and behaviors through a short questionnaire.

In addition, we will be examining two student projects that used substantial portions of primary research:

Derek Laan, a nutrition major at Purdue University, wanted to learn more about student eating habits on campus. His primary research included observations of the campus food courts, student behavior while in the food courts, and a survey of students' daily food intake. His secondary research included looking at national student eating trends on college campuses, information from the United States Food and Drug Administration, and books on healthy eating.

Jared Schwab, an agricultural and biological engineering major at Purdue, was interested in learning more about how writing and communication took place in his field. His primary research included interviewing a professional engineer and a student who was a senior majoring in engineering. His secondary research included examining journals, books, professional organizations, and writing guides within the field of engineering.

ETHICS OF PRIMARY RESEARCH

Both projects listed above included primary research on human participants; therefore, Derek and Jared both had to consider research ethics throughout their primary research process. As Earl Babbie writes in *The Practice of Social Research,* throughout the early and middle parts of the twentieth century researchers took advantage of participants and treated them unethically. During World War II, Nazi doctors performed heinous experiments on prisoners without their consent, while in the U.S., a number of medical and psychological experiments on caused patients undue mental and physical trauma and, in some cases, death. Because of these and other similar events, many nations have established ethical laws and guidelines for researchers who work with human participants. In the United States, the guidelines for the ethical treatment of human research participants are described in *The Belmont Report,* released in 1979. Today, universities have Institutional Review Boards (or IRBs) that oversee research. Students conducting research as part of a class may not need permission from the university's IRB, although they still need to ensure that they follow ethical guidelines in research. The following provides a brief overview of ethical considerations:

- *Voluntary participation. The Belmont Report* suggests that, in most cases, you need to get permission from people before you involve them in any primary research you are conducting. If you are doing a survey or interview, your participants must first agree to fill out your survey or to be interviewed. Consent for observations can be more complicated, and is discussed later in the essay.

- *Confidentiality and anonymity.* Your participants may reveal embarrassing or potentially damaging information such as racist comments or unconventional behavior. In these cases, you should keep your participants' identities anonymous when writing your results. An easy way to do this is to create a "pseudonym" (or false name) for them so that their identity is protected.
- *Researcher bias.* There is little point in collecting data and learning about something if you already think you know the answer! Bias might be present in the way you ask questions, the way you take notes, or the conclusions you draw from the data you collect.

The above are only three of many considerations when involving human participants in your primary research. For a complete understanding of ethical considerations please refer to *The Belmont Report.*

Now that we have considered the ethical implications of research, we will examine how to formulate research questions and plan your primary research project.

PLANNING YOUR PRIMARY RESEARCH PROJECT

The primary research process is quite similar to the writing process, and you can draw upon your knowledge of the writing process to understand the steps involved in a primary research project. Just like in the writing process, a successful primary research project begins with careful planning and background research. This section first describes how to create a research timeline to help plan your research. It then walks you through the planning stages by examining when primary research is useful or appropriate for your first year composition course, narrowing down a topic, and developing research questions.

The Research Timeline

When you begin to conduct any kind of primary research, creating a timeline will help keep you on task. Because students conducting primary research usually focus on the collection of data itself, they often overlook the equally important areas of planning (invention), analyzing data, and writing. To help manage your time, you should create a research timeline, such as the sample timeline presented here.

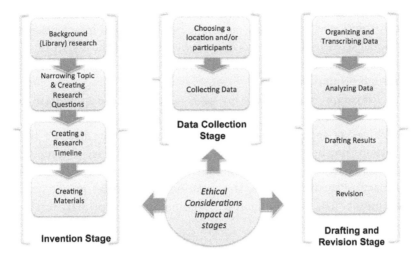

Fig. 1: The Research Process

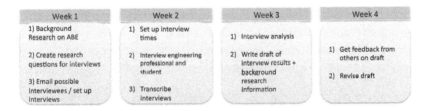

Fig. 2: A sample timeline for Jared's research project.

When Primary Research Is Useful or Appropriate

In *Evaluating Scientific Research: Separating Fact from Fiction,* Fred Leavitt explains that primary research is useful for questions that can be answered through asking others and direct observation. For first year writing courses, primary research is particularly useful when you want to learn about a problem that does not have a wealth of published information. This may be because the problem is a recent event or it is something not commonly studied. For example, if you are writing a paper on a new political issue, such as changes in tax laws or health-care, you might not be able to find a wealth of peer-reviewed research because the issue is only several weeks old. You may find it necessary to collect some of your own data on the issue to supplement what you found at the library. Primary research is also useful when you are studying a local problem or learning how a larger issue plays out at the local level. Although you might be able to find information on national statistics for healthy eating, whether or not those statistics are representative of your college campus is something that you can learn through primary research.

However, not all research questions and topics are appropriate for primary research. As Fred Leavitt writes, questions of an ethical, philosophical, or metaphysical nature are not appropriate because these questions are not testable or observable. For example, the question "Does an afterlife exist?" is not a question that can be answered with primary research. However, the question "How many people in my community believe in an afterlife?" is something that primary research can answer.

Narrowing Your Topic

Just like the writing process, you should start your primary research process with secondary (library) research to learn more about what is already known and what gaps you need to fill with your own data. As you learn more about the topic, you can narrow down your interest area and eventually develop a research question or hypothesis, just as you would with a secondary research paper.

Developing Research Questions or Hypotheses

As John Stuart Mill describes, primary research can use both *inductive* and *deductive* approaches, and the type approach is usually based on the field of inquiry. Some fields use *deductive reasoning*, where researchers start with a hypothesis or general conclusion and then collect specific data to support or refute their hypothesis. Other fields use *inductive reasoning*, where researchers start with a question and collect information that eventually leads to a conclusion.

Once you have spent some time reviewing the secondary research on your topic, you are ready to write a primary research question or hypothesis. A research question or hypothesis should be something that is specific, narrow, and discoverable through primary research methods. Just like a thesis statement for a paper, if your research question or hypothesis is too broad, your research will be unfocused and your data will be difficult to analyze and write about. Here is a set of sample research questions:

> *Poor Research Question:* What do college students think of politics and the economy?

> *Revised Research Question:* What do students at Purdue University believe about the current economic crisis in terms of economic recoverability?

The poor research question is unspecific as to what group of students the researcher is interested in—i.e. students in the U.S.? In a particular state? At their university? The poor research question was also too broad; terms like "politics" and the "economy" cover too much ground for a single project. The revised question narrows down the topic to students at a particular university and focuses on a specific issue related to the economy: economic recoverability. The research question could also be rephrased as a testable hypothesis using deductive reasoning: "Purdue University college students are well informed about economic recoverability plans." Because they were approaching their projects in an exploratory, inductive manner, both Derek and Jared chose to ask research questions:

> Derek: Are students' eating habits at Purdue University healthy or unhealthy? What are the causes of students' eating behavior?

> Jared: What are the major features of writing and communication in agricultural and biological engineering? What are the major controversies?

A final step in working with a research question or hypothesis is determining what key terms you are using and how you will define them. Before conducting his research, Derek had to define the terms "healthy" and "unhealthy"; for this, he used the USDA's Food Pyramid as a guide. Similarly, part of what Jared focused on in his interviews was learning more about how agricultural and biological engineers defined terms like "writing" and "communication." Derek and Jared thought carefully about the terms within their research questions and how these terms might be measured.

Choosing a Data Collection Method

Once you have formulated a research question or hypothesis, you will need to make decisions about what kind of data you can collect that will best address your research topic. Derek chose to examine eating habits by observing both what students ate at lunch and surveying students about eating behavior. Jared decided that in-depth interviews with experienced individuals in his field would provide him with the best information.

To choose a data collection method for your research question, read through the next sections on observations, interviews, and surveys.

OBSERVATIONS

Observations have lead to some of the most important scientific discoveries in human history. Charles Darwin used observations of the animal and marine life at the Galapagos Islands to help him formulate his theory of evolution that he describes in *On the Origin of Species*. Today, social scientists, natural scientists, engineers, computer scientists, educational researchers, and many others use observations as a primary research method.

Observations can be conducted on nearly any subject matter, and the kinds of observations you will do depend on your research question. You might observe traffic or parking patterns on campus to get a sense of what improvements could be made. You might observe clouds, plants, or other natural phenomena. If you choose to observe people, you will have several additional considerations including the manner in which you will observe them and gain their consent.

If you are observing people, you can choose between two common ways to observe: participant observation and unobtrusive observation. Participant observation is a common method within ethnographic research in sociology and anthropology. In this kind of observation, a researcher may interact with participants and become part of their community. Margaret Mead, a famous anthropologist, spent extended periods of time living in, and interacting with, communities that she studied. Conversely, in unobtrusive observation, you do not interact with participants but rather simply record their behavior. Although in most circumstances people must volunteer to be participants in research, in some cases it is acceptable to not let participants know you are observing them. In places that people perceive as public, such as a campus food court or a shopping mall, people do not expect privacy, and so it is generally acceptable to observe without participant consent. In places that people perceive as private, which can include a church, home, classroom, or even an intimate conversation at a restaurant, participant consent should be sought.

The second issue about participant consent in terms of unobtrusive observation is whether or not getting consent is feasible for the study. If you are observing people in a busy airport, bus station, or campus food court, getting participant consent may be next to impossible. In Derek's study of student eating habits on campus, he went to the campus food courts during meal times and observed students purchasing food. Obtaining participant consent for his observations would have been next to impossible because hundreds of students were coming through the food court during meal times. Since Derek's research was in a place that participants would perceive as public, it was not practical to get their consent, and since his data was anonymous, he did not violate their privacy.

Eliminating Bias in Your Observation Notes

The ethical concern of being unbiased is important in recording your observations. You need to be aware of the difference between an observation (recording exactly what you see) and an interpretation (making assumptions and judgments about what you see). When you observe, you should focus first on only the events that are directly observable. Consider the following two example entries in an observation log:

1. The student sitting in the dining hall enjoys his greasy, oil-soaked pizza. He is clearly oblivious of the calorie content and damage it may do to his body.
2. The student sits in the dining hall. As he eats his piece of pizza, which drips oil, he says to a friend, "This pizza is good."

The first entry is biased and demonstrates judgment about the event. First, the observer makes assumptions about the internal state of the student when she writes "enjoys" and "clearly oblivious to the calorie content." From an observer's standpoint, there is no way of ascertaining what the student may or may not know about pizza's nutritional value nor how much the student enjoys the pizza. The second entry provides only the details and facts that are observable.

To avoid bias in your observations, you can use something called a "double-entry notebook." This is a type of observation log that en-

Observations	Thoughts
The student sits in the dining hall. As he eats his piece of pizza, which drips oil, he says to a friend, "This pizza is good."	It seems like the student really enjoys the high-calorie content pizza.
I observed cash register #1 for 15 minutes. During that time 22 students paid for meals. Of those 22 students, 15 grabbed a candy bar or granola bar. 3 of the 22 students had a piece of fruit on their plate.	Fruit is less accessible than candy bars (it is further back in the dining court). Is this why more students are reaching for candy bars?

Figure 3: Two sample entries from a double-entry notebook.

courages you to separate your observations (the facts) from your feelings and judgments about the facts.

Observations are only one strategy in collecting primary research. You may also want to ask people directly about their behaviors, beliefs, or attitudes—and for this you will need to use surveys or interviews.

Surveys and Interviews: Question Creation

Sometimes it is very difficult for a researcher to gain all of the necessary information through observations alone. Along with his observations of the dining halls, Derek wanted to know what students ate in a typical day, and so he used a survey to have them keep track of their eating habits. Likewise, Jared wanted to learn about writing and communication in engineering and decided to draw upon expert knowledge by asking experienced individuals within the field.

Interviews and surveys are two ways that you can gather information about people's beliefs or behaviors. With these methods, the information you collect is not first-hand (like an observation) but rather "self-reported" data, or data collected in an indirect manner. William Shadish, Thomas Cook, and Donald Campbell argued that people are inherently biased about how they see the world and may report their own actions in a more favorable way than they may actually behave. Despite the issues in self-reported data, surveys and interviews are an excellent way to gather data for your primary research project.

Survey or Interview?

How do you choose between conducting a survey or an interview? It depends on what kind of information you are looking for. You should use surveys if you want to learn about a general trend in people's opinions, experiences, and behavior. Surveys are particularly useful to find small amounts of information from a wider selection of people in the hopes of making a general claim. Interviews are best used when you want to learn detailed information from a few specific people. Interviews are also particularly useful if you want to interview experts about their opinions, as Jared did. In sum, use interviews to gain details from a few people, and surveys to learn general patterns from many people.

Writing Good Questions

One of the greatest challenges in conducting surveys and interviews is writing good questions. As a researcher, you are always trying to eliminate bias, and the questions you ask need to be unbiased and clear. Here are some suggestions on writing good questions:

Ask about One Thing at a Time

A poorly written question can contain multiple questions, which can confuse participants or lead them to answer only part of the question you are asking. This is called a "double-barreled question" in journalism. The following questions are taken from Jared's research:

> Poor question: What kinds of problems are being faced in the field today and where do you see the search for solutions to these problems going?

> Revised question #1 : What kinds of problems are being faced in the field today?

> Revised question #2: Where do you see the search for solutions to these problems going?

Avoid Leading Questions

A leading question is one where you prompt the participant to respond in a particular way, which can create bias in the answers given:

> Leading question: The economy is clearly in a crisis, wouldn't you agree?

Revised question: Do you believe the economy is currently in a crisis? Why or why not?

Understand When to Use Open and Closed Questions

Closed questions, or questions that have yes/no or other limited responses, should be used in surveys. However, avoid these kinds of questions in interviews because they discourage the interviewee from going into depth. The question sample above, "Do you believe the economy currently is in a crisis?" could be answered with a simple yes or no, which could keep a participant from talking more about the issue. The "why or why not?" portion of the question asks the participant to elaborate. On a survey, the question "Do you believe the economy currently is in a crisis?" is a useful question because you can easily count the number of yes and no answers and make a general claim about participant responses.

Write Clear Questions

When you write questions, make sure they are clear, concise, and to the point. Questions that are too long, use unfamiliar vocabulary, or are unclear may confuse participants and you will not get quality responses.

Now that question creation has been addressed, we will next examine specific considerations for interviews and surveys.

INTERVIEWS

Interviews, or question and answer sessions with one or more people, are an excellent way to learn in-depth information from a person for your primary research project. This section presents information on how to conduct a successful interview, including choosing the right person, ways of interviewing, recording your interview, interview locations, and transcribing your interview.

Choosing the Right Person

One of the keys to a successful interview is choosing the right person to interview. Think about whom you would like to interview and whom you might know. Do not be afraid to ask people you do not know for interviews. When asking, simply tell them what the interview will be about, what the interview is for, and how much time it will take. Jared used his Purdue University connection to locate both of the individuals that he ended up interviewing—an advanced Purdue student and a Purdue alum working in an Engineering firm.

Face-to-Face and Virtual Interviews

When interviewing, you have a choice of conducting a traditional, face-to-face interview or an interview using technology over the Internet. Face-to-face interviews have the strength that you can ask follow-up questions and use non-verbal communication to your advantage. Individuals are able to say much more in a face-to-face interview than in an email, so you will get more information from a face-to-face interview. However, the Internet provides a host of new possibilities when it comes to interviewing people at a distance. You may choose to do an email interview, where you send questions and ask the person to respond. You may also choose to use a video or audio conferencing program to talk with the person virtually. If you are choosing any Internet-based option, make sure you have a way of recording the interview. You may also use a chat or instant messaging program to interview your participant—the benefit of this is that you can ask follow-up questions during the interview and the interview is already transcribed for you. Because one of his interviewees lived several hours away, Jared chose to interview the Purdue student face-to-face and the Purdue alum via email.

Finding a Suitable Location

If you are conducting an in-person interview, it is essential that you find a quiet place for your interview. Many universities have quiet study rooms that can be reserved (often found in the university library). Do not try to interview someone in a coffee shop, dining hall, or other loud area, as it is difficult to focus and get a clear recording.

Recording Interviews

One way of eliminating bias in your research is to record your interviews rather than rely on your memory. Recording interviews allows you to directly quote the individual and re-read the interview when you are writing. It is recommended that you have two recording devices for the interview in case one recording device fails. Most computers, MP3 players, and even cell phones come with recording equipment built in. Many universities also offer equipment that students can check out and use, including computers and recorders. Before you record any interview, be sure that you have permission from your participant.

Transcribing Your Interview

Once your interview is over, you will need to transcribe your interview to prepare it for analysis. The term transcribing means creating a written record that is exactly what was said—i.e. typing up your interviews. If you have conducted an email or chat interview, you already have a transcription and can move on to your analysis stage.

SURVEYS

Other than the fact that they both involve asking people questions, interviews and surveys are quite different data collection methods. Creating a survey may seem easy at first, but developing a quality survey can be quite challenging. When conducting a survey, you need to focus on the following areas: survey creation, survey testing, survey sampling, and distributing your survey.

Survey Creation: Length and Types of Questions

One of the keys to creating a successful survey is to keep your survey short and focused. Participants are unlikely to fill out a survey that is lengthy, and you'll have a more difficult time during your analysis if your survey contains too many questions. In most cases, you want your survey to be something that can be filled out within a few minutes. The target length of the survey also depends on how you will distribute the survey. If you are giving your survey to other students in your dorm or classes, they will have more time to complete the survey. Therefore, five to ten minutes to complete the survey is reasonable. If you are asking students as they are walking to class to fill out your survey, keep it limited to several questions that can be answered in thirty seconds or less. Derek's survey took about ten minutes and asked students to describe what they ate for a day, along with some demographic information like class level and gender.

Use closed questions to your advantage when creating your survey. A closed question is any set of questions that gives a limited amount of choices (yes/no, a 1–5 scale, choose the statement that best describes you). When creating closed questions, be sure that you are accounting for all reasonable answers in your question creation. For example, asking someone "Do you believe you eat healthy?" and providing them only "yes" and "no" options means that a "neutral" or "undecided" option does not exist, even though the survey respondent may not feel strongly either way. Therefore, on closed questions you may find it helpful to include an "other" category where participants can fill in an answer. It is also a good idea to have a few open-ended questions where participants can elaborate on certain points or earlier responses. However, open-ended questions take much longer to fill out than closed questions.

Survey Creation: Testing Your Survey

To make sure your survey is an appropriate length and that your questions are clear, you can "pilot test" your survey. Prior to administering your survey on a larger scale, ask several classmates or friends to fill it out and give you feedback on the survey. Keep track of how long the survey takes to complete. Ask them if the questions are clear and make sense. Look at their answers to see if the answers match what you wanted to learn. You can revise your survey questions and the length of your survey as necessary.

Sampling and Access to Survey Populations

"Sampling" is a term used within survey research to describe the subset of people that are included in your study. Derek's first research question was: "Are students' eating habits at Purdue University healthy or unhealthy?" Because it was impossible for Derek to survey all 38,000 students on Purdue's campus, he had to choose a representative sample of students. Derek chose to survey students who lived in the dorms because of the wide variety of student class levels and majors in the dorms and his easy access to this group. By making this choice, however, he did not account for commuter students, graduate students, or those who live off campus. As Derek's case demonstrates, it is very challenging to get a truly representative sample.

Part of the reason that sampling is a challenge is that you may find difficulty in finding enough people to take your survey. In thinking about how get people to take your survey, consider both your everyday surroundings and also technological solutions. Derek had access to many students in the dorms, but he also considered surveying students in his classes in order to reach as many people as possible. Another possibility is to conduct an online survey. Online surveys greatly increase your access to different kinds of people from across the globe, but may decrease your chances of having a high survey response rate. An email or private message survey request is more likely to be ignored due to the impersonal quality and high volume of emails most people receive.

ANALYZING AND WRITING ABOUT PRIMARY RESEARCH

Once you collect primary research data, you will need to analyze what you have found so that you can write about it. The purpose of analyzing your data is to look at what you collected (survey responses, interview answers to questions, observations) and to create a cohesive, systematic interpretation to help answer your research question or examine the validity of your hypothesis.

When you are analyzing and presenting your findings, remember to work to eliminate bias by being truthful and as accurate as possible about what you found, even if it differs from what you expected to find. You should see your data as sources of information, just like sources you find in the library, and you should work to represent them accurately.

The following are suggestions for analyzing different types of data.

Observations

If you've counted anything you were observing, you can simply add up what you counted and report the results. If you've collected descriptions using a double-entry notebook, you might work to write thick descriptions of what you observed into your writing. This could include descriptions of the scene, behaviors you observed, and your overall conclusions about events. Be sure that your readers are clear on what were your actual observations versus your thoughts or interpretations of those observations.

Interviews

If you've interviewed one or two people, then you can use your summary, paraphrasing, and quotation skills to help you accurately describe what was said in the interview. Just like in secondary research when working with sources, you should introduce your interviewees and choose clear and relevant quotes from the interviews to use in your writing. An easy way to find the important information in an interview is to print out your transcription and take a highlighter and mark the important parts that you might use in your paper. If you have conducted a large number of interviews, it will be helpful for you to create a spreadsheet of responses to each question and compare the responses, choosing representative answers for each area you want to describe.

Surveys

Surveys can contain quantitative (numerical) and qualitative (written answers/descriptions) data. Quantitative data can be analyzed using a spreadsheet program like Microsoft Excel to calculate the mean (average) answer or to calculate the percentage of people who responded in a certain way. You can display this information in a chart or a graph and also describe it in writing in your paper. If you have qualitative responses, you might choose to group them into categories and/or you may choose to quote several representative responses.

WRITING ABOUT PRIMARY RESEARCH

In formal research writing in a variety of fields, it is common for research to be presented in the following format: introduction/background; methods; results; discussions; conclusion. Not all first year writing classes will require such an organizational structure, although it is likely that you will be required to present many of these elements in your paper. Because of this, the next section examines each of these in depth.

Introduction (Review of Literature)

The purpose of an introduction and review of literature in a research paper is to provide readers with information that helps them understand the context, purpose, and relevancy of your research. The introduction is where you provide most of your background (library) research that you did earlier in the process. You can include articles, statistics, research studies, and quotes that are pertinent to the issues at hand. A second purpose in an introduction is to establish your own credibility (ethos) as a writer by showing that you have researched your topic thoroughly. This kind of background discussion is required in nearly every field of inquiry when presenting research in oral or written formats.

Derek provided information from the Food and Drug Administration on healthy eating and national statistics about eating habits as part of his background information. He also made the case for healthy eating on campus to show relevancy:

> Currently Americans are more overweight than ever. This is coming at a huge cost to the economy and government. If current trends in increasing rates of overweight and obesity continue it is likely that this generation will be the first one to live shorter lives than their parents did. Looking at the habits of university students is a good way to see how a new generation behaves when they are living out on their own for the first time.

Describing What You Did (Methods)

When writing, you need to provide enough information to your readers about your primary research process for them to understand what you collected and how you collected it. In formal research papers, this is often called a methods section. Providing information on your study methods also adds to your credibility as a writer. For surveys, your methods would include describing who you surveyed, how many surveys you collected, decisions you made about your survey sample, and relevant demographic information about your participants (age, class level, major). For interviews, introduce whom you interviewed and any other relevant information about interviewees such as their career or expertise area. For observations, list the locations and times you observed and how you recorded your observations (i.e. double-entry notebook). For all data types, you should describe how you analyzed your data.

The following is a sample from Jared about his participants:

> In order to gain a better understanding of the discourse community in environmental and resource engineering, I interviewed Anne Dare, a senior in environmental and natural resource engineering, and Alyson Keaton an alumnus of Purdue University. Alyson is a current employee of the Natural

Resource Conservation Service (NRCS), which is a division
of the United States Department of Agriculture (USDA).

Here is a sample from Derek's methods section:

> I conducted a survey so that I could find out what students
> at Purdue actually eat on a typical day. I handed out surveys
> asking students to record what they ate for a day . . . I received
> 29 back and averaged the results based on average number of
> servings from each food group on the old food guide pyramid.
> The group included students from the freshman to the gradu-
> ate level and had 8 women and 21 men respond.

Describing Your Study Findings (Results)

In a formal research paper, the results section is where you describe
what you found. The results section can include charts, graphs, lists,
direct quotes, and overviews of findings. Readers find it helpful if you
are able to provide the information in different formats. For example,
if you have any kind of numbers or percentages, you can talk about
them in your written description and then present a graph or chart
showing them visually. You should provide specific details as supporting evidence to back up your findings. These details can be in the
form of direct quotations, numbers, or observations.

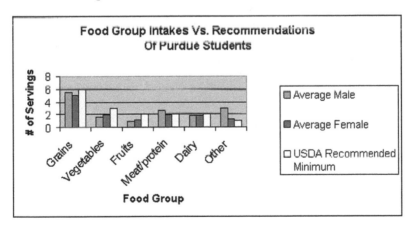

Fig. 4: Graphic from Derek's results section.

Jared describes some of his interview results:

Alyson also mentioned the need for phone conversation. She stated, "The phone is a large part of my job. I am communicating with other NRCS offices daily to find out the status of our jobs." She needs to be in constant contact in order to insure that everything is running smoothly. This is common with those overseeing projects. In these cases, the wait for a response to an email or a memo can be too long to be effective.

Interpreting What You Learned (Discussion)

In formal research papers, the discussion section presents your own interpretation of your results. This may include what you think the results mean or how they are useful to your larger argument. If you are making a proposal for change or a call to action, this is where you make it. For example, in Derek's project about healthy eating on campus, Derek used his primary research on students' unhealthy eating and observations of the food courts to argue that the campus food courts needed serious changes. Derek writes, "Make healthy food options the most accessible in every dining hall while making unhealthy foods the least. Put nutrition facts for everything that is served in the dining halls near the food so that students can make more informed decisions on what to eat."

Jared used the individuals he interviewed as informants that helped him learn more about writing in agricultural and biological engineering. He integrated the interviews he conducted with secondary research to form a complete picture of writing and communication in agricultural and biological engineering. He concludes:

> Writing takes so many forms, and it is important to know about all these forms in one way or another. The more forms of writing you can achieve, the more flexible you can be. This ability to be flexible can make all the difference in writing when you are dealing with a field as complex as engineering.

Primary Research and Works Cited or References Pages

The last part of presenting your primary research project is a works cited or references page. In general, since you are working with data you collected yourself, there is no source to cite an external source. Your methods section should describe in detail to the readers how and where the data presented was obtained. However, if you are working with interviews, you can cite these as "personal communication." The MLA and APA handbooks both provide clear listings of how to cite personal communication in a works cited/references page.

CONCLUSION

This essay has presented an overview to three commonly used methods of primary research in first year writing courses: observations, interviews, and surveys. By using these methods, you can learn more about the world around you and craft meaningful written discussions of your findings.

DISCUSSION

1. Primary research techniques show up in more places than just first year writing courses. Where else might interviews, surveys, or observations be used? Where have you seen them used?
2. The chapter provides a brief discussion of the ethical considerations of research. Can you think of any additional ethical considerations when conducting primary research? Can you think of ethical considerations unique to your own research project?
3. Primary research is most useful for first year writing students if it is based in your local community or campus. What are some current issues on your campus or in your community that could be investigated using primary research methods?
4. In groups or as a class, make a list of potential primary research topics. After each topic on the list, consider what method of inquiry (observation, interview, or survey) you would use to study the topic and answer why that method is a good choice.

SUGGESTED RESOURCES

For more information on the primary methods of inquiry described here, please see the following sources:

Babbie, Earl. *The Practice of Social Research*. 10th edition. Wadsworth Publishing, 2003. Print.

Creswell, John. *Research Design: Qualitative, Quantitative, and Mixed Methods Approaches*. 3rd ed. Sage publications, 2008. Print.

Rubin, Herbert and Irene Rubin. *Qualitative Interviewing: The Art of Hearing Data*. 2nd edition. Thousand Oaks, CA: Sage Publications, 2004. Print.

Fink, Arlene. *How to Conduct Surveys: A Step-by-Step Guide*. 4th ed. Thousand Oaks, CA: Sage Publications, 2008. Print.

Sanger, Jack. *Compleat Observer? A Field Research Guide to Observation*. New York: Routledge, 1996. Print.

The National Commission for the Protection of Human Subjects of Biomedical and Behavioral Research. *The Belmont Report*. 18 April 1979. Web. <http://ohsr.od.nih.gov/guidelines/belmont.html>.

WORKS CITED

Babbie, Earl. *The Practice of Social Research*. 10th ed. Belmont, CA: Wadsworth publishing, 2003. Print.

Creswell, John. *Research Design: Qualitative, Quantitative, and Mixed Methods Approaches*. 3rd ed. Thousand Oaks, CA: Sage publications, 2008. Print.

Shadish, William, Thomas, Cook and Donald Campbell. *Quasi-Experimentation: Design and Analysis Issues*. Boston, MA: Houghton Mifflin Company, 1979. Print.

Darwin, Charles. *On the Origin of Species by Means of Natural Selection*. New York: L Hurst and Company, No date. Print.

Lauer, Janice and William Asher. *Composition Research: Empirical Designs*. Oxford: Oxford University Press, 1988. Print.

Leavitt, Fred. *Evaluating Scientific Research: Separating Fact from Fiction*. Long Grove, IL: Waveland Press, 2004. Print.

Mead, Margaret. *Growing Up in New Guinea: A Comparative Study of Primitive Education*. New York: Morrow, 193. Print.

Mill, John Stuart. *John Stuart Mill's Philosophy of Scientific Method*. Ernest Nagel, Ed. New York: Hafner Publishing Co, 1950. Print.

Rubin, Herbert and Irene Rubin. *Qualitative Interviewing: The Art of Hearing Data*. 2nd ed. Thousand Oaks, CA: Sage Publications, 2004. Print.

Putting Ethnographic Writing in Context

Seth Kahn

If you're like most students, you may wonder why your writing instructor is asking you to do *ethnographic writing.** You may have a vague idea of what ethnography is—what anthropologists do when they live in faraway places for long stretches of time, trying to understand what makes a culture unique or interesting. You may wonder what studying cultures in detail, conducting fieldwork and interviews, has to do with writing papers for your college classes.

Anthropologists James Spradley and David McCurdy answer the question concisely when they say, "A good writer must be a good ethnographer" (4). Ethnographic writing challenges you to consider everything that's interesting and difficult about writing; it pushes you to *generate, collect, analyze,* and *synthesize* more material than you've probably had to work with in one paper before. Moreover, because ethnographies are about actual people, the assignment makes you think about *ethics* (how you're presenting information, how that information might affect people if made public, being as accurate as you can) and *knowledge* (what it is you really know at the end of the project and how you present that knowledge without sounding more confident than you should). And finally, because these projects generally take a long time and you write constantly while doing them, you'll have plenty of time to reflect on and understand how you're learning and changing as writers along the way.

Along with the benefits to your writing, ethnography really highlights and emphasizes human relationships: between participants and researchers; between writers and readers of ethnographic narratives/reports; between students and teachers in classrooms. If all goes well, you'll find that your writing helps you navigate those relationships. That is, ethnographic writing can, when it works well, do more than produce interesting papers: it can improve your understanding of people and their ways of thinking/talking; it can improve the lives of the people you write about; it can help you reflect on your own positions within cultures.

One big lesson you should learn is that ethnographic writing, when it works well, does not—in fact cannot—follow a conventional formula for essays. It requires you to experiment with style, voice, structure, and purpose in ways you probably haven't before. To help you see what I mean by that, I'll at times evoke my own experiences as an ethnographer and teacher of ethnographic writing; the mixture of narrative and analysis should give you an idea—not necessarily a model—of the ways that traditional and non-traditional academic writing conventions work for this kind of project.

SOME NUTS AND BOLTS: WHAT ETHNOGRAPHERS DO

The term most synonymous with *ethnography* is *participant-observation research*. Ethnographers study *cultures,* i.e., the relationships, rituals, values, and habits that make people understand themselves as members of a group (or society, or what have you). We do so by spending lots of time in the cultures we study, interacting with members, watching and learning from how they act and talk, participating in their activities, and talking with them about how they understand their groups and their lives. That is, we adopt a stance that's both distanced (observing) and interactive (participatory), and good ethnographic writing emerges from the juxtaposition of those stances. Good ethnographic writing also acknowledges the effects we have on the cultures we study—which, I'll contend below, is both inevitable and desirable—and the effects those cultures have on us.

Put simply then, ethnographers: observe, participate, interact, analyze, reflect, write, rethink, and describe cultures, their members, and our own involvements with them. What pins together all these ways of thinking and seeing is that they all either happen in—or directly lead to—*writing*. I can't even pretend to generate an exhaustive list of all the writing you'll do for your project, but here's some of it:

1. Pre-writing: reflections on what you know about the culture you'll study, what you think you know, your biases and predispositions towards its members, the questions you're interested in trying to answer, and more.

2. Introductions/consent forms: letters/emails to group members explaining your project and asking for permission to do it; consent forms for participants to sign, indicating that they understand your project and agree to be involved in it.

3. Fieldnotes/interview notes/transcripts: notes on your visits to the group/research site; notes taken during interviews with participants; transcripts of interviews with participants; descriptions of physical locations, settings, physical artifacts, and so on.

4. Journal: a running internal monologue, so to speak, of your thinking throughout the project—what you're seeing, what you think is important, what you need to pursue further, what you're confused about, who you need to make sure you interview, and/or anything else that helps you keep track of your ideas; some instructors might require occasional "progress reports," which are slightly more elaborated, formal versions of journal entries.

5. Drafts and revisions of ethnographies: your write-up of the project will require multiple drafts and major overhauls in organization/structure, voice, and content, all of which should help you understand your own points as much as they help your readers. Your instructor might even require that you share drafts of your paper with participants in your study.

If you're still wondering what this assignment can teach you about writing, then understand also that this list is not only incomplete, but also not in any necessary order. You'll probably find that your process is *recursive*, e.g., that a journal entry near the end of the project might call on you to re-interview a participant, or that something you'd forgotten about in your fieldnotes makes you rethink your analysis in a third draft of the paper. And, just as importantly, you may find that sharing your notes, transcripts, and drafts with participants in your project heightens your awareness of what some of us call the *ethics of representation*, i.e., the responsibility to our participants to ensure that what we say about them is fair, reasonable, and accurate.

Learning from Experience

One of the driving forces behind assigning ethnographic writing is that people learn more from direct experience than from second-hand experience (e.g., reading, lectures). When we ask you to go out into the field to do your participant-observation research, we're expecting you to learn a lot more about the culture you study than you could by reading about it, or listening to somebody else talk about it. We're also expecting that all the writing you do about it will help you come to terms with what you know, both by making you make sense for yourselves about what you're experiencing, and by making you make sense of it for readers.

If you've written personal reflective essays (like many college admission essays, as well as assignments you might have done for courses), then you've done some of what I'm describing; you've written a narrative in order to help you reflect on an experience, to help you learn or understand something about yourself, and to make that as clear as you can to somebody else. Ethnography also requires you to do this kind of *inductive reasoning,* which means that you collect and consider evidence and experience without a hypothesis or conclusion in mind; your analysis and descriptions explain what you've learned, rather than confirming or disconfirming what somebody else already claimed or knew. But ethnography is different from personal reflective writing in at least these two ways. First, rather than writing about experiences you've *already had,* most of the writing you'll do is about experiences *you're having.* That is, your writing can actually change your situation in ways that reflecting on the past can't. Second, while you're certainly part of the story you're experiencing and writing, you're also writing about *other people,* which comes with a set of responsibilities that can become very complex very quickly.

LEARNING FROM SOMEBODY ELSE'S EXPERIENCE

You can, of course, learn from other people's experiences, too. I want to tell you the story of my first ethnographic project. The project, a study of a graduate-level literature course, should help you see in concrete terms what I've been describing: the kinds of writing involved, and some of the ethical issues that arise from talking about real people and real events, with real implications.

Fall 1996 semester: for a research methods course (most graduate students are required to take at least one methods course, in which we learn to do the professional scholarship we'll have to do as faculty), our major assignment, which would span about eight weeks, was to pick a course in our department, negotiate access to the course with the professor, and do participant-observation research for about five weeks, leaving the last three weeks to write an ethnographic description of fifteen to twenty pages.

The first half of the research methods course had gone smoothly. We studied ethnographic techniques: negotiating access (convincing participants to let us study their cultures), interview strategies, ways of taking fieldnotes, and types of data analysis. We read two full-length ethnographic studies—Elizabeth Chiseri-Strater's *Academic Literacies* and Bonnie Sunstein's *Composing a Culture*—as well as two books that theorize the importance of *writing* to ethnographic research: anthropologist Clifford Geertz's *Works and Lives: The Anthropologist as Author* and sociologist John Van Maanen's *Tales of the Field: On Writing Ethnography*. I'll return to the Geertz text later; for now, suffice it to say that our entire class believed we'd been well trained to do participant-observation research, and to write interesting and ethically responsible accounts of our experiences.

I decided to approach a professor I had taken a course from before; the course I wanted to study examined relationships between jazz music and literature in the 1950s. I had really enjoyed working with him, and he had some teaching habits I wanted to examine while I wasn't a student in his course. He was intrigued by the idea, and because we'd developed a solid working relationship, he quickly granted access. His only request, one you shouldn't be surprised to encounter, was that I share the final paper with him.

The fieldwork went fine. Over five weeks, I attended class three times each week for fifty minutes; took fieldnotes on the nine students and the professor (an average of five handwritten pages per day); interviewed everybody, some more than once (a total of fifteen interviews, averaging about twenty minutes). The professor gave me copies of his syllabus and all the assignments, as well as examples of work students had done earlier in the semester so I could see the kinds of topics they were interested in researching. In all, I had hundreds of pages of notes, course documents, students' work, and my own journals.

By the time I was done with the fieldwork, I knew how I would focus my description and analysis—which, in retrospect, was part of the problem. What I found, in brief, from my research was what I thought I'd find—a professor who knew his material inside-out, who worked hard to involve students in conversations, who cared as much as anybody I've ever known about his students, but who at times responded to students' comments in ways that seemed dismissive or sarcastic. As a result, the students were sometimes confused about how to respond to the professor's questions and discussion prompts, which frustrated the professor into sometimes sounding even more sarcastic, hoping to lighten the mood but often doing just the opposite.

I had plenty of evidence to write a good paper demonstrating what I'd learned.

We spent two weeks drafting and revising the papers, and receiving extensive feedback from classmates and the professor of the research methods course. All the feedback emphasized readers' needs for more direct evidence: anecdotes from class meetings; sections of interview transcripts; relevant pieces of the syllabus and course materials. By the time I submitted the final draft, I believed I had represented the central issue of the class in a readable, interesting, and believable way. My professor, Wendy, (mostly) agreed. She gave me an A- on the paper, an A in the course, and I thought I'd had a positive learning experience.

I had, but not the one I anticipated. Here's what Wendy wrote about my study in a textbook that incorporates a lot of the work and experiences of graduate students in her courses:

> I have had a classroom mini-ethnography cause consternation to a colleague who had allowed one of my students to study him. Consent forms were signed. Classroom reports were drafted and commented on and shared: novice work, much learning. The teacher who was portrayed in the classroom study was—with some reason—much dismayed to read his portrait. I was able to assure him that the student had no intention of publishing that work. (He didn't, particularly

> after talking to the teacher, whose work he actually admired
> no matter how his report played out, and he had even less in-
> tention of doing so when he realized his informant was upset.)
> (Bishop 122)

Wendy's description is much more careful and rational than mine was;
I wrote in my journal, after the professor reacted to what I'd written:

> I can't believe this guy! I can't believe he called me, at home,
> after midnight last night to yell at me about my paper. We
> were on the phone for an hour while he disputed everything
> I said, except the actual facts! Was I wrong when I said [. . .
>], or when I described his way of [. . .], or [. . .]? [I'm leav-
> ing out specific details to protect his identity]. Everything I
> said was right! It's not my fault if he's offended by his own
> behaviors.

Once I calmed down (a few days later!), I began to understand the
professor's reaction: not so much that I'd included specific unflatter-
ing details, but that I'd made him look unprofessional (while I thought
he looked quirky and interesting). He was an award-winning faculty
member, understandably concerned that a published version of my
paper could harm his reputation—an example of what I meant before when I talked about some of the ethical problems that arise from
ethnographic writing. In retrospect, I wish I had shown him a draft
of the paper while I was working on it so that he'd had a chance to
respond, and perhaps clarify, what he believed were misrepresentations
and misunderstandings on my part. I also learned a hard lesson about
seeing situations from the perspectives of *all* participants; while my
paper represented the students' frustrations at length, it didn't account
for the professor's nearly well enough.

RISKS AND BENEFITS FOR PARTICIPANTS

Because you're writing about real people in real life in your ethnography, your words have potentially profound consequences for the
people you write about. I was devastated by the professor's response
to my paper. Somebody I respected was very upset about what I'd
written, and beyond his hurt feelings, he was concerned that my piece
might affect his professional life. And I would soon teach my first
research-writing course, having just experienced first-hand what hap-

pens when an ethnographic writer upsets a participant. The professor whose course I'd studied made it quite clear that we were no longer friends, and only once since then have we had any contact at all. He felt *betrayed,* a term I borrow from composition researcher Thomas Newkirk's essay, "Seduction and Betrayal in Qualitative Research." Newkirk contends that because qualitative research is inductive (we don't know what we'll see until it happens), there's no sure way to ensure that participants won't be unhappy about what researchers find; moreover, informed consent not only can't stop this from happening, but also may lull participants into a false sense of security during the project.

Because I wrote the paper for a class with no intention of ever publishing it, the professional consequences for the professor were minimal; that's not to say, of course, that his feelings weren't hurt by the experience. However, even your fieldnotes can have consequences, and you need to be very careful to protect the identities of your participants, even if you don't expect anybody else to see what you write. One former student of mine left his notebook on a table at his site one afternoon, and when he returned five minutes later, two of his participants were reading it. One of them discovered that her boyfriend was cheating on her with another group member; within two days the group had disbanded, and one participant wound up in the hospital with injuries from the ensuing fight.

Situations this dramatic are rare; I've read about 700 ethnographies and count fewer than ten with the potential to endanger any of the participants. The point is that they can be, and you should take steps to minimize the danger: never use anybody's real name or anything that easily identifies them; ask participants to check your notes about them for accuracy, and respect requests not to reveal certain details; make sure participants have signed consent forms. None of these is fail-safe, but they should all be habitual.

Your ethnographic research and writing can, of course, be beneficial for you and your participants, too. Several of my students have discovered, during their projects, significant ways to help their groups. One student, who studied a dance troupe at the university where I did my doctorate, found that the biggest problem they faced was the absence of a regular practice space; she used the evidence she developed in her research—specifically the time members spent worrying about and looking for practice space instead of practicing, and the number

of prospective members they lost because they looked disorganized—
to argue for a dedicated room, and the group still uses the room to
this day. Another studied a university office that provided escorts to
students crossing campus late at night. His thesis in the first draft of
his paper was that the service was under-utilized, largely because it
was understaffed and underfunded. When he showed the draft to the
office's director, however, he learned the office had been well-funded
and well-advertised for many years, but had slipped off the university's
radar. His study, particularly evidence that the staff didn't take its
public relations responsibilities very seriously because they didn't have
enough people to serve more students, helped the office's director develop a convincing argument to resume funding and public relations
work so that the service got the resources it needed.

   These projects helped their writers to see the significance of their
own writing in very direct terms. One reason their papers worked so
well is the *authority* (a somewhat different kind of authority than conventional academic writing demonstrates, a distinction that will be
clearer shortly) with which they represented the cultures and the issues. Earlier, I mentioned anthropologist Clifford Geertz and sociologist John Van Maanen, both of whom have been extremely influential
among ethnographers in helping us understand what ethnographic
writing is good for. Geertz especially, in a book called *Works and Lives:
The Anthropologist as Author,* develops two concepts that have become
crucial to my understanding of ethnographic writing. First is *ethnographic authority.* In simple terms, the problem is that for decades,
anthropologists and sociologists had treated ethnography as if it were
a science, i.e., as if it could/should result in objective descriptions of
cultures. By the 1960s, ethnographers had begun to realize that objectivity isn't possible in this kind of research; when I said in the second paragraph that ethnography makes you think about the kind of
knowledge you make from doing it, this is what I was introducing. To
be taken seriously as research, the writing has to demonstrate a level
of rigor that many academic disciplines believe is best represented by
scientific reportage (like chemistry lab reports—very thoroughly detailed, step-by-step descriptions of processes; careful analysis of results;
style that excludes any mention of the researcher; etc.). But with the
realization that ethnography doesn't work like a science, ethnographic
writers had to think about other ways to establish authority for their
work.

Geertz presents the second major concept from *Works and Lives* in the deceptively simple phrase, "being there":

> The ability of anthropologists to get us to take what they say seriously has less to do with either a factual look or an air of conceptual elegance than it has with their capacity to convince us that what they say is a result of their having actually penetrated (or, if you prefer, been penetrated by) another form of life, of having, one way or another, truly 'been there.' (4–5)

As he unpacks this phrase throughout the book, it becomes possible to paraphrase it in another deceptively simple way, i.e., ethnographic authority results from being able to present details and insights that only the writer would know, because the writer was there and readers weren't.

The logic here is circular (authority comes from sounding like an authority)—mostly. Geertz's goal is a little more complicated than I've put it. We haven't explored yet his assertion (or recognition) that issues of writers' *voices* and *styles* are as relevant to ethnographic authority as the writers' *content*. Let me be clear here: nobody would argue that strong voice and style can override bad content; the data/findings/results have to be strong (in the sense that they're specific, concrete, and analyzed carefully) before presentation matters. But, whereas traditional scientific discourse assumes that personal voice and style are distractions from content, Geertz posits that content, by itself, doesn't really accomplish anything; the knowledge that ethnography produces emerges from the relationships formed among writers and readers. The students in my classes whose projects directly benefited their cultures were all able to construct relationships of trust with their readers—exactly what I failed to do in my project I described earlier—helping the data make the case that something needed to change on behalf of their groups. It's hard to imagine that happening if they hadn't "been there."

Another way that ethnographers can benefit participants in our research is by establishing a relationship of *reciprocity*. The principle, in the abstract, is simple—in return for inviting us into their worlds and letting us take information from them, we agree to return the favor by performing services of various kinds for community members. Literacy researcher Ellen Cushman, in her book *The Struggle and the Tools*, describes this exchange between members of a black Muslim mosque and herself as an example:

> [A]rea residents invited me to attend the mosque with them
> (this group of Muslims happened to be particularly private
> and only allowed Whites to attend if invited by a member).
> With their invitation, I was granted entry into a religious
> arena that I would have been hard pressed to enter otherwise
> [. . .]. In like fashion, I invited residents [participants in her
> study] to use the computer facilities of the private university
> I attended. Because this institute was private, residents would
> have been hard pressed to use the computers without my in-
> vitation. (23)

Much of her work with the residents of an inner city neighborhood
also involved helping them deal with government agencies, advising
high school students on college prospects, and similar activities.

Further, the principle of reciprocity signifies a commitment ethnographers make to developing personal relationships with research
participants. Not only does reciprocity establish a relationship that
goes beyond *taking;* it also allows ethnographers and participants to
collaborate in the process of learning about each other, and learning
about themselves. As ethnographers, we aren't watching lab rats run
through mazes or observing processes in laboratories. We are real people, involving ourselves in the lives of other real people, with real consequences for all of us.

The takeaway value of these concepts (consent, reciprocity) is
that you need to respect your participants and make sure you're not
exploiting them and their goodwill just for the sake of your grades.
Along with heightened attention to writerly authority (the discussion
of Geertz earlier), concern for participants as a primary feature of ethnography is the most important shift following from the realization
that ethnography isn't a science.

Putting Ethnographic Writing
in Historical Context

If ethnography isn't science, then what is it? Why do we talk about
it as *research?* If its primary goal—as least as I've been putting it—is
to benefit the cultures and participants in studies, then why do ethnographers pay so much attention to procedures, kinds of data, style,
voice, authority—all the academic-sounding concerns I'm raising in
this essay? The answer, at least my answer, to that question is compli-

cated. To understand it well, it's helpful to know some history of where ethnography and ethnographic writing came from.

Most scholars in Anthropology (ethnography's "home" discipline) agree on two predecessors of ethnography: missionary work and travel writing, beginning as early as the seventeenth and eighteenth centuries. Anthropologist Dell Hymes traces the tradition back to ancient Greece, marked by the beginnings of sea-faring international commerce (21), contending that trade couldn't happen successfully unless traders understood the cultures they were trading with. Other anthropologists (Clifford Geertz; James Clifford; George Marcus; many more) likewise describe the peak of European/Christian missionary work, claiming that missionaries had to study and document the cultures in which they worked, and that the texts they produced were often extremely detailed descriptions of cultures—structures, membership, hierarchies, value systems, rituals, customs. Missionaries' purposes weren't *academic,* i.e., their task wasn't primarily scholarly, but they established the habit of *writing up* their findings.

Their writing, however, didn't need to appeal to an especially wide audience, or an audience that needed to be convinced that the "findings" were rigorous. Their audience was themselves, their churches, and other missionaries who would follow them into similar regions. As people began traveling more in the nineteenth century, many of whom were traveling in lands that missionaries had explored and written about, a new kind of cultural document emerged: travel writing. Nineteenth-century travel writing borrowed from missionary writing the habit of presenting detailed accounts of places, people, customs, rituals, and so on, but more with an eye towards representing the exotic, exciting elements of those cultures. The purpose was to highlight the *otherness* of foreign cultures in order to encourage people to visit them, or to feel like they'd shared the experience of visiting them, without recognizing (or caring about) the risk of stereotyping or marginalizing those cultures.

These forms of pre-ethnographic writing were crucial to developing the discipline of Anthropology, establishing the habits of writing detailed and (ideally) interesting texts about cultures other than the writers.' But missionary and travel writing also laid the seeds for two major ethical problems plaguing ethnographers since: the *imperial* and *colonial* critiques. The *imperial* critique contends that ethnographers bring cultural assumptions and agendas with us when we enter new cultures, and (almost) inevitably try to impose those agendas and values on those cultures—which is, by definition, what missionaries do. I'm not accusing missionaries of anything insidious; I'm making the point that their understandings of other cultures are instrumental (they serve specific purposes) rather than intellectual. As an ethnographer, you'll discover, if you haven't already, that it's very hard not to do this. You can't help but see cultures in terms you're comfortable with. For now, as long as you're not trying to convince members of the cultures you're studying to *think like you do,* to share your beliefs instead of your trying to understand theirs, you're on the right track.

The *colonial* critique emerges more directly from the habits of travel writing, positing that simply taking data from a culture without giving anything back exploits the members of those cultures for personal gain (for academics, that usually means publications and conference presentations; for you, it means course credit and a good grade), leaving the cultures in the same conditions we found them. For many decades, anthropologists studied cultures that were isolated, pre-industrial, and very often on the brink of disappearing or being controlled by powerful nations. My earlier discussions of risks and benefits, especially the notions of respect and reciprocity, developed in direct response to these critiques.

With the shift away from seeing ethnography as science, possibilities for its usefulness have expanded significantly. No longer is ethnography a direct descendent of missionary work, an effort to romanticize the voyeurism of wealthy travelers, or a scientific effort to document different cultures—although it still wrestles with all of those influences. Instead, ethnography is a means of engaging and understanding cultures and cultural differences with respect and care for the members of those cultures.

LEARNING FROM A BETTER EXPERIENCE

Most of what I've discussed in the last two sections (Risks and Benefits; Historical Context) I learned after I'd struggled with the research project I described earlier. Although I couldn't know then what I know now, at least you can know some of it. In the same spirit but on a happier note, I'll finish this essay by describing a—not to put too fine a point on it—better ethnographic project, one that embodies what I learned. The goal is for you to see what these concepts look like in practice. Although this project was much bigger and more complex than what you're doing, you should be able to see what it looks like to design and conduct a study that incorporates the kinds of care and respect for participants I'm calling for, and to see how various forms of writing contribute to making that happen.

My PhD dissertation, called *Grassroots Democracy in Process: Ethnographic Writing as Democratic Action,* merged my interests in *doing* and *teaching* ethnographic writing. I had taught ethnographic writing in my courses for years, studied what other ethnographic writing teachers do, and studied ethnographic theory and practice in other disciplines. What would happen if I did ethnography in a course where I was teaching ethnography? How would what I'd learned about research ethics, collaborative knowledge-making, and authority play out as I tried both to enact and teach them? I was also interested, as a teacher whose scholarly work speaks primarily to other teachers, in exploring the difficulties of being both the instructor and the researcher in the same setting.

In order to do what I'd learned—and, because I'd already started publishing articles about research ethics, to practice what I preached—a key goal of the project was making sure that the students' needs never became subordinate to mine. I needed to collect data: fieldnotes from every class and conference, transcripts of interviews, the students' writing, course materials, and so on. I also needed not to to push their projects in ways that fit my expectations. Most importantly, I needed to make sure that the students' learning was always the focus of our activities.

For the most part, we could say that I was trying to build the kind of *reciprocal* relationship that Ellen Cushman calls for. Anthropologist Robert Jay probably describes what I was after a little more precisely: a relationship of collaboration and trust. The goal, that is, wasn't simply to return favors to participants, but to establish a relationship in which we all worked together on a common project that benefitted all of us equally as a result. As early as 1969, anthropologists were beginning (and I can't overemphasize that word—even forty years later many anthropologists don't fully subscribe to this position) to privilege the well-being of their research participants above even their own research agendas. Jay declares:

> In future field work I shall place first a mutual responsibility to my whole self and to those I go to learn from, in agreement

with my desire to relate to them as full equals, personal and intellectual. I shall try to use my relationships with them to find out what topics are relevant to each of us, to be investigated through what questions and what modes of questioning, and for what kinds of knowledge. I should wish to make the first report for them, in fact with them; indeed it may be that written reports would seem to us redundant. (379)

Jay might sound preachy (he does to me), but his point is important. Ethnographers always have to remember that our work can have serious implications for our participants. As such, we share the responsibility to make those implications: (1) as positive as possible; and (2) collaboratively determined with our participants. By engaging our participants as collaborators, we make sure their needs are just as important as ours; our studies serve their aims as much as ours; and they benefit from participating in them as much as we do.

In my project, students collaborated as fellow researchers primarily by reading, responding to, and discussing every word of my fieldnotes during the semester. Every two weeks, I'd distribute all my notes. They'd read them for homework, and then we'd discuss them. They corrected any mistakes or misattributions in the notes. The discussions would focus on issues they saw recurring or emerging, what they found interesting or anomalous, and questions they had either about the method or the data. Thinking through all this information with the students was stimulating; they had ideas and noticed patterns I wouldn't have, which I carefully credited them with in the dissertation. More important than the direct benefit to me was the sense of collaboration this practice generated among them. Because the group really understood the project as a collaboration rather than an imposition, they spoke candidly about contentious issues, and were willing to trust that when I asked them to do seemingly strange activities, I wasn't just experimenting on them.

I also designed the course so that everything students did for my study helped them with their ethnographies; everything we did served two purposes at once. When they read and commented on fieldnotes, for example, they were collaborating and helping me understand our class, but they were also learning valuable lessons about fieldnote-taking and data presentation. About halfway through the semester, I asked them to interview each other about our class; the transcripts provided me with insights into their thoughts about the semester, while at the same time allowing them to practice interviewing techniques. An exercise late in the semester, in which they reflected on what they thought somebody would need to know in order to do well in the course, helped them learn to synthesize and make claims about vast amounts of data, while showing me what struck them as important, annoying, useful, and distracting about the way we conducted ourselves in class.

By the end of the semester, I had a pretty good idea what my ethnography would say. Its central claim, that involving my students in my project helped them do theirs better, seemed clear and supportable. However, I also knew from my last experience that the obvious claim certainly wasn't all there was to it, and I needed to write and think a lot more about what I'd learned. I was lucky I had lots of time—more than a year—to write slowly and revise extensively; also, I was lucky to have two readers who worked very hard to provide feedback. The upshot of that long process was a project that made a much better claim than the one I'd started with. Yes, the ethnographies from that semester were better than ones I'd read before, but there was more to it than simply that they'd participated in somebody else's study while doing their own. I realized, after months of writing and rewriting, that all the writing we'd done (fieldnotes, comments on fieldnotes, interviews, in-class exercises) had been the catalyst for the students' improved work. That is, the fact that we wrote with, for, and about each other all semester long had helped the students understand what they were engaged in much more richly than they would have otherwise.

You shouldn't be taking my project as a model for yours. But you will, I hope, see one way of working with and through the major concepts I've laid out in the essay (the lessons to be learned about writing: the significant ethical issues that arise from representing other people; and the possible benefits of ethnographic research and writing). Rather than seeing this part of the text as instructions, I'd rather you feel inspired, or provoked—either way, prepared—to think your way through your own projects. The best feature of ethnographic writing is that whatever happens, it's important and interesting as long as you make it so by writing well about it. That's the hardest thing about it, too; nobody can provide you with a precise formula for the writing. You have to work that out by drafting, working with feedback, and revising.

Conclusions and (In)Conclusions

I hope you've learned enough about ethnography's problems and possibilities to understand *why* we ask you to do it. It's connecting events with how you understand them; with how your understanding connects to your participants' understandings; how all of those understandings interrelate, conflict with, and affirm each other; how you expect your readers to make sense of all that in a way that's meaningful for them; and how all that contributes to the lives of your participants and yourself.

Those are lofty goals. You may have noticed that I said little about writing any of my own ethnographic texts; that's partially because this collection limits texts to a certain length, but more importantly because you can only sort through these problems of representation and authority, and of collaboration and mutual respect, by writing your own way through them. Your writing, the feedback you get, and your revision processes will all make you see these problems as connected and complicated; keep writing, and you'll find your way.

Discussion

1. Perhaps the most complex problem facing ethnographic writers is the problem of representing your research participants ethically. How have the theoretical and anecdotal evidence in this chapter helped you think about how to do that?
2. As I was drafting and revising this essay, I asked several classes to read it. There was strong disagreement among my students over which sections they found most convincing: the more traditionally academic, or the more narrative/anecdotal. How would you answer that question, and why?
3. Based on any fieldwork you've already done (if you've begun), or you can imagine doing, what specific strategies can you suggest for avoiding imperial and/or colonial critiques of your own research?
4. What lessons that you're learning about ethnographic research can you imagine applying to other kinds of research and writing that you do as college students, or beyond?

Works Cited

Bishop, Wendy. *Ethnographic Writing Research: Writing It Down, Writing It Up, and Reading It.* Portsmouth, NH: Boynton-Cook/Heinemann, 1999. Print.

Chiseri-Strater, Elizabeth. *Academic Literacies: The Public and Private Discourse of University Students.* Portsmouth, NH: Boynton-Cook/Heinemann, 1991. Print.

Clifford, James. "Introduction: Partial Truths." *Writing Culture: The Poetics and Politics of Ethnography.* Ed. James Clifford and George E. Marcus. Berkeley, CA: U of California P, 1986. 1–26. Print.

Cushman, Ellen. *The Struggle and the Tools: Oral and Literate Strategies in an Inner City Community.* Albany, NY: State U of New York P, 1998. Print.

Geertz, Clifford. *Works and Lives: The Anthropologist as Author.* Stanford, CA: Stanford UP, 1988. Print.

Hymes, Dell, ed. *Reinventing Anthropology.* New York: Pantheon, 1972. Print.

Marcus, George. *Ethnography through Thick and Thin.* Princeton, NJ: Princeton UP, 1998. Print.

Newkirk, Thomas. "Seduction and Betrayal in Qualitative Research." *Ethics and Representation in Qualitative Studies of Literacy.* Ed. Peter Mortensen and Gesa E. Kirsch. Urbana, IL: National Council of Teachers of English, 1996. 3–16. Print.

Spradley, James, and David A. McCurdy. *The Cultural Experience: Ethnography in Complex Society.* Chicago: Science Research Associates, 1972. Print.

Sunstein, Bonnie. *Composing a Culture: Inside a Summer Writing Program with High School Teachers.* Portsmouth, NH: Boynton-Cook/Heinemann, 1994. Print.

Van Maanen, John. *Tales of the Field: On Writing Ethnography.* Chicago: U of Chicago P, 1988. Print.

Walk, Talk, Cook, Eat: A Guide to Using Sources

Cynthia R. Haller

Marvin, a college student at Any University, sits down at his computer.[*]
He logs in to the "Online Professor," an interactive advice site for students.
After setting up a chat, he begins tapping the keys.

Marvin: Hi. I'm a student in the physician assistant program. The major paper for my health and environment class is due in five weeks, and I need some advice. The professor says the paper has to be 6–8 pages, and I have to cite and document my sources.

O-Prof: Congratulations on getting started early! Tell me a bit about your assignment. What's the purpose? Who's it intended for?

Marvin: Well, the professor said it should talk about a health problem caused by water pollution and suggest ways to solve it. We've read some articles, plus my professor gave us statistics on groundwater contamination in different areas.

O-Prof: What's been most interesting so far?

Marvin: I'm amazed at how much water pollution there is. It seems like it would be healthier to drink bottled water, but the plastic bottles hurt the environment.

O-Prof: Who else might be interested in this?

Marvin: Lots of people are worried about bad water. I might even get questions about it from my clients once I finish my program.

O-Prof: OK. So what information do you need to make a good recommendation?

Marvin thinks for a moment.

Marvin: I don't know much about the health problems caused by contaminated drinking water. Whether the tap water is safe depends on where you live, I guess. The professors talked about arsenic poisoning in Bangladesh, but what about the water in the U.S.? For my paper, maybe I should focus on a particular location? I also need to find out more about what companies do to make sure bottled water is pure.

O-Prof: Good! Now that you know what you need to learn, you can start looking for sources.

Marvin: When my professors talk about sources, they usually mean books or articles about my topic. Is that what you mean?

O-Prof: Books and articles do make good sources, but you might think about sources more generally as "forms of meaning you use to make new meaning." It's like your bottled water. The water exists already in some location but is processed by the company before it goes to the consumer. Similarly, a source provides information and knowledge that you process to produce new meaning, which other people can then use to make their own meaning.

A bit confused, Marvin scratches his head.

Marvin: I thought I knew what a source was, but now I'm not so sure.

O-Prof: Think about it. Sources of meaning are literally everywhere—for example, your own observations or experiences, the content of other people's brains, visuals and graphics, experiment results, TV and radio broadcasts, and written texts. And, there are many ways to make new meaning from sources. You can give an oral presentation, design a web page, paint a picture, or, as in your case, write a paper.

Marvin: I get it. But how do I decide which sources to use for my paper?

O-Prof: It depends on the meaning you want to make, which is why it's *so* important to figure out the purpose of your paper and who will read it. You might think about using sources as *walking, talking, cooking, and eating.* These aren't the only possible metaphors, but they do capture some important things about using sources.

Marvin: Hey! I thought we were talking about writing!

O-Prof: We are, but these metaphors can shed some light on writing with sources. Let's start with the first one: *walking.* To use sources well, you first have to go where they are. What if you were writing an article on student clubs for the school newspaper? Where would you go for information?

Marvin: I'd probably walk down to the Student Activities office and get some brochures about student clubs. Then I'd attend a few club meetings and maybe interview the club leaders and some members about their club activities.

O-Prof: OK, so you'd *walk* to where you could find relevant information for your article. That's what I mean by *walking.* You have to get to the sources you need.

Marvin: Wait a minute. For the article on student clubs, maybe I could save some walking. Maybe the list of clubs and the club descriptions are on the Student Activities web page. That'd save me a trip.

O-Prof: Yes, the Internet has cut down on the amount of physical walking you need to do to find sources. Before the Internet, you had to either travel to a source's physical location, or bring that source to your location. Think about your project on bottled water. To get information about the quality of a city's tap water in the 1950s, you would have had to figure out who'd have that information, then call or write to request a copy or *walk* to wherever the information was stored. Today, if you type "local water quality" into Google, the Environmental Protection Agency page comes up as one of the first hits. Its home page links to water quality reports for local areas.

Marvin pauses for a second before responding, thinking he's found a good short cut for his paper.

Marvin: So can I just use Google or Bing to find sources?

O-Prof: Internet search engines can help you find sources, but they aren't always the best route to getting to a good source. Try entering the search term "bottled water quality" into Google, without quotation marks around the term. How many hits do you get?

Marvin types it in.

Marvin: 5,760,000. That's pretty much what I get whenever I do an Internet search. Too many results.

O-Prof: Which is one of the drawbacks of using only Internet search engines. The Internet may have cut down on the physical *walking* needed to find good sources, but it's made up for the time savings by pointing you to more places than you could possibly go! But there are some ways you can narrow your search to get fewer, more focused results.

Marvin: Yeah, I know. Sometimes I add extra words in and it helps weed down the hits.

O-Prof: By combining search terms with certain words or symbols, you can control what the search engine looks for. If you put more than one term into a Google search box, the search engine will only give you sites that include both terms, since it uses the Boolean operator AND as the default for its searches. If you put OR between two search terms, you'll end up getting even more results, because Google will look for all websites containing either of the terms. Using a minus sign in front of a term eliminates things you're not interested in. It's the Google equivalent of the Boolean operator NOT. Try entering bottled water quality health -teeth.

Marvin types in the words, remembering suddenly that he has to make an appointment with the dentist.

Marvin: 329,000 hits.

O-Prof: Still a lot. You can also put quotation marks around groups
          of words and the search engine will look only for sites that
          contain all of those words in the exact order you've given.
          And you can combine this strategy with the other ways of
          limiting your search. Try "bottled water quality" (in quota-
          tion marks) health teeth.

Marvin: Only 333. That's more like it.

O-Prof: Yes, but you don't want to narrow it so far that you miss use-
          ful sources. You have to play around with your search terms
          to get to what you need. A bigger problem with Internet
          search engines, though, is that they won't necessarily lead
          you to the sources considered most valuable for college writ-
          ing.

Marvin: My professor said something about using peer-reviewed ar-
          ticles in scholarly journals.

O-Prof: Professors will often want you to use such sources. Articles
          in scholarly journals are written by experts; and if a journal's
          peer-reviewed, its articles have been screened by other ex-
          perts (the authors' peers) before being published.

Marvin: So that would make peer-reviewed articles pretty reliable.
          Where do I find them?

O-Prof: Google's got a specialized search engine, Google Scholar, that
          will search for scholarly articles that might be useful (www.
          googlescholar.com). But often the best place is the college
          library's bibliographic databases. A database is a collection of
          related data, usually electronic, set up for easy access to items
          in the collection. Library bibliographic databases contain ar-
          ticles from newspapers, magazines, scholarly journals, and
          other publications. They can be very large, but they're a lot
          smaller than the whole Internet, and they generally contain
          reliable information. The Internet, on the other hand, con-
          tains both good and bad information.

Marvin looks down at his feet.

Marvin: Sounds sort of like looking for shoes. When I was buying my
          running shoes, I went to a specialty running shop instead of
          a regular shoe store. The specialty shop had all the brands I

was looking for, and I didn't have to weed through sandals and dress shoes. Is that kind of like a library's bibliographic database?

O-Prof: Exactly. But remember, a database search engine can only find what's actually in the database. If you're looking for information on drinking water, you won't find much in a database full of art history publications. The library has some subject guides that can tell you the best databases to use for your topic.

Marvin: What about books? I did check out the library catalog and found a couple of good books on my topic.

O-Prof: Yes, don't forget about books. You generally have to walk physically to get information that's only in print form, or have someone else bring it to you. Even though Google has now scanned many of the world's books into its database, they won't give you access to the entire book if the book is still under copyright.

Marvin: So I'm back to real walking again.

O-Prof: Yes. Don't forget to ask for help when you're looking around for sources. Reference librarians make very good guides; it's their job to keep up on where various kinds of knowledge are located and help people find that knowledge. Professors also make good guides, but they're most familiar with where to find knowledge in their own fields.

Marvin: I could ask my health and environment professor for help, of course, and maybe my geology and chemistry professors. I'm guessing my music teacher would be less helpful.

O-Prof: One last hint about finding sources. If you find an article or book that's helpful for your paper, look at its reference list. There might be some useful sources listed there.

Marvin: Thanks, Professor. I think I can do some good *walking* now. What about that *talking* metaphor?

O-Prof: Before we move on, there's an important aspect of *walking* with sources that you need to be aware of. In college writing, if you use a source in a paper, you're expected to let the reader know exactly how to find that source as well. Providing this "source address" information for your sources is known as *documenting your sources.*

Marvin: What do you mean by a "source address"?

O-Prof: It's directions for finding the source. A mailing address tells you how to find a person: the house number, street, city, state, and zip code. To help your readers find your sources, it's customary to give them the name of the author; the title of the book or article or website; and other information such as date, location of publication, publisher, even the database in which a source is located. Or, if it's a website, you might give the name of the site and/or the date on which you accessed it. Source documentation can be complicated, because the necessary source address information differs for different types of sources (e.g., books vs. journal articles, electronic vs. print). Additionally, different disciplines (e.g., history, philosophy, psychology, literature, etc.) use different "address" formats. Eventually, you'll become familiar with the documentation conventions for your own academic major, but source documentation takes a lot of practice. In the meantime, your teachers and various writing handbooks can provide instructions on what information you'll need.

Marvin: Do I really need to include all that information? A lot of times, the sources I use are readings my teachers have assigned, so they already know where to find them.

O-Prof: Your teachers don't always know where all your sources are from, and they also want you to get into the habit of source documentation. And what about your other readers? If they're deeply interested in your topic, they may want to find more information than you've included in your paper. Your source documentation allows them to find the original source. And there are other reasons for documenting sources. It can help readers understand your own position on a topic, because they can see which authors you agree with and which you don't. It also shows readers you've taken time to investigate your topic and aren't just writing off the top of your head. If readers see that your ideas are based on trustworthy sources, they're more likely to trust what you say.

Marvin: Like, if I used a university or government website on bottled water quality, they'd trust me more than if I just used a bottled water company website.

O-Prof: Yes. But to dig deeper into the question of trust, let's move on to a second metaphor: *talking*. Although the metaphor of *walking* is useful for understanding how to find and document sources, it can give the impression that sources are separate, inert, and neutral things, waiting to be snatched up like gold nuggets and plugged into your writing. In reality, sources are parts of overlapping knowledge networks that connect meanings and the people that make and use them. Knowledge networks are always in flux, since people are always making new meaning. Let's go back to your health and environment project. Refresh my memory. What kinds of questions do you need answers to before you can write your paper?

Marvin: Well, I need to know if bottled water is truly healthier, like the beverage companies claim. Or would I be just as well off drinking tap water?

O-Prof: To answer this question, you'll want to find out who's *talking* about these issues. As Kenneth Burke put it, you can think of sources as voices in an ongoing conversation about the world:

> Imagine that you enter a parlor. You come late. When you arrive, others have long preceded you, and they are engaged in a heated discussion, a discussion too heated for them to pause and tell you exactly what it is about. In fact, the discussion had already begun long before any of them got there, so that no one present is qualified to retrace for you all the steps that had gone before. You listen for a while, until you decide that you have caught the tenor of the argument; then you put in your oar. Someone answers; you answer him; another comes to your defense; another aligns himself against you, to either the embarrassment or gratification of your opponent, depending upon the quality of your ally's assistance. However, the discussion is interminable. The hour grows late, you must depart. And you do depart, with the discussion still vigorously in progress. (110–111)

The authors of texts aren't speaking aloud, of course, but they're making written statements that others can "listen" and "respond" to. Knowing which texts you can trust means understanding which authors you can trust.

Marvin: How do I figure that out?

O-Prof: It helps to know who the authors are. What they're saying. Where, when, and to whom they're saying it. And what their purposes are. Imagine the world as divided into many parlors like the one Kenneth Burke described. You'd want to go to the parlors where people who really know something are *talking* about the topics you're interested in. Let's go back to your initial Google search for a minute. Did any Wikipedia articles come up for bottled water?

Marvin: Yeah, and I took a quick look at one of them. But some of my professors say I shouldn't use Wikipedia.

O-Prof: That's because the quality of information in Wikipedia varies. It's monitored by volunteer writers and editors rather than experts, so you should double-check information you find in Wikipedia with other sources. But Wikipedia articles are often good places to get background info and good places to connect with more reliable sources. Did anything in the Wikipedia article seem useful for finding sources on bottled water?

Marvin clicks back to the Wikipedia site.

Marvin: It does mention that the National Resources Defense Council and the Drinking Water Research Foundation have done some studies on the health effects of bottled water ("Bottled Water").

O-Prof: So, you could go to the websites for these organizations to find out more about the studies. They might even have links to the full reports of these studies, as well as other resources on your topic. Who else might have something to say about the healthfulness of bottled and tap water?

Marvin: Maybe doctors and other health professionals? But I don't know any I could ask.

O-Prof: You can look in the library's subject guides or ask the librarian about databases for health professionals. The Cumulative Index to Nursing & Allied Health Literature (CINAHL) database is a good one. Are you logged in to the library? Can you try that one?

Marvin logs in, finds the database, and types in "bottled water AND health."

Marvin: Here's an article called "Health Risks and Benefits of Bottled Water." It's in the journal *Primary Care Clinical Office Practice* (Napier and Kodner).

O-Prof: If that's a peer-reviewed journal, it might be a good source for your paper.

Marvin: Here's another one: "Socio-Demographic Features and Fluoride Technologies Contributing to Higher Fluorosis Scores in Permanent Teeth of Canadian Children" (Maupome et al.). That one sounds pretty technical.

O-Prof: And pretty narrow, too. When you start using sources written by experts, you move beyond the huge porch of public discourse, where everyone *talks* about all questions on a general level, into some smaller conversational parlors, where groups of specialists *talk* about more narrow questions in greater depth. You generally find more detailed and trustworthy knowledge in these smaller parlors. But sometimes the conversation may be too narrow for your needs and difficult to understand because it's experts *talking* to experts.

Way ahead of the professor, Marvin's already started reading about the health risks and benefits of bottled water.

Marvin: Here's something confusing. The summary of this article on risks and benefits of bottled water says tap water is fine if you're in a location where there's good water. Then it says that you should use bottled water if the purity of your water source is in question. So which is better, tap or bottled?

O-Prof: As you read more sources, you begin to realize there's not always a simple answer to questions. As the CINAHL article points out, the answer depends on whether your tap water is pure enough to drink. Not everyone agrees on the answers, either. When you're advising your future clients (or in this case, writing your paper), you'll need to "listen" to what different people who *talk* about the healthfulness of bottled and tap water have to say. Then you'll be equipped to make your own recommendation.

Marvin: Is that when I start writing?

O-Prof: You've really been writing all along. Asking questions and gathering ideas from sources is all part of the process. As we think about the actual drafting, though, it's helpful to move on to that third metaphor: *cooking*. When you *cook* with sources, you process them in new ways. Cooking, like writing, involves a lot of decisions. For instance, you might decide to combine ingredients in a way that keeps the full flavor and character of each ingredient.

Marvin: Kind of like chili cheese fries? I can taste the flavor of the chili, the cheese, and the fries separately.

O-Prof: Yes. But other food preparation processes can change the character of the various ingredients. You probably wouldn't enjoy gobbling down a stick of butter, two raw eggs, a cup of flour, or a cup of sugar (well, maybe the sugar!). But if you mix these ingredients and expose them to a 375-degree temperature, chemical reactions transform them into something good to eat, like a cake.

Marvin reaches into his backpack and pulls out a snack.

Marvin: You're making me hungry. But what do chili cheese fries and cakes have to do with writing?

O-Prof: Sometimes, you might use verbatim quotations from your sources, as if you were throwing walnuts whole into a salad. The reader will definitely "taste" your original source. Other times, you might paraphrase ideas and combine them into an intricate argument. The flavor of the original source might be more subtle in the latter case, with only your source documentation indicating where your ideas came from. In some ways, the writing assignments your professors give you are like recipes. As an apprentice writing *cook,* you should analyze your assignments to determine what "ingredients" (sources) to use, what "cooking processes" to follow, and what the final "dish" (paper) should look like. Let's try a few sample assignments. Here's one:

Assignment 1: Critique (given in a human development course)

We've read and studied Freud's theory of how the human psyche develops; now it's time to evaluate the theory. Read at least two articles that critique Freud's theory, chosen from the list I provided in class. Then, write an essay discussing the strengths and weaknesses of Freud's theory.

Assume you're a student in this course. Given this assignment, how would you describe the required ingredients, processes, and product?

Marvin thinks for a minute, while chewing and swallowing a mouthful of apple.

Marvin: Let's see if I can break it down:

Ingredients:

- everything we've read about Freud's theory
- our class discussions about the theory
- two articles of my choice taken from the list provided by the instructor

Processes: I have to read those two articles to see their criticisms of Freud's theory. I can also review my notes from class, since we discussed various critiques. I have to think about what aspects of Freud's theory explain human development well, and where the theory falls short—like in class, we discussed how Freud's theory reduces human development to sexuality alone.

Product: The final essay needs to include both strengths and weaknesses of Freud's theory. The professor didn't specifically say this, but it's also clear I need to incorporate some ideas from the two articles I read—otherwise why would she have assigned those articles?

O-Prof: Good. How about this one?

> **Assignment 2: Business Plan** (given in an entrepreneurship course)
>
> As your major project for this course, your group will develop a business plan for a student-run business that meets some need on this campus. Be sure to include all aspects of a business plan. During the last few weeks of class, each group will present the plan to the class, using appropriate visuals.

Marvin: I'll give it a try.

> **Ingredients**: Hmm . . . It's hard to tell the sources I'll need. Obviously, whatever the teacher teaches us about business plans in the course will be important—hope she goes into detail about this and provides examples. What if she doesn't? What sources could my group use? Our textbook has a chapter on business plans that will probably help, and maybe we can go to the library and look for books about writing business plans. Some sample business plans would be helpful—I wonder if the Center for Small Business Support on our campus would have some?
>
> **Processes**: Well, maybe we could have each member of the group look for sources about business plans and then meet together to discuss what we need to do, or talk online. Don't know how we'll break down the writing—maybe we could divide up the various sections of the plan, or discuss each section together, then someone could write it up?
>
> **Product**: It's clear that we have to include all the information that business owners put in a business plan, and we'll have to follow the organization of a typical plan. But we can't tell exactly what that organization should be until we've done some research.

O-Prof: Here's one last assignment to try out.

> **Assignment 3: Research Paper** (given in a health and environment course)
>
> Write a 6–8-page paper in which you explain a health problem related to water pollution (e.g., arsenic poisoning, gastrointestinal illness, skin disease, etc.). Recommend a potential

way or ways this health problem might be addressed. Be sure to cite and document the sources you use for your paper.

Marvin: Oho, trick question! That one sounds familiar.

Ingredients: No specific guidance here, except that sources have to relate to water pollution and health. I've already decided I'm interested in how bottled water might help with health where there's water pollution. I'll have to pick a health problem and find sources about how water pollution can cause that problem. Gastrointestinal illness sounds promising. I'll ask the reference librarian where I'd be likely to find good articles about water pollution, bottled water, and gastrointestinal illness.

Process: There's not very specific information here about what process to use, but our conversation's given me some ideas. I'll use scholarly articles to find the connection between water pollution and gastrointestinal problems, and whether bottled water could prevent those problems.

Product: Obviously, my paper will explain the connection between water and gastrointestinal health. It'll evaluate whether bottled water provides a good option in places where the water's polluted, then give a recommendation about what people should do. The professor did say I should address any objections readers might raise—for instance, bottled water may turn out to be a good option, but it's a lot more expensive than tap water. Finally, I'll need to provide in-text citations and document my sources in a reference list.

O-Prof: You're on your way. Think for a minute about these three assignments. Did you notice that the "recipes" varied in their specificity?

Marvin: Yeah. The first assignment gave me very specific information about exactly what source "ingredients" to use. But in the second and third assignments, I had to figure it out on my own. And the processes varied, too. For the business plan, the groups will use sources to figure out how to organize the plan, but the actual content will be drawn from their own ideas for their business and any market research they do. But in the third assignment—my own assignment—I'll have to use content from my sources to support my recommendation.

O-Prof: Different professors provide different levels of specificity in their writing assignments. If you have trouble figuring out the "recipe," ask the professor for more information.

Marvin: Sometimes it can be really frustrating not to have enough information. Last semester, I sat around being frustrated and put off doing an assignment as long as possible, then rushed to finish it. I didn't do very well on the rough draft, but then I met with my professor and talked to him. Also, the class read each other's papers. Getting feedback and looking at what other students had done gave me some new ideas for my final draft.

O-Prof: When it comes to "cooking with sources," no one expects you to be an executive chef the first day you get to college. Over time, you'll become more expert at writing with sources, more able to choose and use sources on your own. You'll probably need less guidance for writing in your senior year than in your freshman year. Which brings me to the last metaphor for using sources.

Marvin: *Eating*, right?

O-Prof: Good memory. In fact, this last metaphor is about memory, which is how sources become a part of who you are. You've probably heard the expression, "you are what you eat." When you *eat* sources—that is, think about things, experiment, read, write, talk to others—you yourself change. What you learn stays with you.

Marvin: Not always. It's hard for me to remember the things I learn in class until the final exam, not to mention after the class is over.

O-Prof: Of course. We all forget a lot of the things we learn, especially those we seldom or never use again; but what you learn and use over a long period of time will affect you deeply and shape the way you see the world. Take a look at this quote from Mark Twain in *Life on the Mississippi*, where the narrator's talking about his apprenticeship as a steamboat pilot. When he first began his apprenticeship, the Mississippi River looked the same as any other river. But after he made many long trips up and down it, with the captain and others explaining things along the way, he began to see it in all its complexity.

> The face of the water, in time, became a wonderful book—a book that was a dead language to the uneducated passenger, but which told its mind to me without reserve, delivering its most cherished secrets as clearly as if it uttered them with a voice. (77–78)

Eventually, the narrator could identify each of the river's bends, knew how its currents were running, and could estimate how deep it was just by looking at the surface. It was the same river, but he was a different man. Your bottled water project isn't as involved as learning to pilot a steamship. But once you start reading your sources, your experience of bottled water will shift. It'll still be the same water you used to drink, but it won't be the same you.

Marvin: I can sort of see that already. I've learned a lot about anatomy and physiology in the physician assistant program. Now, when I see a soccer player, I think about how the shin guard is protecting her tibia, not her shin. If I see someone with yellowish eyeballs, I think about bilirubin levels. And I always read the health section of the newspaper first.

O-Prof: Right. And a journalism major, who takes courses on beat reporting and feature writing, thinks about what will make a good story. A geology major does field work, looks at maps, learns about geological history, and sees rocks everywhere. Over time, through much exposure to a field and practice in it, a person's identity gradually becomes intertwined with his or her profession. Not entirely, of course. All of us are many things. A doctor may have an interest in calligraphy. A business manager might study poetry in her spare time. In both work and leisure activities, you'll keep on learning and making meaning from sources like other people, writing, books, websites, videos, articles, and your own experience. College is about learning *how* to make meaning. Learn how to *walk* (find the sources you need); *talk* (converse with source authors); *cook* (integrate sources to make new meaning); and *eat* (allow sources to change your life). You won't ever finish using sources to make meaning—not in your health and environment course, not while you're in college, not even after you've been working and living for a long time.

Marvin glances at his watch.

Marvin: Speaking of time, I should probably grab some dinner before the cafeteria closes. Thanks, Professor, for all your help.

O-Prof: Anytime. Good luck with your paper, and with the rest of your writing life.

DISCUSSION

1. What writing assignments have you received from your various professors? How many of them involve working with sources? What kinds of sources do your professors ask you to use?
2. What difficulties have you encountered in finding good sources for writing assignments? How have you overcome those difficulties?
3. How helpful is the "recipe analysis" technique for understanding how to go about your assignments? What other analysis techniques have you used to understand writing assignments?
4. The metaphors in this dialogue explain some aspects of using sources, but not others. What other metaphors can you think of for working with sources? How would those other metaphors add to an understanding of writing with sources?

WORKS CITED

"Bottled Water." *Wikipedia.* Web. 12 Sept. 2009.

Burke, Kenneth. *The Philosophy of Literary Form.* Berkeley: U of California P, 1941. Print.

Maupome, G., et al. "Socio-Demographic Features and Fluoride Technologies Contributing to Higher Fluorosis Scores in Permanent Teeth of Canadian Children." *Caries Research* 37.5 (2003): 327–334. CINAHL. Web. 10 Oct. 2010.

Napier, Gena, and Charles Kodner. "Health Risks and Benefits of Bottled Water." *Primary Care Clinical Office Practice* 35.4 (2008): 789–802. CINAHL. Web. 10 Oct. 2010.

Twain, Mark. *Life on the Mississippi.* New York: Harper & Row, 1951. Print.

Reading Games: Strategies for Reading Scholarly Sources

Karen Rosenberg

IF AT FIRST YOU FALL ASLEEP . . .

During my first year in college, I feared many things: calculus, cafeteria food, the stained, sweet smelling mattress in the basement of my dorm.* But I did not fear reading. I didn't really think about reading at all, that automatic making of meaning from symbols in books, newspapers, on cereal boxes. And, indeed, some of my coziest memories of that bewildering first year involved reading. I adopted an overstuffed red chair in the library that enveloped me like the lap of a department store Santa. I curled up many evenings during that first, brilliant autumn with my English homework: Toni Morrison's *The Bluest Eye*, Gloria Naylor's *Mama Day*, Sandra Cisneros' *The House on Mango Street*. I'd read a gorgeous passage, snuggle deeper into my chair, and glance out to the sunset and fall leaves outside of the library window. This felt deeply, unmistakably collegiate.

But English was a requirement—I planned to major in political science. I took an intro course my first semester and brought my readings to that same chair. I curled up, opened a book on the Chinese Revolution, started reading, and fell asleep. I woke up a little drooly, surprised at the harsh fluorescent light, the sudden pitch outside. Not to be deterred, I bit my lip and started over. I'd hold on for a paragraph or two, and then suddenly I'd be thinking about my classmate Joel's elbows, the casual way he'd put them on the desk when our professor lectured, sometimes resting his chin in his hands. He was a long limbed runner and smelled scrubbed—a mixture of laundry detergent and shampoo. He had black hair and startling blue eyes. Did I find him sexy?

Crap! How many paragraphs had my eyes grazed over while I was thinking about Joel's stupid elbows? By the end of that first semester, I abandoned ideas of majoring in political science. I vacillated between intense irritation with my assigned readings and a sneaking suspicion that perhaps the problem was me—I was too dumb to read academic texts. Whichever it was—a problem with the readings or with me—I carefully chose my classes so that I could read novels, poetry, and plays for credit. But even in my English classes, I discovered, I had to read dense scholarly articles. By my Junior year, I trained myself to spend days from dawn until dusk hunkered over a carrel in the library's basement armed with a dictionary and a rainbow of highlighters. Enjoying my reading seemed hopelessly naïve—an indulgence best reserved for beach blankets and bathtubs. A combination of obstinacy, butt-numbingly hard chairs, and caffeine helped me survive my scholarly reading assignments. But it wasn't fun.

Seven years later I entered graduate school. I was also working and living on my own, cooking for myself instead of eating off cafeteria trays. In short, I had a life. My days were not the blank canvas they had been when I was an undergraduate and could sequester myself in the dungeon of the library basement. And so, I finally learned how to read smarter, not harder. Perhaps the strangest part of my reading transformation was that I came to *like* reading those dense scholarly articles; I came to crave the process of sucking the marrow from the texts. If you can relate to this, if you also love wrestling with academic journal articles, take joy in arguing with authors in the margins of the page, I am not writing for you.

However, if your reading assignments confound you, if they send you into slumber, or you avoid them, or they seem to take you *way* too long, then pay attention. Based on my experience as a frustrated student and now as a teacher of reading strategies, I have some insights to share with you designed to make the reading process more productive, more interesting, and more enjoyable.

JOINING THE CONVERSATION[1]

Even though it may seem like a solitary, isolated activity, when you read a scholarly work, you are participating in a conversation. Academic writers do not make up their arguments off the top of their heads (or solely from creative inspiration). Rather, they look at how others have approached similar issues and problems. Your job—and one for which you'll get plenty of help from your professors and your peers—is to locate the writer and yourself in this larger conversation. Reading academic texts is a deeply social activity; talking with your professors and peers about texts can not only help you understand your readings better, but it can push your thinking and clarify your own stances on issues that really matter to you.

In your college courses, you may have come across the term "rhetorical reading."[2] Rhetoric in this context refers to how texts work to persuade readers—a bit different from the common connotation of empty, misleading, or puffed up speech. Rhetorical reading refers to a set of practices designed to help us understand how texts work and to engage more deeply and fully in a conversation that extends beyond the boundaries of any particular reading. Rhetorical reading practices ask us to think deliberately about the role and relationship between the writer, reader, and text.

When thinking about the writer, we are particularly interested in clues about the writer's motivation and agenda. If we know something about what the writer cares about and is trying to accomplish, it can help orient us to the reading and understand some of the choices the writer makes in his or her work.

As readers, our role is quite active. We pay attention to our own motivation and agenda for each reading. On one level, our motivation may be as simple as wanting to do well in a class, and our agenda may involve wanting to understand as much as necessary in order to complete our assignments. In order to meet these goals, we need to go deeper, asking, "Why is my professor asking me to read this piece?" You may find clues in your course syllabus, comments your professor makes in class, or comments from your classmates. If you aren't sure why you are being asked to read something, ask! Most professors will be more than happy to discuss in general terms what "work" they want a reading to do—for example, to introduce you to a set of debates, to provide information on a specific topic, or to challenge conventional thinking on an issue.

Finally, there is the text—the thing that the writer wrote and that you are reading. In addition to figuring out *what* the text says, rhetorical reading strategies ask us to focus on *how* the text delivers its message. In this way of thinking about texts, there is not one right and perfect meaning for the diligent reader to uncover; rather, interpretations of the reading will differ depending on the questions and contexts readers bring to the text.

STRATEGIES FOR RHETORICAL READING

Here are some ways to approach your reading that better equip you for the larger conversation. First, consider the **audience**. When the writer sat down to write your assigned reading, to whom was he or she implicitly talking? Textbooks, for the most part, have students like you in mind. They may be boring, but you've probably learned what to do with them: pay attention to the goals of the chapter, check out the summary at the end, ignore the text in the boxes because it's usually more of a "fun fact" than something that will be on the test, and so on. Magazines in the checkout line at the supermarket also have you in mind: you can't help but notice headlines about who is cheating or fat or anorexic or suicidal. Writers of scholarly sources, on the other hand, likely don't think much about you at all when they sit down to write. Often, academics write primarily for other academics. But just because it's people with PhDs writing for other people with PhDs doesn't mean that you should throw in the towel. There's a formula for these types of texts, just like there's a formula for all the *Cosmo* articles that beckon with titles that involve the words "hot," "sex tips," "your man," and "naughty" in different configurations.

It's just that the formula is a little more complicated.

The formula also changes depending on the flavor of study (physics, management, sociology, English, etc.) and the venue. However, if you determine that the audience for your reading is other academics, recognize that you are in foreign territory. You won't understand all of the chatter you hear on street corners, you may not be able to read the menus in the restaurants, but, with a little practice, you will be able to find and understand the major road signs, go in the right direction, and find your way.

How can you figure out the primary audience? First, look at the publication venue. (Here, to some extent, you can judge a book by its cover). If the reading comes from an academic journal, then chances are good that the primary audience is other academics. Clues that a journal is academic (as opposed to popular, like *Time* or *Newsweek*) include a citation format that refers to a volume number and an issue number, and often this information appears at the top or bottom of every page. Sometimes you can tell if a reading comes from an academic journal based on the title—e.g., do the *Journal for Research in Mathematics Education* or *Qualitative Research in Psychology* sound like they are written for a popular audience? What if you're still not sure? Ask your reference librarians, classmates, your instructor, or friends and family who have more experience with these types of readings than you do.

There are two implications that you should be aware of if you are not the primary audience for a text. First, the author will assume prior knowledge that you likely don't have. You can expect sentences like "as Durkheim has so famously argued . . ." or "much ink has been spilled on the implications of the modernization hypothesis" where you have no idea who Durkheim is or what the modernization hypothesis says. That's OK. It might even be OK to not look these things up at all and still get what you need from the reading (but you won't know that yet). In the first reading of an article, it's smart to hold off on looking too many things up. Just be prepared to face a wall of references that don't mean a whole lot to you.

Second, if you're not the primary audience, don't be surprised if you find that the writing isn't appealing to you. Whereas a novelist or a magazine writer works hard to draw us in as readers, many academic authors don't use strategies to keep us hooked. In fact, many of these strategies (use of sensory language, suspense, etc.) would never get published in academic venues. By the same token, you'll use very different strategies to read these scholarly texts.

You may be wondering, if you're not the intended audience for the text, why do you have to read it in the first place? This is an excellent question, and one that you need to answer before you do your reading. As I mentioned earlier in the discussion of the role of the reader, you may need to do a little sleuthing to figure this out. In addition to the suggestions I provided earlier, look to your course notes and syllabus for answers. Often professors will tell you why they assign specific readings. Pay attention—they will likely offer insights on the context of the reading and the most important points. If after all of this, you still have no idea why you're supposed to read six articles on the history of Newtonian physics, then ask your professor. Use the answers to help you focus on the really important aspects of the texts and to gloss over the parts that are less relevant to your coursework. If you remain confused, continue to ask for clarification. Ask questions in class (your classmates will be grateful). Go to office hours. Most faculty love the opportunity to talk about readings that they have chosen with care.

Once you have an idea who the intended audience is for the article and why you are assigned to read it, don't sit down and read the article from start to finish, like a good mystery. Get a lay of the land before you go too deep. One way to do this is to study the architecture of the article. Here are some key components to look for:

The title. As obvious as it sounds, pay attention to the title because it can convey a lot of information that can help you figure out how to read the rest of the article more efficiently. Let's say that I know my reading will be about the Russian Revolution. Let's say I even know that it will be about the role of music in the Russian Revolution. Let's say the title is "'Like the beating of my heart': A discourse analysis of Muscovite musicians' letters during the Russian Revolution." This tells me not only the subject matter of the article (something about letters Russian musicians wrote during the Revolution) but it also tells me something about the methodology, or the way that the author approaches the subject matter. I might not know exactly what discourse analysis is, but I can guess that you can do it to letters and that I should pay particular attention to it when the author mentions it in the article. On the other hand, if the title of the article were "Garbage cans and metal pipes: Bolshevik music and the politics of proletariat propaganda" I would know to look out for very different words and concepts. Note, also, that the convention within some academic disciplines to have a pretty long title separated by a colon usually follows a predictable pattern. The text to the left of the colon serves as a teaser, or as something to grab a reader's attention (remember that the author is likely not trying to grab your attention, so you may not find these teasers particularly effective—though it is probably packed with phrases that would entice someone who already studies the topic). The information to the right of the colon typically is a more straightforward explanation of what the article is about.

The abstract. Not all of your readings will come with abstracts, but when they do, pay close attention. An abstract is like an executive summary. Usually one paragraph at the beginning of an article, the abstract serves to encapsulate the main points of the article. It's generally a pretty specialized summary that seeks to answer specific questions. These include: the main problem or question, the approach (how did the author(s) do the work they write about in the article?), the shiny new thing that this article does (more on this later, but to be published in an academic journal you often need to argue that you are doing something that has not been done before), and why people who are already invested in this field should care (in other words, you should be able to figure out why another academic should find the article important). The abstract often appears in database searches, and helps scholars decide if they want to seek out the full article.

That's a whole lot to accomplish in one paragraph.

As a result, authors often use specialized jargon to convey complex ideas in few words, make assumptions of prior knowledge, and don't worry much about general readability. Abstracts, thus, are generally dense, and it's not uncommon to read through an abstract and not have a clue about what you just read. This is a good place to re-read, highlight, underline, look up what you don't know. You still may not have a firm grasp on everything in the abstract, but treat the key terms in the abstract like parts of a map when you see them in the main text, leading you to treasure: understanding the main argument.

The introduction. The introduction serves some of the same functions as the abstract, but there is a lot more breathing room here. When I started reading academic texts, I'd breeze through the introduction to get to the "meat" of the text. This was exactly the wrong thing to do. I can't remember how many times I'd find myself in the middle of some dense reading, perhaps understanding the content of a particular paragraph, but completely unable to connect that paragraph with the overall structure of the article. I'd jump from the lily pad of one paragraph to the next, continually fearful that I'd slip off and lose myself in a sea of total confusion (and I often did slip).

If the author is doing her/his job well, the introduction will not only summarize the whole piece, present the main idea, and tell us why we should care, but it will also often offer a road map for the rest of the article. Sometimes, the introduction will be called "introduction," which makes things easy. Sometimes, it's not. Generally, treat the first section of an article as the introduction, regardless if it's explicitly called that or not.

There are times where your reading will have the introduction chopped off. This makes your work harder. The two most common instances of introduction-less readings are assigned excerpts of articles and lone book chapters. In the first case, you only have a portion of an article so you cannot take advantage of many of the context clues the writer set out for readers. You will need to rely more heavily on the context of your course in general and your assignment in particular to find your bearings here. If the reading is high stakes (e.g., if you have to write a paper or take an exam on it), you may want to ask your professor how you can get the whole article. In the second case, your professor assigns a chapter or two from the middle of an academic book. The chapter will hopefully contain some introductory material (and generally will include much more than the middle of a journal article), but you will likely be missing some context clues that the author included in the introduction to the whole book. If you have trouble finding your footing here, and it's important that you grasp the meaning and significance of the chapter, seek out the book itself and skim the introductory chapter to ground you in the larger questions that the author is addressing. Oddly, even though you'll be doing more reading, it may save you time because you can read your assigned chapter(s) more efficiently.

Roadmaps included in the introduction are often surprisingly straightforward. They often are as simple as "in the first section, we examine . . . in the second section we argue . . ." etc. Search for these maps. Underline them. Highlight them. Go back to them when you find your comprehension slipping.

Section headings. A section heading serves as a title for a particular part of an article. Read all of these to get a sense of the trajectory of the text before delving into the content in each section (with the exception of the introduction and the conclusion which you should read in detail). Get a passing familiarity with the meanings of the words in the section headings—they are likely important to understanding the main argument of the text.

Conclusion. When writing papers, you've likely heard the cliché "in the introduction, write what you will say, then say it, then write what you just said." With this formula, it would seem logical to gloss over the conclusion, because, essentially, you've already read it already. However, this is not the case. Instead, pay close attention to the conclusion. It can help you make sure you understood the introduction.

Sometimes a slight re-phrasing can help you understand the author's arguments in an important, new way. In addition, the conclusion is often where authors indicate the limitations of their work, the unanswered questions, the horizons left unexplored. And this is often the land of exam and essay questions . . . asking you to extend the author's analysis beyond its own shores.

At this point, you have pored over the title, the introduction, the section headings, and the conclusion. You haven't really read the body of the article yet. Your next step is to see if you can answer the question: what is the **main argument or idea** in this text?

Figuring out the main argument is *the* key to reading the text effectively and efficiently. Once you can identify the main argument, you can determine how much energy to spend on various parts of the reading. For example, if I am drowning in details about the temperance movement in the United States in the 19th Century, I need to know the main argument of the text to know if I need to slow down or if a swift skim will do. If the main argument is that women's organizing has taken different forms in different times, it will probably be enough for me to understand that women organized against the sale and consumption of alcohol. That might involve me looking up "temperance" and getting the gist of women's organizing. However, if the main argument were that scholars have misunderstood the role of upper class white women in temperance organizing in Boston from 1840–1865, then I would probably need to slow down and pay closer attention.

Unless the reading is billed as a review or a synthesis, the only way that an academic text can even get published is if it claims to argue something new or different. However, unlike laundry detergent or soft drinks, academic articles don't advertise what makes them new and different in block letters inside cartoon bubbles. In fact, finding the main argument can sometimes be tricky. Mostly, though, it's just a matter of knowing where to look. The abstract and the introduction are the best places to look first. With complicated texts, do this work with your classmates, visit your campus writing center (many of them help with reading assignments), or drag a friend into it.

Once you understand the different parts of the text and the writer's main argument, use this information to see how and where you can enter the conversation. In addition, keep your own agenda as a reader in mind as you do this work.

PUTTING IT ALL TOGETHER

Collectively, these suggestions and guidelines will help you read and understand academic texts. They ask you to bring a great deal of awareness and preparation to your reading—for example, figuring out who the primary audience is for the text and, if you are not that audience, why your professor is asking you to read it anyway. Then, instead of passively reading the text from start to finish, my suggestions encourage you to pull the reading into its constituent parts—the abstract, the introduction, the section headings, conclusion, etc.—and read them unevenly and out of order to look for the holy grail of the main argument. Once you have the main argument you can make wise decisions about which parts of the text you need to pore over and which you can blithely skim. The final key to reading smarter, not harder is to make it social. When you have questions, ask. Start conversations with your professors about the reading. Ask your classmates to work with you to find the main arguments. Offer a hand to your peers who are drowning in dense details. Academics write to join scholarly conversations. Your professors assign you their texts so that you can join them too.

DISCUSSION

1. Pick one reading strategy above that you may have used in reading a text previously (like paying close attention to the introduction of a book, chapter, or article). Discuss the ways in which this strategy worked for you and/or didn't work for you. Would you recommend friends use this strategy? (How) might you amend it, and when might you use it again?

2. The author writes in several places about reading academic texts as entering a conversation. What does this mean to you? How can you have a conversation with a text?

3. How might the reading strategies discussed in this article have an impact on your writing? Will you be more aware of your introduction, conclusion, and clues you leave throughout the text for readers? Talk with other writers to see what they may have learned about writing from this article on reading strategies.

Notes

1. In this discussion I draw on Norgaard's excellent discussion of reading as joining a conversation (1–28). By letting you, the reader, know this in a footnote, I am not only citing my source (I'd be plagiarizing if I didn't mention this somewhere), but I'm also showing how I enter this conversation and give you a trail to follow if you want to learn more about the metaphor of the conversation. Following standard academic convention, I put the full reference to Norgaard's text at the end of this article, in the references.

2. I draw on—and recommend—Rounsaville et al.'s discussion of rhetorical sensitivity, critical reading and rhetorical reading (1–35).

Works Cited

Norgaard, Rolf. *Composing Knowledge: Readings for College Writers*. Boston: Bedford/St. Martin's, 2007. Print.

Rounsaville, Angela, Rachel Goldberg, Keith Feldman, Cathryn Cabral, and Anis Bawarshi, eds. *Situating Inquiry: An Introduction to Reading, Research, and Writing at the University of Washington*. Boston: Bedford/St. Martin's, 2008. Print.

Googlepedia: Turning Information Behaviors into Research Skills

Randall McClure

INTRODUCTION

The ways in which most writers find, evaluate, and use information have changed significantly over the past ten years.[*] A recent study, for example, has shown that as many as nine out of every ten students begin the process of searching for information on the Web, either using a search engine, particularly Google, or an online encyclopedia, notably Wikipedia (Nicholas, Rowlands and Huntington 7). I believe this finding is true of most writers, not just students like you; the Web is our research home.

To illustrate for you how the Web has changed the nature of research and, as a result, the shape of research-based writing, I trace in this chapter the early research decisions of two first year composition students, Susan and Edward, one who begins research in Google and another who starts in Wikipedia. Part narrative, part analysis, part reflection, and part instruction, this chapter blends the voices of the student researchers with me, in the process of seeking a new way to research.

Please understand that I do not plan to dismiss the use of what I call "Googlepedia" in seeking information. As James P. Purdy writes in his essay on Wikipedia in Volume 1 of *Writing Spaces*, "[Y]ou are going to use [Google and] Wikipedia as a source for writing assignments regardless of cautions against [them], so it is more helpful to address ways to use [them] than to ignore [them]" (205). Therefore, my goal in this chapter is to suggest a blended research process that begins with the initial tendency to use Google and Wikipedia and ends in the university library. While Susan and Edward find Googlepedia to be "good enough" for conducting research, this chapter shows you why that's not true and why the resources provided by your school library are still much more effective for conducting research. In doing so, I include comments from Susan and Edward on developing their existing information behaviors into academic research skills, and I offer questions to help you consider your own information behaviors and research skills.

UNDERSTANDING INFORMATION LITERACY

Before I work with you to move your information behaviors inside the online academic library, you need to understand the concept of information literacy. The American Library Association (ALA) and the Association of College and Research Libraries (ACRL) define information literacy "a set of abilities requiring individuals to recognize when information is needed and have the ability to locate, evaluate, and use effectively the needed information" (American Library Association). The ACRL further acknowledges that information literacy is "increasingly important in the contemporary environment of rapid technological change and proliferating information resources. Because of the escalating complexity of this environment, individuals are faced with diverse, abundant information choices" (Association of College and Research Libraries). In short, information literacy is a set of skills you need to understand, find, and use information.

I am certain that you are already familiar with conducting research on the Web, and I admit that finding information quickly and effortlessly is certainly alluring. But what about the reliability of the information you find? Do you ever question if the information you find is really accurate or true? If you have, then please know that you are not alone in your questions. You might even find some comfort in my belief that conducting sound academic research is more challenging now than at any other time in the history of the modern university.

Writing in a Googlepedia World

Teachers Tiffany J. Hunt and Bud Hunt explain that the web-based encyclopedia Wikipedia is not just a collection of web pages built on *wiki* technology[1], it is a web-based community of readers and writers, and a trusted one at that. Whereas most student users of Wikipedia trust the community of writers that contribute to the development of its pages of information, many teachers still criticize or disregard Wikipedia because of its open participation in the writing process, possible unreliability, and at times shallow coverage (Purdy 209), since "anyone, at any time, can modify by simply clicking on an 'edit this page' button found at the top of every Web entry" (Hunt and Hunt 91). However, the disregard for Wikipedia appears to be on the decline, and more and more users each day believe the "information is trustworthy and useful because, over time, many, many people have contributed their ideas, thoughts, passions, and the facts they learned both in school and in the world" (91). Wikipedia and Google are so much a part of the research process for writers today that to ignore their role and refuse to work with these tools seems ludicrous.

Still, the accuracy and verifiability of information are not as clear and consistent in many sources identified through Wikipedia and Google as they are with sources found in most libraries. For this reason, I am sure you have been steered away at least once from information obtained from search engines like Yahoo and Google as well as online encyclopedias like Answers.com and Wikipedia. Despite the resistance that's out there, Alison J. Head and Michael Eisenberg from *Project Information Literacy* report from their interviews with groups of students on six college campuses that "Wikipedia was a unique and indispensible research source for students . . . there was a strong consensus among students that their research process began with [it]" (11). The suggestion by Head and Eisenberg that many students go to Google and Wikipedia first, and that many of them go to these websites in order to get a sense of the big picture (11), is confirmed in the advice offered by Purdy when he writes that Wikipedia allows you to "get a sense of the multiple aspects or angles" on a topic (209). Wikipedia brings ideas together on a single page as well as provides an accompanying narrative or summary that writers are often looking for during their research, particularly in the early stages of it. Head and Eisenberg term this Googlepedia-based information behavior "presearch," specifically pre-researching a topic before moving onto more focused, serious, and often library-based research.

The concept of presearch is an important one for this chapter; Edward's reliance on Wikipedia and Susan's reliance on Google are not research crutches, but useful presearch tools. However, Edward and Susan admit they would not have made the research move into the virtual library to conduct database-oriented research without my intervention in the research process. Both students originally viewed this move like many students do, as simply unnecessary for most writing situations.

Talkin' Bout This Generation

Wikipedia might be the starting point for some writers; however, Google remains the starting point for most students I know. In fact, one group of researchers believes this information behavior—students' affinity for all things "search engine"—is so prominent that it has dubbed the current generation of students "the Google Generation." Citing not only a 2006 article from *EDUCAUSE Review* but also, interestingly enough, the Wikipedia discussion of the term, a group of researchers from University College London (UCL) note the "first port of call for knowledge [for the Google Generation] is the [I]nternet and a search engine, Google being the most popular" (Nicholas, Rowlands and Huntington 7). In other words, the UCL researchers argue that "students have already developed an ingrained coping behavior: they have learned to 'get by' with Google" (23). I believe we all are immersed and comfortable in the information world created by Googlepedia, yet there is much more to research than this.

Despite the fact that it would be easy and understandable to dismiss your information behaviors or to just tell you never to use Google or Wikipedia, I agree with teacher and author Troy Swanson when he argues, "We [teachers] need to recognize that our students enter our [college] classrooms with their own experiences as users of information" (265). In my attempt though to show you that research is more than just a five-minute stroll through Googlepedia, I first acknowledge what you already do when conducting research. I then use these behaviors as part of a process that is still quick, but much more efficient. By mirroring what writers do with Googlepedia and building on that process, this essay will significantly improve your research skills and assist you with writing projects in college and your professional career.

The Wikipedia Hoax

At this point in the chapter, let me pause to provide an example of why learning to be information literate and research savvy is so important. In his discussion of the "Wikipedia Hoax," Associated Press writer Shawn Pogatchnik tells the story of University College Dublin student Shane Fitzgerald who "posted a poetic but phony" quote supposedly by French composer Maurice Jarre in order to test how the "Internet-dependent media was upholding accuracy and accountability." Fitzgerald posted his fake quote on Wikipedia within hours of the composer's death, and later found that several newspaper outlets had picked up and published the quote, even though the administrators of Wikipedia recognized and removed the bogus post. The administrators removed it quickly, "but not quickly enough to keep some journalists from cutting and pasting it first."

It can safely be assumed these journalists exhibited nearly all of the information behaviors that most teachers and librarians find disconcerting:

- searching in Wikipedia or Google
- power browsing quickly through websites for ideas and quotes
- cutting-and-pasting information from the Web into one's own writing without providing proper attribution for it
- viewing information as free, accurate, and trustworthy
- treating online information as equal to print information

Of course, it is impossible to actually prove the journalists used these behaviors without direct observation of their research processes, but it seems likely. In the end, their Googlepedia research hurt not only their writing, but also their credibility as journalists.

EDWARD, SUSAN, AND GOOGLEPEDIA

Edward and Susan are two students comfortable in the world of Googlepedia, beginning and, in most cases, ending their research with a search engine (both students claimed to use Google over any other search engine) or online encyclopedia (both were only aware of Wikipedia). Interestingly, Edward and Susan often move between Google and Wikipedia in the process of conducting their research, switching back and forth between the two sources of information when they believe the need exists.

For an upcoming research writing project on the topic of outsourcing American jobs, Susan chooses to begin her preliminary research with Google while Edward chooses to start with Wikipedia. The students engage in preliminary research, research at the beginning of the research writing process; yet, they work with a limited amount of information about the assignment, a situation still common in many college courses. The students know they have to write an argumentative essay of several pages and use at least five sources of information, sources they are required to find on their own. The students know the research-based essay is a major assignment for a college course, and they begin their searches in Googlepedia despite the sources available to them through the university library.

Edward

Edward begins his research in Wikipedia, spending less than one minute to find and skim the summary paragraph on the main page for "outsourcing." After reading the summary paragraph[2] to, in Edward's words, "make sure I had a good understanding of the topic," and scanning the rest of the main page (interestingly) from bottom to top, Edward focuses his reading on the page section titled "criticism." Edward explains his focus,

> Since I am writing an argumentative paper, I first skimmed the whole page for ideas that stood out. I then looked at the references for a clearly opinionated essay to see what other people are talking about and to compare my ideas [on the subject] to theirs,' preferably if they have an opposing view.

This search for public opinion leads Edward to examine polls as well as skim related web pages linked to the Wikipedia page on outsourcing, and Edward quickly settles on the "reasons for outsourcing" in the criticism section of the Wikipedia page. Edward explains, "I am examining the pros of outsourcing as I am against it, and it seems that companies do not want to take responsibility for [outsourcing]."

It is at this point, barely fifteen minutes into his research, that Edward returns to the top of the Wikipedia main page on outsourcing to re-read the opening summary on the topic, as I stop him to discuss the thesis he is developing on corporate responsibility for the outsourcing problem. We discuss what I make of Edward's early research; Edward relies on Wikipedia for a broad overview, to verify his understanding on a subject.

Presearch into Research

Analysis: Some teachers and librarians might argue against it, but I believe starting a search for information in Wikipedia has its benefits. It is difficult enough to write a college-level argumentative essay on a topic you know well. For a topic you know little about, you need to first learn more about it. Getting a basic understanding of the topic or issue through an encyclopedia, even an online one, has been a recommended practice for decades. Some librarians and teachers question the reliability of online encyclopedias like Wikipedia, but this is not the point of the instruction I am offering to you. I want you to keep going, to not stop your search after consulting Wikipedia. To use it as a starting point, not a final destination.

Recommendation: Deepen your understanding. Formulate a working thesis. Reread the pages as Edward has done here. This is recursive preliminary research, a process that will strengthen your research and your writing.

After our brief discussion to flush out his process in conducting research for an argumentative essay, I ask Edward to continue his research. Though he seems to identify a research focus, corporate responsibility, and working thesis—that American corporations should be held responsible for jobs they ship overseas—Edward still chooses to stay on the outsourcing page in Wikipedia to search for additional information.

He then searches the Wikipedia page for what he believes are links to expert opinions along with more specific sources that interest him and, in his approach to argumentative writing, contradict his opinion on the subject. Unlike Susan who later chooses to side with the majority opinion, Edward wants to turn his essay into a debate, regardless of where his ideas fall on the spectrum of public opinion.

Research and Critical/Creative Thinking

Analysis: Edward's reliance on Wikipedia at this point is still not a concern. He is starting to link out to other resources, just as you should do. I, however, suggest that you spend more time at this point in your research to build your knowledge foundation. Your position on the issue should become clearer with the more you read, the more you talk to teachers and peers, and the more you explore the library and the open Web.

Recommendation: Keep exploring and branching out. Don't focus your research at this point. Let your research help focus your thinking.

Staying in Wikipedia leads Edward to texts such as "Outsourcing Bogeyman" and "Outsourcing Job Killer." Edward explains that his choices are largely based on the titles of the texts (clearly evident from these examples), not the authors, their credentials, the websites or sources that contain the texts, the URLs, or perhaps their domain names (e.g. .org, .edu, .net, .com)—characteristics of Web-based sources that most academic researchers consider. Even though Edward acknowledges that the source of the "Bogeyman" text is the journal *Business Week,* for example, he admits selecting the text based on the title alone, claiming "I don't read [*Business Week*], so I can't judge the source's quality."

Research and Credibility

Analysis: Understanding the credentials of the author or source is particularly important in conducting sound academic research and especially during the age of the open Web. We live a world where most anyone with an Internet connection can post ideas and information to the Web. Therefore, it is always a good idea to understand and verify the sources of the information you use in your writing. Would you want to use, even unintentionally, incorrect information for a report you were writing at your job? Of course not. Understanding the credibility of a source is a habit of mind that should be practiced in your first year composition course and has value way beyond it.

Recommendation: Take a few minutes to establish the credibility of your sources. Knowing who said or wrote it, what credentials he or she has, what respect the publication, website, or source has where you found the ideas and information, and discussing these concepts with your peers, librarian, and writing teacher should dramatically improve the essays and reports that result from your research.

What Edward trusts are the ideas contained in the text, believing the writer uses trustworthy information, thereby deferring source evaluation to the author of the text. For example, Edward comments of the "Job Killer" text, "After reading the first three paragraphs, I knew I was going to use this source." Edward adds that the convincing factor is the author's apparent reliance on two studies conducted at Duke University, each attempting to validate a different side of the outsourcing debate and the roles of corporations in it. From Edward's statement, it is clear he needs help to better understand the criteria most scholars use for evaluating and selecting Web-based sources:

- Check the purpose of the website (the extension ".edu," ".org," ".gov," ".com" can often indicate the orientation or purpose of the site).
- Locate and consider the author's credentials to establish credibility.
- Look for recent updates to establish currency or relevancy.
- Examine the visual elements of the site such as links to establish relationships with other sources of information. (Clines and Cobb 2)

A Text's Credibility Is Your Credibility

Analysis: Viewed one way, Edward is trying to establish the credibility of his source. However, he doesn't dig deep enough or perhaps is too easily convinced. What if the studies at Duke, for instance, were conducted by undergraduate students and not faculty members? Would that influence the quality of the research projects and their findings?

Recommendation: Know as much as you can about your source and do your best to present his or her credentials in your writing. As I tell my own students, give "props" to your sources when and where you can in the text of your essays and reports that incorporate source material. Lead-ins such as "Joe Smith, Professor of Art at Syracuse University, writes that . . ." are especially helpful in giving props. Ask your teacher for more strategies to acknowledge your sources.

Edward's next step in his research process reveals more understanding than you might think. Interested in the Duke University studies cited in the "Job Killer" text, Edward moves from Wikipedia to Google in an attempt to find, in his words, "the original source and all its facts." This research move is not for the reason that I would have searched for the original text (I would be looking to verify the studies and validate their findings); still, Edward indicates that he always searches for and uses the original texts, what many teachers would agree is a wise decision. Finding the original studies in his initial Google query, Edward's research move here also reminds us of a new research reality: many original sources previously, and often only, available through campus libraries are now available through search engines like Google and Google Scholar.

After only thirty minutes into his preliminary research, it's the appropriate time for Edward to move his Googlepedia-based approach significantly into the academic world, specifically to the online library.

Before working with Edward to bring his Googlepedia-based research process together with a more traditional academic one, I ask Edward about library-based sources, particularly online databases. His response is the following: "I am more familiar with the Internet, so there is no reason [to use the library databases]. It is not that the library and databases are a hassle or the library is an uncomfortable space, but I can get this research done in bed." Edward's response is interesting here as it conflicts with the many reports that students often find the college library to be an intimidating place. Edward doesn't find the library to be overwhelming or intimidating; he finds the information in it *unnecessary* given the amount of information available via Googlepedia.

> But what if researching in the online library could be a more reliable and more efficient way to do research?

Susan

Susan begins her research where most students do, on Google. Interestingly, Susan does not start with the general topic of outsourcing, opting instead to let the search engine recommend related search terms. As Susan types in the term "outsourcing," Google as a search engine builds on character recognition software providing several "suggestions" or related search terms, terms that Susan expects to be provided for her, and one—"outsourcing pros and cons"—quickly catches her attention. Commenting on this choice instead of searching by the general concept of outsourcing, Susan notes, "I would have to sort through too much stuff [on Google] before deciding what to do." She selects "pros and cons" from the many related and limiting search terms suggested to her; Susan states, "I want both sides of the story because I don't know much about it."

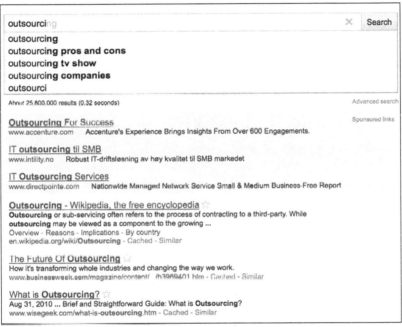

Fig. 1. Outsourcing suggestions from Google.

Susan next moves into examining the top ten returns provided on the first page of her Google search for outsourcing pros and cons. Doing what is now common practice for most Web users, Susan immediately selects the link for the first item returned in the query. I believe most search engine users are wired this way, even though they are likely familiar with the emphasis given to commercial sites on Google and other search engines. Quickly unsatisfied with this source, Susan jumps around on the first page of returns, stopping on the first visual she encounters on a linked page: a table illustrating pros and cons.

Asked why she likes the visual, Susan responds that she is trying to find out how many arguments exist for and against outsourcing. On this page, Susan notes the author provides seven pros and four cons for outsourcing. This finding leads Susan to believe that more pros likely exist and that her essay should be in support of outsourcing.

"Visual" Research

Analysis: There are at least two points worthy of your attention here. First, Susan's information behavior shows how attracted we all are to visuals (maps, charts, tables, diagrams, photos, images, etc.), particularly when they appear on a printed page or screen. Second, she fails to acknowledge a basic fact of research—that visual information of most any kind can be misleading. In the above example, Susan quickly deduces that more (7 pros vs. 4 cons) means more important or more convincing. Couldn't it be possible that all or even any one of the cons is more significant than all of the pros taken together?

Recommendation: Consider using visuals as both researching and writing aids. However, analyze them as closely as you would a printed source. Also, examine the data for more than just the numbers. It might be a truism that numbers don't lie, but it is up to you, as a writer, to explain what the numbers really mean.

Like Edward, Susan is not (initially) concerned about the credibility of the text (author's credentials, source, sponsoring/hosting website, URL or domain, etc.); she appears only concerned with the information itself. When prodded, Susan mentions the text appears to be some form of press release, the URL seems legitimate, and the site appears credible. She fails to mention that the author's information is not included on the text, but Susan quickly dismisses this: "The lack of author doesn't bother me. It would only be a name anyway." Susan adds that her goal is to get the research done "the easiest and fastest way I can." These attitudes—there is so much information available in the Googlepedia world that the information stands on its own and the research process itself doesn't need to take much time—appear to be a common misconception among students today, and the behaviors that result from them could possibly lead to flimsy arguments based on the multiplicity rather than the quality of information.

Research and CRAAP

Analysis: I have referenced criteria for evaluating sources throughout this chapter. If you do not fully understand them, you should consult the resources below and talk with your teacher or a reference librarian.

Recommendation: Learn to put your sources to the CRAAP test (easy to remember, huh?):

- *"Currency:* The timeliness of the information."
- *"Relevance:* The importance of the information for your needs."
- *"Authority:* The source of the information."
- *"Accuracy:* The reliability, truthfulness, and correctness of the informational content."
- *"Purpose:* The reason the information exists." (Meriam Library)

- For specific questions to pose of your sources to evaluate each of these, visit the website for the developers of the CRAAP test at http://www.csuchico.edu/lins/handouts/evalsites.html. Another useful site is http://www.gettysburg.edu/library/research/tips/webeval/index.dot.

Unlike Edward, Susan is not concerned with engaging in a debate on the subject of outsourcing, regardless of her opinions on it. Susan views the assignment as I think many students would, another "get it done" research paper. Further, she believes the majority opinion, at least as it is discussed in the initial source she locates, should be *her* opinion in her essay. Susan explains, "I tend to take the side that I think I can make the stronger argument for . . . If it was a personal issue or an issue I was really interested in, like abortion, I wouldn't do this. This topic doesn't affect me though."

Good Search Terms=Good Research Options

Analysis: Susan needs to understand why being overly reliant on sources uncovered early on in the research process is a problem (particularly here where the search term pros comes before the search term cons likely leading to the results Susan has received). I hope you also share my concerns with the working thesis she appears to be constructing, though I recognize that many students approach research papers just this way.

Recommendation: Improve your research by attempting at least a handful of Web searches using different key terms. If necessary, work with the search phrases and terms provided by the search engine. Also, place your search terms inside quotes on occasion to help vary and focus your search returns. Looking at the subject from different perspectives should help you gain a better sense of the topic and should lead you to a thesis and the development of an essay that is more convincing to your readers.

To her credit, Susan understands the need to validate the information provided by her first source, and she examines the original ten search returns for another text that might indicate the number of advantages and disadvantages to outsourcing. This search behavior of relying on the first page of returns provided by a search engine query has been widely documented, if nowhere else but in the experience of nearly every computer user. When was the last time you went to say the fourth or fifth page of returns on Google? Such a research move contradicts the power browsing nature of most of today's computer users, teachers and students alike. As Susan (perhaps, to some degree, rightly) explains, "The farther away from the first page, the less topic appropriate the articles become." I would contend this might be true of the thirty-seventh page of returns; yet, please understand that you should explore beyond the first page of returns when seeking out information via a search engine. Google your own name (last name first as well) some day to see just how curiously search returns are prioritized.

Next, Susan identifies a subsequent source, www.outsource2india. com. This website provides the confirmation that Susan is looking for, noting sixteen pros and only twelve cons for outsourcing. At this point, Susan confirms her process for gathering source material for argumentative essays: she looks for two to three web-based articles that share similar views, particularly views that provide her with arguments, counterarguments, and rebuttals. Once she has an adequate list of points and has determined which side of a debate can be more effectively supported, Susan refines her Google search to focus only on that side of the debate.

Don't Rush to Argument

Analysis: There are two concerns with Susan's research at this point: (1) her rush to research and (2) her rush to judgment.

Recommendation: In addition to reworking your research process with the help of the ideas presented in this chapter, consider building your understanding of writing academic arguments. In addition to your writing teacher and composition textbook, two sources to consult are http://www.dartmouth.edu/~writing/materials/student/ac_paper/what.shtml#argument and http://www.unc.edu/depts/wcweb/handouts/argument.html#2.

Similar to the way she began searching for information only fifteen minutes earlier, Susan uses Google's "suggestions" to help her identify additional sources that support the side of the debate she has chosen to argue. As she types in "pros outsourcing," Susan identifies and selects "pro outsourcing statistics" from the recommended list of searches provided by Google in a drop-down menu. Like Edward, Susan is interested in validating the points she wants to use in her essay with research studies and scientific findings. Susan comments, "Statistics. Data. Science. They all make an argument stronger and not just opinion." Susan again relies on the first page of search results and focuses on title and URL to make her selections. As she finds information, she copies and pastes it along with the URL to a Word document, noting once she has her five sources with a blend of ideas and statistics together in a Word file that she will stop her research and start her writing.

Track Your Research/Give Props

Analysis: Susan demonstrates here the common information behavior of cutting-and-pasting text or visuals from Web pages. She also demonstrates some understanding of the value of quantitative research and scientific proof. She also appears to use Word to create a working bibliography. These behaviors are far from perfect, but they can be of some help to you.

Recommendation: Learn to use an annotated bibliography. This type of research document will help you with both remembering and citing your sources. For more information on building an annotated bibliography, visit http://www.ehow.com/how_4806881_construct-annotated-bibliography.html. There

are also many software and online applications such as Zotero
and RefWorks that can help you collect and cite your sources.
Next, make sure to do more than just cut-and-paste the ideas of
others and the information you find on the Web into an essay
or report of yours.[3] Learn to use paraphrases and summaries in
addition to word-for-word passages and quotes. The Purdue
OWL, a great resource for all things research and writing, explains options for incorporating research into your own writing:
http://owl.english.purdue.edu/owl/resource/563/1/. Finally, realize the value and limitations of statistics/numerical data and
scientific findings. This type of research can be quite convincing as support for an argument, but it takes your explanations of
the numbers and findings to make it so. You need to explain
how the ideas of others relate to your thesis (and don't forget to
give props).

Edward and Susan: Remix

As you know by now, I certainly have concerns with Susan's and
Edward's research process; however, I recognize that the process used
by each of these students is not uncommon for many student researchers. More importantly, each process includes strategies which could be
easily reworked in the digital library.

Yes, I am concerned that Susan doesn't recognize that you can find
two or three sources on the Web that agree on just about anything, no
matter how crazy that thing might be. Yes, I am concerned that Susan
opts out of forming an argument that she truly believes in. Yes, I am
concerned that both Susan and Edward trust information so quickly
and fail to see a need to question their sources. Despite my concerns,
and perhaps your own, their Googlepedia-based research process can
provide the terms they need to complete the research in more sound
and productive ways, and the process can be easily replicated in an
online library.

Based on their Googlepedia research to this point, I suggest to Edward that he construct his essay as a rebuttal argument and that he
use the search terms "outsourcing" and "corporate responsibility" to
explore sources available to him from the library. For Susan, I suggest
that she too construct a rebuttal argument and that she use the search
string "outsourcing statistics" to explore sources in the university's vir-

tual library. (For more information on writing rebuttal arguments, visit http://www.engl.niu.edu/wac/rebuttal.html.)

Given the influence and value of using search engines like Google and online encyclopedias like Wikipedia in the research process, I recommend the following eight step research process to move from relying on instinctive information behaviors to acquiring solid research skills:

1. Use Wikipedia to get a sense of the topic and identify additional search terms.
2. Use Google to get a broader sense of the topic as well as verify information and test out search terms you found in Wikipedia.
3. Search Google again using quotation marks around your "search terms" to manage the number of results and identify more useful search terms.
4. Search Google Scholar (scholar.google.com) to apply the search terms in an environment of mostly academic and professional resources.
5. Do a limited search of "recent results or "since 2000" on Google Scholar to manage the number of results and identify the most current resources.
6. Search your college's library research databases using your college library's web portal: to apply the search terms in an environment of the most trusted academic and professional resources.
7. Focus your search within at least one general academic database such as Academic Search Premier, Proquest Complete, Lexis/Nexis Academic Universe, or CQ Researcher to apply the search terms in a trusted environment and manage the number of results.
8. Do a limited search by year and "full text" returns using the same general academic database(s) you used in step 7 to reduce the number of results and identify the most current resources.

I admit that this process will certainly seem like a lot of work to you, but I want to emphasize that Edward and Susan completed this sequence in less than thirty minutes. After doing so, Edward even commented, "If someone had shown me this in high school, I wouldn't be going to Wikipedia and Google like I do." Susan added that even with her search terms, Google still presented challenges in terms of the number of potential sources: "Google had thousands of hits while Galileo might have less than 100." For students who value speed and ease, this remixed process resonated with them, and I believe it will with you.

More importantly, the remixed process addresses some of the concerns that could have hindered the research and writing of both students if they only worked with Googlepedia. By remixing and sequencing research this way, they worked with issues of currency, credibility, accuracy and bias among others, criteria vital to conducting sound research. This is not to say that Susan and Edward failed to understand or could not apply these concepts, particularly given that our research time was limited to sixty minutes total (thirty minutes researching alone plus thirty minutes for cooperative research). However, any student who makes this research move will find a more viable and valuable research path. As Edward said, "[The library sources] produced a narrowed search pattern and created less results based on a more reliable pool from which to pull the information."

The research approach I am suggesting can be quick and easy, and it can also be more connected to the values of researchers and the skills of adept information users. Don't take just my word for it though. Consider Susan's closing comment from the questionnaire she completed after our research session:

> I really hadn't ever thought of using library sources in looking up information because I've always used open Web resources. I now know the benefits of using library sources and how they can simplify my search. I found being able to categorize articles by date and relevancy very helpful . . . I am inclined to change the way I research papers from using the open Web to using library sources because they are more valid and it's as easy to use as Google.

In just a single one-hour-long preliminary research session, Susan and Edward were able to utilize the research behaviors they were comfortable with, were encouraged to continue starting their research in Googlepedia, and learned to remix their behaviors inside the online library. Working on your own or with a teacher or librarian to make the research move from Googlepedia to the library, as I suggest in this chapter, should help to improve the quality of your research and your writing based upon it.

CONCLUSION

Susan Blum notes that "if we want to teach students to comply with academic norms of [research], it may be helpful to contrast their ordinary textual practices—rich, varied, intersecting, constant, ephemeral, speedy—with the slower and more careful practices required in the academy" (16). Working through the research process as we have in this chapter, we are moving away from *the* research process to a combination of *our* process, as librarians and teachers, with *your* process—a process that blends technological comfort and savvy with academic standards and rigor. I believe this combination makes for an intellectual, real, and honest approach for researching in the digital age. Blum comments, "By the time we punish students, we have failed. So let's talk. These text-savvy students may surprise us" (16). Susan and Edward have done just that for me, and I hope you have learned a little from them, too.

DISCUSSION

1. In the discussion of Edward's preliminary research, several characteristics of a Web-based source that most academic researchers consider are mentioned including the title of the webtext, the author, his or her credentials, the website or source that contains the webtext, the URL, and the domain name (e.g. .org, .edu, .net, .com). What characteristic or characteristics do you examine if any? Which ones do you believe are the most important? Why?

2. Susan mentions that she "would have to sift through too much stuff" when searching for information on Google. Do you agree that Google provides too much information to examine? Why or why not? In addition to Susan's approach of using a search term suggested by Google, what strategies do you have for limiting the information returned to you when seeking information using a search engine?

3. Type your name or your favorite subject into a search engine, such as Google or Yahoo. What do you notice about the search

returns? How do the returns appear to be prioritized? From the results you see, consider how the rankings of returns could help and hurt your research for an academic paper if you relied only on a search engine for your information. Discuss your response with a group of classmates.

4. Try working with Susan's search terms in reverse—the "cons" and "pros" of outsourcing. Use a search engine like Google or Yahoo to compare the results when you switch the order of search terms. How are the results for the "cons and pros of outsourcing" similar to and different from the results for the search for the "pros and cons of outsourcing"? Discuss your findings with a group of classmates.

NOTES

1. Wikis are websites that allow a user to add new web pages or edit any page and have the changes he or she makes integrated into that page.

2. See pages 209–211 in Purdy for more discussion on the value of Wikipedia in preliminary research.

3. See pages 217–218 in Purdy for an example of a student engaging in written conversation with her sources rather than just "parroting" them.

WORKS CITED

American Library Association. Presidential Committee on Information Literacy. Chicago: ALA, 1989. Print.

Association of College and Research Libraries. *Information Literacy Competency Standards for Higher Education.* 2000. Web. 17 May 2010.

Blum, Susan D. "Swimming in a Sea of Texts: Attribution in the Age of the Internet." *On Campus.* 29.1 (Sept/Oct 2009): 16. Print.

Clines, Raymond H. and Elizabeth R. Cobb. *Research Writing Simplified: A Documentation Guide.* 6th ed. NY: Pearson, 2010. Print.

Head, Alison J. and Michael B. Eisenberg. *Lessons Learned: How College Students Seek Information in the Digital Age.* U of Washington: Project Information Literacy Progress Report. 1 Dec 2009. Print.

Hunt, Tiffany J. and Bud Hunt. "Research and Authority in an Online World: Who Knows? Who Decides?" *English Journal.* 95.4 (Mar 2006): 89–92. Print.

Meriam Library. "Evaluating Information—Applying the CRAAP Test." California State U, Chico. 29 Sept 2009. Web. 9 Sept 2010.

Nicholas, David, Ian Rowlands and Paul Huntington. *Information Behaviour of the Researcher of the Future.* 2008. Web. 4 Apr 2009.

Pogatchnik, Shawn. "Student Hoaxes World's Media on Wikipedia." *msnbc. com.* 12 May 2009. Web. 13 May 2009.

Purdy, James P. "Wikipedia Is Good for You!?" *Writing Spaces: Readings on Writing.* Vol. 1. West Lafayette, IN: Parlor P, 2010. 205–224. Print.

Swanson, Troy. "A Radical Step: Implementing a Critical Information Literacy Model." *portal: Libraries and the Academy.* 4.2 (2004): 259–273. Print.

Annoying Ways People Use Sources

Kyle D. Stedman

How Slow Driving Is Like Sloppy Writing

I hate slow drivers.* When I'm driving in the fast lane, maintaining the speed limit exactly, and I find myself behind someone who thinks the fast lane is for people who drive ten miles per hour *below* the speed limit, I get an annoyed feeling in my chest like hot water filling a heavy bucket. I wave my arms around and yell, "What . . . ? But, hey . . . oh come *on!*" There are at least two explanations for why some slow drivers fail to move out of the way:

1. They don't know that the generally accepted practice of high-way driving in the U.S. is to move to the right if an upcoming car wants to pass. Or,
2. They know the guidelines but don't care.

But here's the thing: writers can forget that their readers are sometimes just as annoyed at writing that fails to follow conventions as drivers are when stuck behind a car that fails to move over. In other words, there's something similar between these two people: the knowledge-able driver who thinks, "I thought all drivers *knew* that the left lane is for the fastest cars," and the reader who thinks, "I thought all writers *knew* that outside sources should be introduced, punctuated, and cited according to a set of standards."

One day, you may discover that something you've written has just been read by a reader who, unfortunately, was annoyed at some of the ways you integrated sources. She was reading along and then suddenly exclaimed, "What . . . ? But, hey . . . oh come *on!*" If you're lucky, this reader will try to imagine why you typed things the way you did, giving you the benefit of the doubt. But sometimes you'll be slotted into positions that might not really be accurate. When this frustrated reader walks away from your work, trying to figure out, say, why you used so many quotations, or why you kept starting and ending paragraphs with them, she may come to the same conclusions I do about slow drivers:

1. You don't know the generally accepted practices of using sourc es (especially in academic writing) in the U.S. Or,
2. You know the guidelines but don't care.

And it will be a lot harder for readers to take you seriously if they think you're ignorant or rude.

This judgment, of course, will often be unfair. These readers might completely ignore the merits of your insightful, stylistically beautiful, or revolutionarily important language—just as my anger at another driver makes me fail to admire his custom paint job. But readers and writers don't always see eye to eye on the same text. In fact, some things I write about in this essay will only bother your pickiest readers (some teachers, some editors, some snobby friends), while many other readers might zoom past how you use sources without blinking. But in my experience, I find that teachers do a disservice when we fail to alert students to the kind of things that some readers might be annoyed at—however illogical these things sometimes seem. People are often unreasonably picky, and writers have to deal with that—which they do by trying to anticipate and preemptively fix whatever might annoy a broad range of readers. Plus, the more effectively you anticipate that pickiness, the more likely it is that readers will interpret your quotations and paraphrases in the way you want them to—critically or acceptingly, depending on your writing context.

It helps me to remember that the conventions of writing have a fundamentally *rhetorical* nature. That is, I follow different conventions depending on the purpose and audience of my writing, because I know that I'll come across differently to different people depending on how well I follow the conventions expected in any particular writing space. In a blog, I cite a source by hyperlinking; in an academic essay, I use a parenthetical citation that refers to a list of references at the end of the essay. One of the fundamental ideas of rhetoric is that speakers/writers/composers shape what they say/write/create based on what they want it to do, where they're publishing it, and what they know about their audience/readers. And those decisions include nitty-gritty things like introducing quotations and citing paraphrases clearly: not everyone in the entire world approaches these things the same way, but when I strategically learn the expectations of my U.S. academic audience, what I really want to say comes across smoothly, without little annoying blips in my readers' experience. Notice that I'm not saying that there's a particular *right* or *wrong* way to use conventions in my writing—if the modern U.S. academic system had evolved from a primarily African or Asian or Latin American cultural consciousness instead of a European one, conventions for writing would probably be very different. That's why they're *conventions* and not *rules*.

The Annoyances

Because I'm not here to tell you *rules, decrees,* or *laws,* it makes sense to call my classifications *annoyances*. In the examples that follow, I wrote all of the annoying examples myself, but all the examples I use of good writing come from actual student papers in first year composition classes at my university; I have their permission to quote them.

Armadillo Roadkill

Everyone in the car hears it: buh-BUMP. The driver insists to the passengers, "But that armadillo—I didn't see it! It just came out of nowhere!"

Armadillo Roadkill: dropping in a quotation without introducing it first

Sadly, a poorly introduced quotation can lead readers to a similar exclamation: "It just came out of nowhere!" And though readers probably won't experience the same level of grief and regret when surprised by a quotation as opposed to an armadillo, I submit that there's a kinship between the experiences: both involve a normal, pleasant activity (driving; reading) stopped suddenly short by an unexpected barrier (a sudden armadillo; a sudden quotation).

Here's an example of what I'm talking about:

> We should all be prepared with a backup plan if a zombie invasion occurs. "Unlike its human counterparts, an army of zombies is completely independent of support" (Brooks 155). Preparations should be made in the following areas. . . .

Did you notice how the quotation is dropped in without any kind of warning? (Buh-BUMP.)

The Fix: The easiest way to effectively massage in quotations is by purposefully returning to each one in your draft to see if you set the stage for your readers—often, by signaling that a quote is about to come, stating who the quote came from, and showing how your readers should interpret it. In the above example, that could be done by introducing the quotation with something like this (new text bolded):

> We should all be prepared with a backup plan if a zombie invasion occurs. **Max Brooks suggests a number of ways to prepare for zombies' particular traits, though he underestimates the ability of humans to survive in harsh environments. For example, he writes,** "Unlike its human counterparts, an army of zombies is completely independent of support" (155). **His shortsightedness could have a number of consequences. . . .**

In this version, I know a quotation is coming ("For example"), I know it's going to be written by Max Brooks, and I know I'm being asked to read the quote rather skeptically ("he underestimates"). The sentence with the quotation itself also now begins with a "tag" that eases us into it ("he writes").

Here's an actual example from Alexsandra. Notice the way she builds up to the quotation and then explains it:

> In the first two paragraphs, the author takes a defensive position when explaining the perception that the public has about scientists by saying that "there is anxiety that scientists lack both wisdom and social responsibility and are so motivated by ambition . . ." and "scientists are repeatedly referred to as 'playing God'" (Wolpert 345). With this last sentence especially, his tone seems to demonstrate how he uses the ethos

appeal to initially set a tone of someone that is tired of being misunderstood.

Alexsandra prepares us for the quotation, quotes, and then analyzes it. I love it. This isn't a hard and fast rule—I've seen it broken by the best of writers, I admit—but it's a wise standard to hold yourself to unless you have a reason not to.

Dating Spider-Man

An annoyance that's closely connected to Armadillo Roadkill is the tendency writers sometimes have of starting or ending paragraphs with quotations. This isn't technically *wrong,* and there are situations when the effect of surprise is what you're going for. But often, a paragraph-beginning or paragraph-closing quotation feels rushed, unexplained, disjointed.

Dating Spider-Man: starting or ending a paragraph with a quotation

It's like dating Spider-Man. You're walking along with him and he says something remarkably interesting—but then he tilts his head, hearing something far away, and suddenly shoots a web onto the nearest building and *zooms* away through the air. As if you had just read an interesting quotation dangling at the end of a paragraph, you wanted to hear more of his opinion, but it's too late—he's already moved on. Later, he suddenly jumps off a balcony and is by your side again, and he starts talking about something you don't understand. You're confused because he just dropped in and expected you to understand the context of what was on his mind at that moment, much like when readers step into a paragraph that begins with a quotation. Here's an example:

> *[End of a preceding paragraph:]* . . . Therefore, the evidence clearly suggests that we should be exceptionally careful about deciding when and where to rest.
>
> "When taking a nap, always rest your elbow on your desk and keep your arm perpendicular to your desktop" (Piven and Borgenicht 98). After all, consider the following scenario. . . .

There's a perfectly good reason why this feels odd—which should feel familiar after reading about the Armadillo Roadkill annoyance above. When you got to the quotation in the second paragraph, you didn't know what you were supposed to think about it; there was no guidance.

The Fix is the same: in the majority of situations, readers appreciate being guided to and led away from a quotation by the writer doing the quoting. Readers get a sense of pleasure from the safe flow of hearing how to read an upcoming quotation, reading it, and then being told one way to interpret it. Prepare, quote, analyze.

I mentioned above that there can be situations where starting a paragraph with a quotation can have a strong effect. Personally, I usually enjoy this most at the beginning of essays or the beginning of sections—like in this example from the very beginning of Jennifer's essay:

> "Nothing is ever simple: Racism and nobility can exist in the same man, hate and love in the same woman, fear and loyalty, compromise and idealism, all the yin-yang dichotomies that make the human species so utterly confounding, yet so utterly fascinating" (Hunter). The hypocrisy and complexity that Stephen Hunter from the *Washington Post* describes is the basis of the movie *Crash* (2004).

Instantly, her quotation hooks me. It doesn't feel thoughtless, like it would feel if I continued to be whisked to quotations without preparation throughout the essay. But please don't overdo it; any quotation that opens an essay or section ought to be integrally related to your topic (as is Jennifer's), not just a cheap gimmick.

Uncle Barry and His Encyclopedia of Useless Information

Uncle Barry and his Encyclopedia of Useless Information: using too many quotations in a row

You probably know someone like this: a person (for me, my Uncle Barry) who constantly tries to impress me with how much he knows about just about everything. I might casually bring up something in the news ("Wow, these health care debates are getting really heated, aren't they?") and then find myself barraged by all of Uncle Barry's ideas on government-sponsored health care—which *then* drifts into a story about how his cousin Maxine died in an underfunded hospice center, which had a parking lot that he could have designed better, which reminds him of how good he is at fixing things, just like the garage door at my parents' house, which probably only needs a little. . . . You get the idea. I might even think to myself, "Wait, I want to know more about that topic, but you're zooming on before you contextualize your information at all."

This is something like reading an essay that relies too much on quotations. Readers get the feeling that they're moving from one quotation to the next without ever quite getting to hear the *real* point of what the author wants to say, never getting any time to form an opinion about the claims. In fact, this often makes it sound as if the author has almost no authority at all. You may have been annoyed by paragraphs like this before:

> Addressing this issue, David M. Potter comments, "Whether Seward meant this literally or not, it was in fact a singularly accurate forecast for territorial Kansas" (199). Of course, Potter's view is contested, even though he claims, "Soon, the Missourians began to perceive the advantages of operating without publicity" (200). Interestingly, "The election was bound to be irregular in any case" (201).

Wait—huh? This author feels like Uncle Barry to me: grabbing right and left for topics (or quotes) in an effort to sound authoritative.

The Fix is to return to each quotation and decide why it's there and then massage it in accordingly. If you just want to use a quote to cite a *fact,* then consider paraphrasing or summarizing the source material (which I find is usually harder than it sounds but is usually worth it for the smoothness my paragraph gains). But if you quoted because you want to draw attention to the source's particular phrasing, or if you want to respond to something you agree with or disagree with in the source, then consider taking the time to surround *each* quotation with guidance to your readers about what you want them to think about that quote.

In the following passage, I think Jessica demonstrates a balance between source and analysis well. Notice that she only uses a single quotation, even though she surely could have chosen more. But instead, Jessica relies on her instincts and remains the primary voice of authority in the passage:

> Robin Toner's article, "Feminist Pitch by a Democrat named Obama," was written a week after the video became public and is partially a response to it. She writes, "The Obama campaign is, in some ways, subtly marketing its candidate as a post-feminist man, a generation beyond the gender conflicts

of the boomers." Subtly is the key word. Obama is a passive character throughout the video, never directly addressing the camera. Rather, he is shown indirectly through speeches, intimate conversations with supporters and candid interaction with family. This creates a sense of intimacy, which in turn creates a feeling of trust.

Toner's response to the Obama video is like a diving board that Jessica bounces off of before she gets to the really interesting stuff: the pool (her own observations). A bunch of diving boards lined up without a pool (tons of quotes with no analysis) wouldn't please anyone—except maybe Uncle Barry.

Am I in the Right Movie?

When reading drafts of my writing, this is a common experience: I start to read a sentence that seems interesting

> *Am I in the Right Movie?*
> *failing to integrate a quotation into the grammar of the preceding sentence*

and normal, with everything going just the way I expect it to. But then the unexpected happens: a quotation blurts itself into the sentence in a way that doesn't fit with the grammar that built up to quotation. It feels like sitting in a movie theater, everything going as expected, when suddenly the opening credits start for a movie I didn't plan to see. Here are two examples of what I'm talking about. Read them out loud, and you'll see how suddenly wrong they feel.

1. Therefore, the author warns that a zombie's vision "are no different than those of a normal human" (Brooks 6).
2. Sheila Anne Barry advises that "Have you ever wondered what it's like to walk on a tightrope—many feet up in the air?" (50)

In the first example, the quoter's build-up to the quotation uses a singular subject—*a zombie's vision*—which, when paired with the quotation, is annoyingly matched with the plural verb *are*. It would be much less jolting to write, "a zombie's vision *is*," which makes the subject and verb agree. In the second example, the quoter builds up to the quotation with a third-person, declarative independent clause: *Sheila Anne Barry advises*. But then the quotation switches into second person—*you*—and unexpectedly asks a question—completely different from the expectation that was built up by the first part of the sentence.

The Fix is usually easy: you read your essay out loud to someone else, and if you stumble as you enter a quotation, there's probably something you can adjust in your lead-in sentence to make the two fit together well. Maybe you'll need to choose a different subject to make it fit with the quote's verb (*reader* instead of *readers; each* instead of *all*), or maybe you'll have to scrap what you first wrote and start over. On occasion you'll even feel the need to transparently modify the quotation by adding an [s] to one of its verbs, always being certain to use square brackets to show that you adjusted something in the quotation. Maybe you'll even find a way to quote a shorter part of the quotation and squeeze it into the context of a sentence that is mostly your own, a trick that can have a positive effect on readers, who like smooth water slides more than they like bumpy slip-and-slides. Jennifer does this well in the following sentence, for example:

> In *Crash*, no character was allowed to "escape his own hypocrisy" (Muller), and the film itself emphasized that the reason there is so much racial tension among strangers is because of the personal issues one cannot deal with alone.

She saw a phrase that she liked in Muller's article, so she found a way to work it in smoothly, without the need for a major break in her thought. Let's put ourselves in Jennifer's shoes for a moment: it's possible that she started drafting this sentence using the plural subject *characters,* writing "In *Crash*, no characters were allowed. . . ." But then, imagine she looked back at the quote from Muller and saw that it said "escape *his* own hypocrisy," which was a clue that she had to change the first part of her sentence to match the singular construction of the quote.

I Can't Find the Stupid Link

I Can't Find the Stupid Link: no connection between the first letter of a parenthetical citation and the first letter of a works cited entry

You've been in this situation: you're on a website that seems like it might be interesting and you want to learn more about it. But the home page doesn't tell you much, so you look for an "About Us" or "More Information" or "FAQ" link. But no matter where you search—Top of page? Bottom? Left menu?—you can't find the stupid link. This is usually the fault of web designers, who don't always take the time to test their sites as much as they should with actual users.

The communication failure here is simple: you're used to finding certain kinds of basic information in the places people usually put it. If it's not there, you're annoyed.

Similarly, a reader might see a citation and have a quick internal question about it: *What journal was this published in? When was it published? Is this an article I could find online to skim myself? This author has a sexy last name—I wonder what his first name is?* Just like when you look for a link to more information, this reader has a simple, quick question that he or she expects to answer easily. And the most basic way for readers to answer those questions (when they're reading a work written in APA or MLA style) is (1) to look at the information in the citation, and (2) skim the references or works cited section alphabetically, looking for the first letter in the citation. There's an assumption that the first letter of a citation will be the letter to look for in the list of works cited.

In short, the following may annoy readers who want to quickly learn more about the citation:

> *[Essay Text:]* A respected guide on the subject suggests, "If possible, always take the high ground and hold it" (*The Zombie Survival Guide* 135).

> [Works Cited Page:] Brooks, Max. *The Zombie Survival Guide: Complete Protection from the Living Dead.* New York: Three Rivers, 2003. Print.

The reader may wonder when *The Zombie Survival Guide* was published and flip back to the works cited page, but the parenthetical citation sends her straight to the *Z*'s in the works cited list (because initial *A*'s and *The*'s are ignored when alphabetizing). However, the complete works cited entry is actually with the *B*'s (where it belongs).

The Fix is to make sure that the first word of the works cited entry is the word you use in your in-text citation, every time. If the works cited entry starts with Brooks, use (Brooks) in the essay text.

Citations not including last names may seem to complicate this advice, but they all follow the same basic concept. For instance, you might have:

- **A citation that only lists a title.** For instance, your citation might read ("Gray Wolf General Information"). In this case, the assumption is that the citation can be found under the *G* section of the works cited page. Leah cites her paraphrase of a source with no author in the following way, indicating that I should head to the *G*'s if I want to learn more about her source:

> Alaska is the only refuge that is left for the wolves in the United States, and once that is gone, they will more than likely become extinct in this country ("Gray Wolf General Information").

- **A citation that only lists a page number.** Maybe the citation simply says (25). That implies that somewhere in the surrounding text, the essay writer must have made it stupendously clear what name or title to look up in the works cited list. This happens a lot, since it's common to introduce a quotation by naming the person it came from, in which case it would be repetitive to name that author again in the citation.

- **A quotation without a citation at all.** This happens when you cite a work that is both A) from a web page that doesn't number the pages or paragraphs and B) is named in the text surrounding the quotation. Readers will assume that the author is named nearby. Stephanie wisely leaves off any citation in the example below, where it's already clear that I should head to the *O*'s on the works cited page to find information about this source, a web page written by Opotow:

> To further this point, Opotow notes, "Don't imagine you'll be unscathed by the methods you use. The end may justify the means. . . . But there's a price to pay, and the price does tend to be oneself."

I Swear I Did Some Research!

Let's look in depth at this potentially annoying passage from a hypothetical student paper:

> It's possible that a multidisciplinary approach to understanding the universe will open new doors of understanding. If theories from sociology, communication, and philosophy joined with physics, the possibilities would be boundless. This would inspire new research, much like in the

I Swear I Did Some Research: dropping in a citation without making it clear what information came from that source

1970s when scientists changed their focus from grand-scale theories of the universe to the small concerns of quantum physics (Hawking 51).

In at least two ways, this is stellar material. First, the author is actually voicing a point of view; she sounds knowledgeable, strong. Second, and more to the point of this chapter, the author includes a citation, showing that she knows that ethical citation standards ask authors to cite paraphrases and summaries—not just quotations.

But on the other hand, which of these three sentences, exactly, came from Hawking's book? Did *Hawking* claim that physics experts should join up with folks in other academic disciplines, or is that the student writer? In other words, at which point does the author's point of view meld into material taken specifically from Hawking?

I recognize that there often aren't clean answers to a question like that. What we read and what we know sometimes meld together so unnoticeably that we don't know which ideas and pieces of information are "ours" and which aren't. Discussing "patchwriting," a term used to describe writing that blends words and phrases from sources with words and phrases we came up with ourselves, scholar Rebecca Moore Howard writes, "When I believe I am not patchwriting, I am simply doing it so expertly that the seams are no longer visible—or I am doing it so unwittingly that I cannot cite my sources" (91). In other words, *all* the moves we make when writing came from somewhere else at some point, whether we realize it or not. Yikes. But remember our main purpose here: to not look annoying when using sources. And most of your instructors aren't going to say, "I understand that I couldn't tell the difference between your ideas and your source's because we quite naturally patchwrite all the time. That's fine with me. Party on!" They're much more likely to imagine that you plopped in a few extra citations as a way of defensively saying, "I swear I did some research! See? Here's a citation right here! Doesn't that prove I worked really hard?"

The Fix: Write the sentences preceding the citation with *specific words and phrases that will tell readers what information came from where*. Like this (bolded words are new):

> It's possible that a multidisciplinary approach to understanding the universe will open new doors of understanding. **I believe that** if theories from sociology, communication, and

philosophy joined with physics, the possibilities would be boundless. This would inspire new research, much like **the changes Stephen Hawking describes happening** in the 1970s when scientists changed their focus from grand-scale theories of the universe to the small concerns of quantum physics (51).

Perhaps these additions could still use some stylistic editing for wordiness and flow, but the source-related job is done: readers know exactly which claims the essay writer is making and which ones Hawking made in his book. The last sentence and only the last sentence summarizes the ideas Hawking describes on page 51 of his book.

One warning: you'll find that scholars in some disciplines (especially in the sciences and social sciences) use citations in the way I just warned you to avoid. You might see sentences like this one, from page 64 of Glenn Gordon Smith, Ana T. Torres-Ayala, and Allen J. Heindel's article in the *Journal of Distance Education:*

> Some researchers have suggested "curriculum" as a key element in the design of web-based courses (Berge, 1998; Driscoll, 1998; Meyen, Tangen, & Lian, 1999; Wiens & Gunter, 1998).

Whoa—that's a lot of citations. Remember how the writer of my earlier example cited Stephen Hawking because she summarized his ideas? Well, a number of essays describing the results of experiments, like this one, use citations with a different purpose, citing previous studies whose general conclusions support the study described in this new paper, like building blocks. It's like saying to your potentially skeptical readers, "Look, you might be wondering if I'm a quack. But I can prove I'm not! See, all these other people published in similar areas! Are you going to pick fights with all of *them* too?" You might have noticed as well that these citations are in APA format, reflecting the standards of the social sciences journal this passage was published in. Well, in this kind of context APA's requirement to cite the year of a study makes a lot of sense too—after all, the older a study, the less likely it is to still be relevant.

Conclusion: Use Your Turn Signals

You may have guessed the biggest weakness in an essay like this: what's annoying varies from person to person, with some readers happily skimming past awkward introductions to quotations without a blink, while others see a paragraph-opening quotation as something to complain about on Facebook. All I've given you here—all I *can* give you unless I actually get to know you and your various writing contexts—are the basics that will apply in a number of academic writing contexts. Think of these as signals to your readers about your intentions, much as wise drivers rely on their turn signals to communicate their intentions to other drivers. In some cases when driving, signaling is an almost artistic decision, relying on the gut reaction of the driver to interpret what is best in times when the law doesn't mandate use one way or the other. I hope your writing is full of similar signals. Now if I could only convince the guy driving in front of me to use *his* blinker. . . .

DISCUSSION

1. Because so many of these guidelines depend on the writer's purpose, publication space, and audience, it can be difficult to know when to follow them strictly and when to bend them. What are some specific writing situations where a writer is justified to bend the standards of how to incorporate sources?

2. Choose one of the annoyances. Then, look through a number of different pieces of writing from different genres and collect two examples of writers who followed your chosen guideline perfectly and two who didn't. For each source you found, jot a sentence or two describing the context of that source and why you think its writer did or did not follow the guideline.

3. Rank the annoyances in order of most annoying to least annoying, pretending that you are a college professor. Now, rank them from the point of view of a newspaper editor, a popular blogger, and another college student. What changes did you make in your rankings?

WORKS CITED

Barry, Sheila Anne. *Tricks & Pranks to Fool Your Friends*. New York: Sterling, 1984. Print.

Brooks, Max. *The Zombie Survival Guide: Complete Protection from the Living Dead*. New York: Three Rivers, 2003. Print.

"Gray Wolf General Information." *Environmental Conservation Online System.* U.S. Fish and Wildlife Service, 15 Oct. 2008. Web. 23 Oct. 2008.

Hawking, Stephen. *A Brief History of Time: From the Big Bang to Black Holes.* New York: Bantam, 1988. Print.

Howard, Rebecca Moore. "The New Abolitionism Comes to Plagiarism." *Perspectives on Plagiarism and Intellectual Property in a Postmodern World.* Ed. Lisa Buranen and Alice M. Roy. Albany: SUNY P, 1999. 87–95. Print.

Hunter, Stephen. "'Crash': The Collision Of Human Contradictions." *The Washington Post.* The Washington Post Company, 6 May 2005. Web. 21 Feb. 2008.

Muller, Bill. "Crash: LA Tale Confronts, Then Shatters, Stereotypes." *The Arizona Republic.* AZCentral.com, 6 May 2005. Web. 21 Feb. 2008.

Opotow, Susan. "Moral Exclusion and Torture: The Ticking Bomb Scenario and the Slippery Ethical Slope." *Peace and Conflict Studies* 13.4 (2007): 457–61. *PsycINFO.* Web. 27 Sept. 2008.

Piven, Joshua, and David Borgenicht. *The Worst-Case Scenario Survival Handbook: Work.* San Francisco: Chronicle, 2003. Print.

Potter, David M. *The Impending Crisis: 1848–1861.* Ed. Don E. Fehrenbacher. New York: Harper & Row, 1976. Print.

Smith, Glenn Gordon, Ana T. Torres-Ayala, and Allen J. Heindel. "Disciplinary Differences in E-learning Instructional Design: The Case of Mathematics." *Journal of Distance Education* 22.3 (2008): 63–88. Web. 10 Sept. 2009.

Toner, Robin. "Feminist Pitch by a Democrat Named Obama." *The New York Times.* The New York Times Company, 2 Dec. 2007. Web. 22 Oct. 2008.

Wolpert, Lewis. "Is Cell Science Dangerous?" *Journal of Medical Ethics* 33.6 (2007): 345–48. *Academic Search Premier.* Web. 28 Jan. 2009.

Everything Changes, or Why MLA Isn't (Always) Right

Janice R. Walker

"The only thing that doesn't change is the fact that everything changes."* I've heard this saying all my life, but until I wanted to use it for this essay, it never occurred to me to check where it came from. According to Bartleby.com, this pithy saying is attributed to Heraclitus, a Greek philosopher, and should actually read, "Change alone is unchanging." But then Bartleby cites *The Columbia World of Quotations,* edited by Robert Andrews, Mary Biggs, and Michael Seidel, as the source of the information about Heraclitus.

So, now what do I do? Do I change the opening quotation? I like my version better than Heraclitus's (maybe because it's the way I always heard it, right or wrong). Do I cite Heraclitus? Do I cite *Bartleby. com?* Or do I cite *The Columbia World of Quotations?* Or maybe I don't need a citation at all. But then, will I be charged with plagiarism? Of course, if I can argue it's common knowledge, maybe I can get away with leaving it alone?

I'm *so* confused!

When it comes to citation practices, the saying is not only confusing to cite, but apt. Often citing sources for an academic project *is* a bit like trying to hit a moving target: the rules seem to keep changing. What doesn't seem to change, of course, is the need to know where information comes from. Otherwise, how do we (both authors and readers) know if the information is reliable? If we don't know or understand the context from which information is gleaned, how do we know what it means? And, of course, failure to cite words, ideas, or information obtained from other sources is considered plagiarism and can have serious repercussions.

So, in the face of so much turmoil and because the issue can have very high stakes, in the classroom and beyond, most of us are, admittedly, confused. While attempting to clear up this confusion may actually complicate it still further, nonetheless, in this article, I explore citation as a rhetorical practice, one which does not always fit precisely within the boundaries of traditional style guides but that nonetheless follows a logic that does make sense and that can be learned.

CITATION AS A RHETORICAL ACT

Strict attribution of sources has not always been necessary, and indeed in many cultures and contexts, it is still not (necessarily) required. Ancient texts often did not follow any formal rules of attribution, since it was assumed that the audience would already be familiar with the body of scholarly work. I have also heard (somewhere) that in Chinese culture, the words of others are used without attribution as a way of honoring those whose words were considered so important that they needed no attribution[1]. That is, it would insult the reader to tell him or her where a quotation was from as much as it would insult an author to assume that his or her words would not be recognized by a reader without such attribution.

In most Western cultures, the invention of the printing press is often cited as an important turning point, especially in discussions of citation and intellectual property. For one thing, the printing press allowed for texts to extend in both time and space in ways that oral texts could not. Even the elaborately illuminated and hand-copied-by-monks texts were prohibitively expensive and jealously guarded so that it could safely be assumed that the audience for these works would be limited. However, the printing press (eventually) allowed for cheaper yet supposedly perfect copies, making knowledge—or at least making printed works purporting to be knowledge—more readily available to the general public. And, of course, free public education extended that general reading public to, well, anyone who wanted to take the time to read a given work. Thus, it could no longer be assumed that readers would be familiar with the body of work referenced by an author.

Even so, we still don't cite every fact, idea, or quotation. So-called common knowledge, we are taught, does not need to be cited. That is, I can write "the world is round" without needing to provide a source to prove the statement. Of course, there was a time when this statement would have been considered heretical and not common knowledge at all! And, quite frankly, it is not technically true that the world is round at all (see http://wiki.answers.com/Q/Is_the_earth_round). Aphorisms, or famous sayings, such as "A rolling stone gathers no moss," or "A stitch in time saves nine," or even "I'll be back!" may also need no attribution. But academic writing is written (or composed) for audiences who expect strict adherence to guidelines for citation. One reason for this is that the persuasiveness of a work depends upon the information the author herself has relied on. Indeed, in some disciplines, citation of sources is a hallmark of credibility:

> Today, a scientific publication is easily recognized by its footnotes, endnotes and references to other scientific articles or books. This is one of the features which make scientific texts so different from a journalist's story or a novel. A scientist seems to be—at least in his [or her] professional life—an annoyingly precise person, whose claims are painstakingly documented. (Wouters 2)

Outside of academia, of course, citation practices aren't always so formal. Newspapers and magazine articles do not usually include a list of works cited or references after all. But they *do* (usually) cite their sources. The Associated Press allows use of anonymous sources only under condition that

1. The material is information and not opinion or speculation, and is vital to the news report.
2. The information is not available except under the conditions of anonymity imposed by the source.
3. The source is reliable, and in a position to have accurate information. (APME)

Of course, not all news organizations are as careful about their use of sources. Nonetheless, even tabloids often attempt to present information in such a way as to appear credible. For example, an article on

UFOs in *The Sun,* a British tabloid known for sensationalist reporting, does identify its source even if the claims presented may be questionable according to scientific standards: "Dr. Yuri Labvin, president of the Tunguska Spatial Phenomenon Foundation, insists an alien spacecraft sacrificed itself to prevent a gigantic meteor from slamming into us above Siberia on June 30, 1908" (Watson). But what does an average reader know about Dr. Labvin's credentials? Would it matter if his doctorate is in UFOlogy from the University of Mars or if, instead, he holds a Ph.D. in Physics from MIT? And what about the foundation over which he presides?[2] What do we know about it? Well, I think you get my point!

A tongue-in-cheek example of the importance of evaluating the possible biases of one's sources can be seen in the movie trailer advertising the 1959 Peter Sellers film, *The Mouse that Roared* (TCM). "Here's what some of the world's keenest and most objective minds have said about *The Mouse that Roared,*" the advertisement proudly exclaims:

> *"Could not be improved upon!"*
>
> —*The Producer*

> *"Completely delightful!"*
>
> —*The Director*

> *"The title role is exquisitely played!"*
>
> —*The Mouse*

Even if we agree that the Mouse's acting was superb, we probably wouldn't want to cite the Mouse as saying so!

Television commercials and magazine advertisements may include what is often termed *fine print* to qualify the claims they make. One mouthwash claims to be the "#1 Dentist Recommended Brand" but with an asterisked note that modifies the claim: it is the number one brand "among fluoride mouth rinses" (ACT). The ad also includes a note identifying a study to support its claim (and, in the case of this online ad, a link to the study itself). Of course, not all research studies are equal. Publication information is essential to aid scholars in determining the authority of a given source: Where was the study published? Was it a scholarly journal or a book published by a university press? If not, did it undergo peer review? Scholarly and profession-al journals in the field may agree—or not—with the results of such commissioned studies. Thus, it is essential to conduct further research to determine the credibility of such sources before relying on them to make an effective argument. (For more information on evaluating sources, see "Evaluating Sources of Information" at http://owl.english.purdue.edu/owl/resource/553/01/).

Academic writers, in other words, are held to the highest standards of reliability for sources. Thus, academic citation formats include in-formation that will not only help a reader to locate a given source and give credit to others for their work, but that will also help a reader to determine a source's credibility, for example, by identifying authorship and/or publication information. However, just as the printing press made it necessary to develop ways to cite information for unfamiliar readers, the advent of new media has made it necessary to develop new ways to cite them. That is, scholars nowadays may rely equally (or even more) on types of resources that quite simply didn't exist a century—or even a decade—ago.

TRADITIONAL STYLE GUIDELINES AND NEW MEDIA

Just when word processors finally automated the process of footnot-ing, the Modern Language Association (MLA) decided that we should cite sources using parenthetic notes instead. And when *Microsoft Word 2007* included an automatic (sort of) bibliography generator, MLA responded by changing its formats so the generator is useless.[3] Of course, bibliography generators generally aren't very good (they are all GIGO—Garbage In, Garbage Out—after all). Nonetheless, it does seem that whenever a technology emerges that can facilitate the process of documenting sources, MLA changes its rules. Now, MLA has decreed that we have to include the medium of publication, even for books and journal articles (the medium for these, by the way, is "print"). For journal articles accessed through library databases, it is no longer necessary to include the library information (which was silly anyway—if you know the name of the database, you can access it from any library that subscribes to it, but you *can't* access a library's resources if you aren't a patron of that library). Instead, MLA now stipulates that one should designate the medium as "Web" for these resources. Technically, of course, library databases aren't on the web although they are accessed (usually) through a web portal. So, are you confused yet?

To make matters worse, MLA has now decreed that it is no longer necessary to include the Uniform Resource Locator, or URL (the Internet address), for sources that *are* on the web (182). Why? Because many students, teachers, and scholars were trying to type in very long and complex URLs that didn't work anyway, perhaps because they don't understand that many URLs are created dynamically and can't be accessed just by typing them into a browser. In other words, because many people did not seem to be able to figure out how to cite Internet sources, many styles have all but given up. Hey, you can just Google it, right? [4] The American Psychological Association (APA)[5] now contends that, if a scholar has reason to believe that a given source accessed online is the "same" as the printed version, then perhaps citing the print source instead of the version actually consulted might be okay (271). In case you can't tell, I disagree that URLs should be omitted from these entries.

Moreover, if a source happens to be in some format other than "print" or HTML (that is, "Web"), the medium gets, well, even more complicated. MLA now requires that we designate the medium for *all* sources—web, print, *Microsoft Word* document, JPEG, television, radio, DVD, CD, PDF, and so on. In other words, we have to know a lot of things about a given source that most of us don't know—and, quite frankly, usually don't need to know:

> An important feature of electronic files is that they are readily transferable from one medium to another: files may be downloaded from their online homes and saved to disks; CD-ROM titles may be installed on a user's hard drive; and most formats may be printed out. For this reason, identifying the publication medium in the bibliographic reference may be meaningless. It certainly violates the principle of economy in that the protocol or publication information is usually sufficient to locate the source. (Walker and Taylor 57)

Our computers usually know how to handle files—regardless of publication media—from the file extension (the letters after the "dot" in a file name) regardless of whether a given file is online, downloaded to a hard drive or diskette, included on a CD-ROM, or whatever. I do not need to tell my computer what program to use to open a file as long as

I have the software to open it. Of course, if my computer doesn't have the software installed, then, yes, I may need to do some research to find out the type of file and what software to use to open it—but even this process is often automated (try opening a file that your computer doesn't recognize; most operating systems and browsers will offer to search the web for the application for you, for good or ill).

Oh, yeah, and now MLA has (finally) decided to allow students and scholars to use italics instead of underlining. Actually, that isn't quite accurate: MLA always allowed this use, but few people seemed aware that MLA stipulated that underlining indicated text that should be italicized (Gibaldi 94). Now, finally, it's clear that it is okay to use italics to indicate text that should be italicized (MLA 78) and there should be only one space after a period, not two (77).

If you're beginning to think that citation styles are just too complicated, you may be right. However, they don't have to be. There really is a logic to citing sources, whether they are online, in print, or in some other medium, now extant or yet to be developed.

The Logic of Citation

In *The Columbia Guide to Online Style, citation* is defined as "the practice of systematically indicating the origins and thoughts, ideas, knowledge, or words that one uses to author a report, essay, article, speech, book, website, or other work" (Walker and Taylor 29). *The Columbia Guide,* thus, takes a rhetorical approach, including an entire section on the logic of citation, based on the following five principles: access, intellectual property, economy, standardization, and transparency (Walker and Taylor 31).

The *principle of access* is satisfied by providing sufficient information to allow interested readers to locate the sources of information upon which a writer has relied. That information includes the elements of citation discussed in the next section, including author, title, and publication information. The *principle of intellectual property* ensures that proper credit is given for the work of others (hence, avoiding plagiarism), as well as ensuring that a writer's reliance on another's work is not so extensive that it is detrimental to that others' property rights. (For more information on intellectual property in the classroom see http://personal.georgiasouthern.edu/~jwalker/ip/ipdummie. html). The *principle of economy* simply means that citations should provide all of the necessary information in as economical a form as possible, that is, by using a readily recognizable format or code rather than having to stipulate every aspect of a citation. Imagine how obnoxious it would be to read the following:

> The quotation I included in the first paragraph following the sub-heading on page 9 of this essay, wherein I defined "citation" as "the practice of systematically indicating the origins and thoughts, ideas, knowledge, or words that one uses to author a report, essay, article, speech, book, Web site, or other work" is from page 29 of the 2nd edition of *The Columbia Guide to Online Style,* a book written by Janice R. Walker and Todd Taylor, and published in the year 2006 by Columbia University Press, which is located in New York City.

Compare this to the brief parenthetic note inserted in the text which merely lists the authors' last names and the page number (i.e., Walker and Taylor 29). The *principle of standardization* ensures that those readers and scholars within any given discipline will recognize this note as providing important information. In this case, the readers will know to look in the alphabetical list of Works Cited, usually at the end of the essay, under "W" to locate the source authored by Walker and Taylor. Then, if the reader is so inclined, he or she may choose to locate the book in a library or bookstore, and turn to page 29 to check the quotation or to obtain more information. The parenthetic note also helps fulfill the *principle of transparency,* ensuring that the citation is as unobtrusive as possible so as not to interfere with the writer's presentation of his or her own ideas while still providing all of the necessary information.

Like most styles, MLA style is designed to fulfill the needs of a specific discipline. It is thus often difficult to force one style to fit the needs of work in other disciplines. That is, following MLA style to cite work in the hard sciences may be just as awkward as attempting to cite work in languages and literature following IEEE style, which is designed for the needs of those working in electrical and electronic engineering fields. Different disciplines may use slightly different arrangements of the elements of citation in order to facilitate communication of important information. For instance, disciplines in the humanities (MLA and Chicago styles, for instance) often focus on the author; scientific disciplines (for example, APA or the Council of Science Editors) follow what is known as an author-date format. Thus, elements need to be arranged in such a way as to be readily understood and recognized by members of the discipline for or in which one is writing. While most high school and first year college composition classes require students to adhere to MLA format, students will usually find that other styles are required in courses in their majors. And, of course, electronic or electronically accessed sources have further complicated the situation.

Luckily, by using an element approach and understanding the elements of a citation, it is possible to then fit the elements into the various codes that you may be tasked with following. The standard elements of most citations are those elements that will aid a reasonably knowledgeable person to locate the source and help in determining its credibility for a particular context (in our case, a scholarly one). Thus, regardless of which style you choose or are directed to follow—and regardless of how many iterations or changes the styles undergo—noting these elements will ensure that you will be able to adequately cite your work.

- *Author information.* Usually, this is the person or persons primarily responsible for a given work, but this could also include performers, producers, or directors (for plays or films); artists or composers (for works of art or music); editors (for edited collections); and/or corporate, group, or organizational authors (for work-for-hire, government agencies, or unsigned news articles, for example). Don't be too quick to assume that an unsigned article or web page has no author. While this will occasionally be true (in which case, your bibliographic entry will begin with the title of the article rather than an author's name), more often the piece is considered "authored" by the group or organization that sponsored it.
- *Title information.* Generally, an article title is enclosed in quotation marks, and preceded by the name(s) of the author(s); if the article is included in a larger work (for instance, a newspaper or magazine or an edited anthology), you will also need to note the title of the larger work (in italics), and include the name(s) of the editor(s) of the collection, if applicable. Title information for online sources is often confusing, especially for personal web pages or sites. A blog entry may have a title

(if so, enclose it in quotation marks) that is different from the title of the blog itself (formatted in italics). A web page may have a title at the top of the page—and a different title in the title bar (the bar, usually blue, at the very top of your browser or application that provides information about the file you are accessing). Sometimes, an online file will not have a title in any traditional sense, in which case you may choose to include the file name (for instance, kitten.jpg for a graphic file) in place of a title. Title information can be very confusing; remember that the purpose is to help a reasonable person locate the same information you are citing by providing the most explicit information possible.

- *Edition and/or version information.* Include information noting 2nd or subsequent editions or revisions of a book or application, since the information they contain may have changed substantially from previous editions. For web pages and sites, the only information you may be able to locate is a "Last modified" date. Again, remember your purpose: to aid your reader in locating the *same* information you have relied on in your work, if possible.

- *Publication information.* This includes the name of the publisher, place of publication, and date of publication (for most books), or title of journal or other periodical, including volume and issue numbers (if applicable), or online publication information, such as a URL (regardless of what MLA says). You may need to omit the URL from your list of Works Cited or References if your teacher requires strict adherence to MLA or APA guidelines, but having the information will still help if you need to verify information—and many teachers will prefer you include it, regardless of the style you are following.

- *Access information.* For information contained in online databases, in addition to noting the name of the database, note any file numbers, search terms, or other information that will help your reader locate the source. For library databases, these may include DOI (Digital Object Identifier), ISSN (International Standard Serial Number), or AN (Accession Number); reference librarians are especially knowledgeable about how to use this information to locate sources. In the case of information published online that might change frequently and/or without notice, such as personal web pages, blogs, or other such sites, include the date you last accessed the source as well as the date of publication or last revision, if available. Some online sites may provide a URL that offers direct access to a file (a single web page or YouTube video for instance). If the URL is especially long and difficult, however, you may be able to include a URL to the main page (say, to the YouTube home page, for instance) so long as you have provided sufficient information (author, title, date, search terms, or whatever) to allow your reader to locate the specific file or source from that main page.

While some instructors frown on the use of bibliography generators, they may be useful in helping you keep track of information. The real challenge in using them, of course, is the same as the challenge for students using *The MLA Handbook* (or any other style manual, for that matter): you must first determine the type of source you are citing in order to determine the necessary elements to cite it. That is, citing a book is different from citing a web page, which is different from citing a YouTube video, which is different from citing a journal article accessed through an online database . . .

Keeping track of information can be difficult. And it can be difficult to locate the elements you need to keep track of in the first place. However, doing so ensures that you can adequately give credit where it is due, and can save you hours of time if you need to re-locate important information yourself—and, of course, adequately citing your work can help make your own work more credible and persuasive. Luckily, once you understand how the various elements of a citation work, you are well on your way.

In the Works Cited list that follows, I have chosen to follow the formats included in the 6th edition of the *MLA Handbook for Writers of Research Papers* rather than include the (silly) information about the medium of publication that the new edition requires, and I have followed the 2nd edition of *The Columbia Guide to Online Style* for electronic or electronically accessed sources (that is, if the editors of this collection let me get away with doing so!). You may have to follow the requirements of teachers, editors, or others in positions to make these choices for you. Hopefully, this essay has given you some insight into how these choices are made—and how you can work with them if need be! By the way, if you're wondering how I finally chose to cite my opening quotation, do what scholars do: check the list of Works Cited! [6,7]

NOTES

1. Lise Buranen presented information that questions this "lore" (as Stephen North, in *The Making of Composition*, terms such knowledge claims) in "But I *Wasn't* Cheating: Plagiarism and Cross-Cultural Mythology" (*Perspectives on Plagiarism and Intellectual Property in a Postmodern World*, ed. Lise Buranen and Alice M. Roy, Albany: SUNY, 1999, pp. 63–74). In her study of Eastern versus Western views of what constitutes plagiarism, responses to questionnaires showed "no basic difference between what they had been taught in their home country and in this country" (68). However, in a personal interview, at least one of her colleagues believed that it might be true that "since the 'acknowledgment' of the source is in the very use of it, listing them [sic] in a bibliography is at best redundant and at worst an insult to a reader's intelligence" (69). Nonetheless, the respondent also argued that "One still credits one's sources, but what is different is the form in which that 'credit' is given, whether explicit or implied" (69). It was noted, however, that Chinese culture does seem to be moving to a more explicit, e.g., Western, style of citation (69).

2. I conducted a quick Google search for Dr. Labvin and the Tuguska Spatial Phenomenon Foundation and was unable to discover any information about either beyond references to the *Sun* article. Obviously, in order to rely on the claims made in this article, a scholar would need to conduct further research to determine how credible a source he is.

3. I do not mean to imply a cause-and-effect relationship here. There is no conspiracy. More likely, MLA and the developers of new word processing technologies were working independently of each other to solve the same problems and perhaps ended up working at cross purposes.

4. The *MLA Handbook* argues that "Readers are now more likely to find resources on the Web by searching for titles and authors' names than by typing URLs" (182).

5. As I write this, the American Psychological Association has released its new 6th edition. Based on, admittedly, a very quick perusal, it appears that, now that MLA no longer requires inclusion of URLs, APA does, along with strongly recommending inclusion of the DOI (a more stable identifying feature than the URL).

6. In this case, I chose to cite the source I actually used, *Bartleby.com*, rather than the source Bartleby cites. I also chose to include the direct URL since it's short and will take the reader directly to the information I used. I could also have chosen to cite the URL for Bartleby's home page, where users can search for the information, perhaps including the search term(s) or

path(s) in my citation. In other words, there is no one right answer for how to cite many of the sources that scholars may reference. The key, of course, is to provide sufficient information for a reasonable and informed reader to re-locate the same source of information. (NOTE AGAIN—even this may not always be possible. Sometimes sites move or disappear, and even books sometimes go out of print. Online there's the "wayback" machine, Google sometimes offers cached copies or online sites, and Amazon.com can often help readers locate even difficult-to-find and out-of-print books.) Are we having fun yet?

7. Thanks to the editors of this collection, Pavel Zemliansky and Charles Lowe, as well as to Jim Kalmbach and Douglas Eyman whose thoughtful and insightful critiques were so helpful in revising and completing this work.

WORKS CITED

ACT Fluoride Rinse. http://www.actfluoride.com/numberone.html (4 July 2009).

APA. *Publication Manual of the American Psychological Association* 5th ed. Washington, DC: APA, 2001.

APME (Associated Press Managing Editors). "AP Statement on Anonymous Sources." 2009. http://www.apme.com/committees/credibility/052705anonymous.shtml (4 July 2009).

Gibaldi, Joseph. *MLA Handbook for Writers of Research Papers* 6th ed. New York: MLA, 2003.

Heraclitus. *Herakleitos and Diogenes.* Trans. Guy Davenport. *Bartleby.com.* http://www.bartleby.com/66/9/27909.html (24 Mar. 2009).

Modern Language Association. *MLA Handbook for Writers of Research Papers* 7th ed. New York: MLA, 2009.

Turner Classic Movies (TCM). Movie Trailer. *The Mouse that Roared.* 1959. http://www.tcm.com/mediaroom/index/?cid=143554 (16 July 2009).

Walker, Janice R., and Todd Taylor. *The Columbia Guide to Online Style.* 2nd ed. New York: Columbia UP, 2006.

Watson, Leon. "UFO 'Sacrificed Itself for Us.'" *The Sun* 4 July 2009. http://www.thesun.co.uk/sol/homepage/news/ufos/2451627/UFO-sacrificed-itself-for-us.html (4 July 2009).

Wouters, Paul. *The Citation Culture.* Doctoral Thesis, U of Amsterdam, 1999. http://www.garfield.library.upenn.edu/wouters/wouters.pdf (7 June 2009).

Storytelling, Narration, and the "Who I Am" Story

Catherine Ramsdell

Green Eggs and Ham was the story of my life. I wouldn't eat a thing when I was a kid, but Dr. Seuss inspired me to try cauliflower!

—*Jim Carrey*

It's all storytelling, you know. That's what journalism is all about.

—*Tom Brokaw*

People have forgotten how to tell a story. Stories don't have a middle or an end any more. They usually have a beginning that never stops beginning.

—*Steven Spielberg*

INTRODUCTION

Are stories just a form of entertainment—like movies, television shows, books, and video games?* Or are they something more? This chapter takes the stance that stories are a fundamental and primary form of communication, and without them, we would lose an important way to teach our children, to train our employees, to sell our products, and to make information memorable to those of any age.

Consider a Jewish story Annette Simmons references in her book *The Story Factor: Inspiration, Influence, and Persuasion Through the Art of Storytelling:*

> Truth, naked and cold, had been turned away from every door in the village. Her nakedness frightened the people. When Parable found her she was huddled in a corner, shivering and hungry. Taking pity on her, Parable gathered her up and took her home. There, she dressed Truth in story, warmed her and sent her out again. Clothed in story, Truth knocked again at the doors and was readily welcomed into the villagers' houses. They invited her to eat at their tables and warm herself by their fires. (27)

Certainly stories can be a form of entertainment—a book to curl up with on a cold rainy afternoon, a movie to share with a best friend, a video game to conquer—but stories can also be much more and, as will be discussed at the end of the chapter, today stories can be found just about anywhere. Furthermore, because stories can be found anywhere from a movie theatre to a corporate boardroom, everyone should know how to tell a good story.

In her book, *The Story Factor: Inspiration, Influence, and Persuasion Through the Art of Storytelling,* Simmons talks about seven different kinds of stories everyone should learn how to tell. One of them is the "Who I Am" story. Simply put, a Who I Am story shows something about its author, and this type of story fits into the genre of memoir or creative nonfiction. Here is an example from Simmons' book:

> Skip looked into the sea of suspicious stockholders and wondered what might convince them to follow his leadership. He was 35, looked 13 and was third generation rich. He could tell they assumed he would be an unholy disaster as a leader. He decided to tell them a story. "My first job was drawing the electrical engineering plans for a boat building company. The drawings had to be perfect because if the wires were not accurately placed *before* the fiberglass form was poured, a mistake might cost a million dollars, easy. At 25, I already had two masters' degrees. I had been on boats all my life and frankly, I found drawing these plans a bit . . . mindless. One morning I got a call *at home* from a $6/hour worker asking me 'are you sure this is right?' I was incensed. Of course I was *sure*—'just

pour the damn thing.' When his supervisor called me an hour later and woke me up *again* and asked 'are you sure this is right?' I had even less patience. 'I said I was sure an hour ago and I'm still sure.'

It was the phone call from the president of the company that finally got me out of bed and down to the site. If I had to hold these guys by the hand, so be it. I sought out the worker who had called me first. He sat looking at my plans with his head cocked to one side. With exaggerated patience I began to explain the drawing. But after a few words my voice got weaker and *my* head started to cock to the side as well. It seems that I had (being left-handed) transposed starboard and port so that the drawing was an exact mirror image of what it should have been. *Thank God* this $6/hour worker had caught my mistake before it was too late. The next day I found this box on my desk. The crew bought me a remedial pair of tennis shoes for future reference. Just in case I got mixed up again— a red left shoe for port, and a green right one for starboard. These shoes don't just help me remember port and starboard. They help me remember to listen even when I think I know what's going on." As he held up the shoebox with one red and one green shoe, there were smiles and smirks. The stockholders relaxed a bit. If this young upstart had already learned this lesson about arrogance, then he might have learned a few things about running companies, too. (1–2)

This example shows some of the reasons why people tell Who I Am stories. Chances are that if Skip had gone into this meeting and said "Look, I know I'm young, but I've got a lot of experience, I know what I'm doing, I've learned a lot from my mistakes. Just trust me," he would not have won over his audience.

Please keep this example and the basic definition of the Who I Am story in mind while reading through the next section, which provides a little background and theory about the fine art of narration and storytelling.

NARRATIVE THEORY

Roland Barthes was arguably one of the most important literary theorists of the twentieth century. To begin, we'll look at his thoughts on narrative:

The narratives of the world are numberless. Narrative is first and foremost a prodigious variety of genres, themselves distributed amongst different substances—as though any material were fit to receive man's stories. Able to be carried by articulated language, spoken or written, fixed or moving images, gestures, and the ordered mixture of all these substances; narrative is present in myth, legend, fable, tale, novella, epic, history, tragedy, drama, comedy, mime, painting (think Carpaccio's *Saint Ursula*), stained-glass windows, cinema, comics, news items, conversation. Moreover, under this almost infinite discovery of forms, narrative is present in every age, in every place, in every society; it begins with the very history of mankind and there nowhere is nor has been a people without narrative. All classes, all human groups, have their narratives, enjoyment of which is very often shared by men with different even opposing, cultural backgrounds. Caring nothing for the division between good and bad literature, narrative is international, transhistorical, transcultural: it is simply there, like life itself. (qtd. in Abbott 1–2)

In the forty-five years since Barthes penned this passage, nearly every book on storytelling or narrative theory has referenced this quote. Even if this quote is not referenced directly, often authors simply make a similar statement in their own words. For example, twenty-one years after Barthes voiced his thoughts on narrative, Luc Herman and Bart Vervaeck, authors of *The Handbook of Narrative Analysis*, stated:

No single period or society can do without narratives. And, a good number of contemporary thinkers hasten to add, whatever you say and think about a certain time or place becomes a narrative in its own right. From the oldest myths and legends to postmodern fabulation, narration has always been central. Postmodern philosophers . . . also contend that everything amounts to a narrative, including the world and the self. If that is correct, then the study of narrative . . . unveils fundamental culture-specific opinions about reality and humankind, which are narrativized in stories and novels. (1)

Whether authors quote Barthes directly or voice the same sentiment in their own words, one of the few things almost all authors, scholars, and critics can agree on is that narrative is part of humankind, it always has been, and it always will be.

Of course, what Barthes and Herman call narration, many, myself included, call story. H. Porter Abbott notes in *The Cambridge Introduction to Narrative*, "Many speakers of English grow up using story to mean what we [Abbott and Barthes among others] are referring to here as a narrative" (16). Technically, however, there are some differences between the words "story" and "narrative." In his book *The Classical Plot and Invention of Western Narrative*, N. J. Lowe talks about these differences using the terms *fabula* and *sjuzhet*:

> This distinction is a cornerstone of modern narrative theory, even though there has been huge disagreement over the precise definition of the two terms and the boundary between them, and scarcely less over how to present them in English. *Fabula* (in English, usually 'story') is the series of events the work recounts, but imagined stripped of all the artifices of storytelling: a series of actual events in their natural order, in what merely happens to be a fictional world. In contrast, *sjuzhet* is the account of those same events that we actually get, reordered and reshaped in the process of telling to reach and affect the audience or reader in a particular and deliberate way. (5)

As Lowe mentions, scholars and writers have disagreed over the exact meaning of words like story and narrative. Abbot, for example, talks about "three distinctions: narrative is the representation of events consisting of story and narrative discourse; story is the event or sequence of events (the action), and narrative discourse is those events as represented" (16). In this chapter, we'll use these definitions: a story (or *fabula*) encompasses the events or action in the story, and narrative discourse (or *sjuzhet*) is the way these events or actions are related. For example, all stylistic choices or organizational strategies, such as flashback, are part of the narrative discourse. Narrative discourse can encompass numerous things, but story almost always includes two primary parts: events and characters. After all, what story does not have these two characteristics? A story by its very nature includes events, and as Abbott contends, "what are events but the actions or reactions of [characters]?" (17).

Characters and events (or actions) may seem inextricably linked, but which is more important has been debated since Aristotle's time. Aristotle took the stance that action was most important. In *Poetics*, he states: "Now character determines men's qualities, but it is by their actions that they are happy or reverse. Dramatic action, therefore, is not with a view to the representation of Character: character comes in as a subsidiary to the actions" (62–63). Still, character was important to Aristotle; he believed it was the second most important element in a drama and that character brought morality to a text (64). In the twentieth century, however, many authors started to think character was more important. For example, as author Andrew Horton notes, "Flannery O'Conner says 'it is the character's personality that creates the action of the story' and not the other way around." Horton goes on to state that usually the characters connect an audience emotionally to a story (2).

Because the purpose of a Who I Am story is to illustrate something about oneself, some might assume that character is the most important aspect of the Who I Am story, but in truth, as novelist Henry James asserts, both character and action are important in this type of story. James believes: "What is character but the determination of incident? What is incident but the illustration of character? . . . It is an incident for a woman to stand up with her hand resting on the table and look out at you in a certain way; or if it be not an incident I think it will be hard to say what it is. At the same time it is the expression of character" (qtd. in Abbott 124).

Granted, thinking of the people in a Who I Am story as characters may seem odd because most likely they will be real people. However, consider Theodore A. Rees Cheney's thoughts:

> Traditional nonfiction, particularly journalistic nonfiction, never concerned itself with developing characters. Fiction writers worked at characterization; nonfiction writers concentrated on events. Creative nonfiction writers say that because so many events occur as the result of human interactions, the event cannot be fully understood without also understanding something of the people (characters) surrounding it. (134)

So while thinking of yourself, friends, or family as characters may not feel completely natural, remember some similarities do exist between characters and real people in that the people/characters in a Who I Am story need to be developed, interesting, and understandable, just like characters in a fiction work. Of course, some differences exist as well. Since the characters in a Who I Am story are real people, you will not be creating characters, as a fiction writer does; instead, as Cheney notes, you will be revealing them:

> When I write about character development, I'm talking about how the writer goes about revealing a person's character . . . The creative nonfiction writer does not 'create' characters; rather, he or she reveals them to the reader as honestly and accurately as possible. Like most contemporary fiction writers, creative nonfiction writers reveal character much as it happens in real life—bit by bit. (134)

Generally speaking, authors reveal their characters in two ways: direct and indirect characterization. With direct characterization, the author simply tells the audience something about a character. The line "He was 35, looked 13 and was third generation rich" from the Who I Am story at the beginning of this chapter is an example of direct characterization. With indirect characterization, the audience learns about characters by watching or listening to them. Indirect characterization can also include descriptions of characters. The Who I Am story at the start of this chapter primarily utilizes indirect characterization. The entire story Skip tells about his first job, the mindless drawing, being upset about an hourly worker calling him at home—all indirect characterization. Since indirect characterization shows what a character does, indirect characterization often directly relates to the sequence of actions, again showing how character and action can intertwine.

Another important piece of a story and narrative discourse is the difference between real time and narrative time. Consider the following passage:

> Amy dropped a mug of coffee. It shattered on the kitchen floor. Coffee and shattered glass were everywhere. Amy got a towel and began cleaning up the mess.

This is real time, but if a few details are added, we get narrative time:

> Amy dropped a mug of coffee. It shattered with a loud crash onto the kitchen floor. She felt the hot liquid burn through her socks into her feet. Coffee and shattered glass were everywhere. Amy sighed; there was no more coffee in the pot, and she had really needed a caffeine burst. Moving carefully through the mess, Amy grabbed an old towel out of the drawer and began cleaning up the remains of her breakfast.

Abbott explains the difference between real (or clock) time and narrative time:

> Clock time . . . always relates back to itself, so that one speaks in terms of numbers or seconds or their multiples (minutes, hours) and fractions (nanoseconds). Narrative time, in contrast, relates to events or incidents. And while clock time is necessarily marked off by regular intervals of a certain length, narrative time is not necessarily any length at all. (4–5)

Abbott adds that writers can slow the "whole sequence down by simply adding details" and "conversely, we can make narrative time go like the wind" by using phrases like "in the following months" or "a few weeks later" (5).

The universality of narrative, *fabula* and *sjuzhet,* character and action, indirect and direct representation, real time and narrative time are just a few aspects of narrative theory, but these terms and this information will provide a solid foundation as we begin thinking more specifically about the Who I Am story.

STARTING THE "WHO I AM" STORY

Your Who I Am story should start to answer the question "who are you?" However, this story should only focus on one characteristic or aspect of your personality. Think back to Skip and the Who I Am story from the beginning of this chapter. His story helped prove he was ready to be a leader and ready to run a corporation.

As with most other types of writing, brainstorming can be a useful tool. To begin, you might just think about all the ways to finish the sentence "I am . . ." The word you choose to finish this sentence then becomes the subject of your Who I Am story. If a subject is not jumping out at you, think about the way your mother, best friend, significant other, or pet might describe you. Think about a characteristic that only the people closest to you see—for example, has anyone ever told you "when I first met you, I never would have guessed that you were so funny (or competitive or happy)"?

Once you have a characteristic in mind, keep brainstorming and think of one specific example or event that illustrates this characteristic. This example will become your story. Again, much like a topic, sometimes an example, or story, will just jump to mind. However, if you cannot think of an example right away, look through some old pictures, scrapbooks, or yearbooks. Reread journals or listen to favorite songs. All of these things can spark memories, and one of these memories can become the example or event on which your Who I Am story will focus. This event does not have to be exciting or flamboyant. Simple but heartfelt stories often are the most effective. Many things can be faked in life, but sincerity is generally not one of them.

Writing the "Who I Am" Story

Once you have the topic, just start writing. Writing a story is not like baking a cake—there is no formula or recipe that guarantees a perfect story. But here are some steps to consider:

1. Ask some questions about the event you are going to write about. When did this event take place? What are the starting and ending points? Where did this event take place? Who was there? Was there a conflict? A resolution?

2. Write down everything you remember. Of course, there are numerous ways to write a first draft, but for a Who I Am story, simply writing down everything you remember about the event is a good place to start. Usually, it is better to have more writing than what you need. So start by writing everything down in chronological order. Do not worry about any rhetorical strategies or making it sound good. Think about the concept of *fabula* and just write down the entire series of events or actions.

3. Go do something else. Once you have the entire story written down, set it aside. Go take a nap or play with your dog, and come back to the story later. Then reread it and see if you left anything out. Time permitting, go through this process of putting the story aside and then rereading it several times.

4. Summarize the main point of the story in one or two sentences. Go through the story and eliminate everything that does not relate to this main point. Do not worry about length right now. Focus on quality and creating a unified story.

5. Think about creating a dominant impression. Is the story sad, thoughtful, sarcastic, or humorous? If you have trouble deciding on a dominant impression, think about setting the story to music. What song would you pick—Mozart's "Moonlight Sonata," something by the Violent Femmes, a sultry jazz tune—and what emotion does this song conjure up?

6. Keeping the main point and dominant impression in mind, add details and expand the most important parts of your story. Real time should now become narrative time. Add concrete details and imagery. Imagine the different senses to which the story could appeal. We are a very visual culture, but go beyond describing what things look like—consider incorporating smells or sounds. Think about the way something feels when touched. Also think about how these details can help draw a reader in. Consider this an example from a student's Who I Am story:

> At the beginning of every school year, I am obligated to introduce myself to a new sea of adolescent hormones swimming with impulsiveness, curiosity, and unfiltered tourette-like verbal ejaculations. Sure, I could stand before the little urchins, and with trident in hand, I could dictate the rules of my class and cast off a long list of life experiences that made me the immortal that stands before them or I could let them place their expectations upon me creating an environment of perceived equality. Being a believer in a democratic classroom, I always opt for the latter.

Look at the way this student builds on the details: the words "sea," "swimming" and "trident" work beautifully together. And look at the choices the student made: using the words "adolescent hormones" and "urchins" instead of students; "unfiltered tourette-like verbal ejaculations" could have simply been opinions or obnoxious comments. The story includes a lot of visual elements, but the phrase "verbal ejaculations" also appeals to the ears. These words, phrases, and ideas all work together to, as clichéd as it sounds, paint a picture of the author of this story.

The author of this story is a student, but she is also a middle-school teacher. The main point of the story is to show who she is as a teacher. Everything in this paragraph relates to that main point. We do not know the color of her hair, whether she is wearing a shirt or a sweater, or if she is tall or short. After all, none of these things relate to the point of this story. Great detail and description and emotions are very important to the Who I Am story. But they need to be the right details, descriptions, and emotions, and they need to be used at the right time.

8. Make certain the story shows and does not tell. The ultimate success of the Who I Am story depends on how well you show, not tell, who you are (i.e. use more indirect characterization than direct characterization). Have faith in your words and in the story you are telling. Trust that the story works and do not end the story with a statement like "clearly this event shows that I am a trustworthy person." Let the story do its job. Consider two more paragraphs from our middle-school teacher's story:

> On the first day of class last year, I allowed students to take seats at their leisure. I sat on my desk and when everyone was settled, I quietly commanded their attention by placing a large black top hat upon my head. Conversations abruptly stopped as my curious audience took notice. 'If I were to say that hats are a metaphor for the different roles we play in our lives, what do you think that means?' I was met with blank stares. 'What if I said that I play many roles every day? I am a teacher, a mother, a daughter, a coworker, and a friend. Are the expectations for those different roles the same or different?' A hand raises and a girl with pale skin, lively eyes and thick auburn hair answers, 'Of course they're different. I don't act the same around my friends as I do in front of my parents!' She has a smug 'as if' expression.
>
> 'You're absolutely right,' I acknowledge. 'Now what if I were to ask you to define the expectations of my role as your teacher?' Eyebrows rise as the class considers this. 'I'm going to pass out sticky notes and I want each of you to write down a word or phrase that describes what my job is as your teacher. When you are done, I want you to place your note on the strip of blue paper that runs up the wall in the back of the room. Each of you should place your note above the note of the person that went before you so that we create a column of sticky notes. Does everyone understand?' A thin-faced, black boy with large eyes and bright teeth pipes up, "So we get to tell you how to do your job?' I thoughtfully pause before answering, 'Well . . . yah!'

What do we learn about the author from reading this passage? What kind of teacher is she? We could describe her as creative, brave, caring, and dedicated. We could decide that she is not afraid to take some risks. We know that she loves her job. Does she directly state any of these things? No. But her story shows that she is all of these things.

9. Look at the introduction of your story. Will it grab a reader's attention? Think about sitting in a doctor's office or waiting for your car to be repaired. You pick up a magazine and start to thumb through it. How long do you give an article to grab your attention before turning the page? Some people flip to the next page if the title of the article does not interest them; other more generous readers will read the first sentence or two before deciding to continue reading or to move on to the next page. Something in the opening paragraph, hopefully in the first sentence or two, should grab the reader and make him or her want to read on. Here is an example from another student's Who I Am story:

> I thought by the time I was thirty I would know what I wanted to be when I grew up. But here I am on the eve of my thirty-first birthday, and I am still searching, searching for where I fit into the world, amidst all the titles I have been given such as Sydney's Mom, Tripp's Wife, and Janice's Daughter. Then there are all the roles I play: maid, chef, bookkeeper, personal shopper, and teacher. Of course that's just what I do and who I do it for. The real question remains, when you take all of that away, who am I?

This is the first paragraph of the student's Who I Am essay, and it does several things nicely. The conversational tone draws us in. We almost feel as if we are getting to peek inside the author's head. "Tripp's Wife," "Janice's Daughter," "chef," "personal shopper" are lovely specifics, and equally important, these are specifics to which most people can relate. Perhaps we are Bob's son or Suzie's boyfriend instead of a daughter or a wife, but we can still see the similarities between the author's life and our own. And because of that, we want to know how she answers the question "who am I?"

10. Treat this story like any other paper. Have a solid organizational scheme (chronological often works well), keep one main idea per paragraph, use transitional phrasing, vary the sentence structure, and make sure the ideas flow into each other. Reflect on word choice and particularly verb choices. Just think, for example, of all the different synonyms for the word walk. A character could strut, saunter, stroll, sashay, or skip. She could mosey, meander, or march. Powerful verbs are a great way to add panache and detail to a story without making it wordy or slowing the pace.

11. Proofread, edit, and proofread again. Give the story to a friend and ask them to read it. Do not tell them what the paper is about or what you are trying to accomplish. Instead just ask them what they learned or what three words they would use to describe your story.

12. And the last bit of advice—have fun. The best storytellers enjoy telling stories. When you are telling a story, pick a story that matters to you and a story that you really want to share. Let your love for that story come through, and let others see you through your story.

LOOKING FORWARD: STORYTELLING IN THE PROFESSIONAL WORLD

As mentioned in the introduction of this chapter, storytelling is not just for entertainment anymore. It's not just a mindless academic exercise either; storytelling is quickly becoming a cornerstone of the non-profit and corporate worlds. Storytelling can be a part of corporate training, public relations, politics, journalism, and of course, the two industries we are going to focus on: grantwriting and advertising.

Cheryl Clarke's book *Storytelling for Grantseekers: A Creative Guide to Nonprofit Fundraising* has been highly praised by both grantwriters and grant readers. For decades grants have been notoriously boring—both to write and to read. Clarke's book is starting to change all that.

Clarke begins by noting the similarities between grantwriting and storytelling:

> Storytelling is a powerful art form. Stories entertain, educate, and enlighten. They have the ability to transport an audience to another location and teach them about issues and people they may know nothing about. The same is true of grantwriting. (xv)

Clarke continues by breaking down the different parts of the grantwriting process. She relates that often the grantwriting process starts with a letter of intent, a one to two page letter summarizing the request that is sent to the funding organization. If the funding organization thinks your request has merit, they will ask you (or your organization) to submit a full grant proposal. Clarke likens the letter of intent to a short story and the full grant proposal to a novel.

Like short stories and novels, grants should also have heroes, villains (or antagonists) and a conflict. The hero is, of course, the nonprofit agency. As Clarke notes,

> Nonprofit agencies do heroic work, and they are the heroes of every proposal we write. Throughout the world today, nonprofits are working diligently to feed the hungry, shelter the homeless, heal the sick, teach children, conserve the environment, save endangered species, and present music performances and art exhibitions, among other important activities. . . . As grantwriters, we have the opportunity to tell others these amazing stories. (52)

The antagonist is simply the need or problem. Hunger, global warming, abused animals, disease—any one of these could be the villain of the grant proposal. The nonprofit and the need become the characters in the story and supply the conflict and tension. Clarke suggests giving these characters a voice, stating "quotes are especially powerful because through them the proposal reviewer 'hears' directly from your agency's clients in their own words" (81). These quotes become the dialogue in the story. Grant proposals often include other elements traditionally seen in novels, such as setting, back stories, and resolutions.

Clarke clearly shows the advantages of using storytelling techniques in grantwriting, and many believe storytelling is an equally important part of advertising as a close examination of the "1984" Macintosh commercial will indicate. In 1984, Apple was in trouble. As Richard Maxwell and Robert Dickman note in their book *The Elements of Persuasion: Use Storytelling to Pitch Better, Sell Faster and Win More Business:*

> at that time the computer industry was in transition . . . Apple had been a major player when computers were seen as expensive toys for hobbyists or learning platforms for children. But when corporations began seriously going digital, they naturally turned to a name they had come to trust—IBM. IBM PC computers became 'industry standard,' with all the purchasing and advertising muscle that implied. (11)

In response, Apple's CEO Steve Jobs created the Macintosh computer, but he needed an advertisement that would bring attention to this computer. The "1984" commercial did just that. The "1984" commercial (available on YouTube: http://www.youtube.com/watch?v=OYecfV3ubP8) shows a dystopia: a dismal gray world where Big Brother is seen (and heard) on every television screen. Row after row of people stare mindlessly at huge television screens, watching propaganda. A woman in red shorts runs through the crowd and hurls a hammer at the largest screen, destroying it and silencing Big Brother. The commercial closes with the tagline "On January 24, Apple Computer will introduce Macintosh. And you'll see why 1984 won't be like *1984*."

The commercial ran only once nationally (during the 1984 Super Bowl) and is generally credited with two things. The first is saving Apple. As Maxwell and Dickman note, "The result of this ad was explosive. Seven days later there wasn't a Macintosh left unsold on any store shelf in America, and back orders were beginning to stretch out for months" (12). Second, many advertising gurus believe that the "1984" commercial was one of the first advertisements to use a story.

Much like the stories Clarke talks about, the "1984" commercial has a hero: the Macintosh computer, which is personified by the attractive blonde in the short red shorts. The villain is the status quo and corporate America, both of which are supposed to symbolize IBM. The smashing of the television screen ends the conflict and provides resolution. This story also has something else: passion. As Maxwell and Dickman note: "But at its cohesive core, what made this ad white-hot was Steve Job's passionate belief that a computer was meant to be a tool to set people free" (12). And Maxwell and Dickman believe passion is another essential element of story.

This is, of course, only one example; today most commercials tell a story, and we can certainly see why. Maxwell and Dickman explain "A good story plays as well on TV as it does whispered to a guy in the back of a union meeting hall. It's as powerful in the powder room as it is in the boardroom. People love a good story. We can't get enough of them. And a good story is infectious. It spreads like wildfire" (46).

Again, storytelling now appears in many forms of professional and workplace communication; grantwriting and advertising are only two examples. So have fun telling your stories, enjoy them, learn to make them come alive. At the same time, you'll be developing a marketable skill because, appropriately enough, storytelling has become a valuable commodity in corporate America.

DISCUSSION

1. Maxwell and Dickman believe that "a story is a fact, wrapped in an emotion that compels us to take an action that transforms our world." How would you define the term story? What do you think are the most important elements of a good story? What examples help support your thoughts?

2. How could stories and storytelling fit into your major field of study? What types of stories do you think professionals in your field might find useful?

WORKS CITED

"1984 Apple's Macintosh Commercial." Online Posting. YouTube. 2005. Web. 20 December 2010.

Abbott, H. Porter. *The Cambridge Introduction to Narrative*. Cambridge UP: Cambridge, 2002. Print.

Aristotle. *Poetics*. Ed. Francis Fergusson. Hill and Wang: New York, 1997. Print.

Brokaw, Tom. "Tom Brokaw Quotes." *BrainyQuote*. BrainyQuote. 2010. Web. 30 Sept. 2010.

Carrey, Jim. "Jim Carrey Quotes." *BrainyQuote*. BrainyQuote. 2010. Web. 30 Sept. 2010.

Cheney, Theodore A. Rees. *Writing Creative Nonfiction: Fiction Techniques for Crafting Great Nonfiction*. Ten Speed Press: Berkeley, 2001. Print.

Clarke, Cheryl. *Storytelling for Grantseekers*. John Wiley and Songs: San Francisco, 2009. Print.

Horton, Andrew. *Writing the Character-Centered Screen Play*. U of California P: Los Angeles, 1999. Print.

Lowe, N.J. *The Classical Plot and the Invention of Western Narrative*. Cambridge UP: New York, 2000. Print.

Luc, Herman and Bart Vervaeck. *The Handbook of Narrative Analysis*. U of Nebraska P: Lincoln, 2005. Print.

Maxwell, Richard and Robert Dickman. *The Elements of Persuasion: Using Storytelling to Pitch Better, Sell Faster, and Win More Business*. Collins: New York, 2007. Print.

Simmons, Annette. *The Story Factor: Inspiration, Influence, and Persuasion Through the Art of Storytelling*. Basic Books: Cambridge, 2006. Print.

Spielberg, Steven. "Steven Spielberg Quotes." *BrainyQuote*. BrainyQuote. 2010. Web. 30 Sept. 2010.

The Sixth Paragraph: A Re-Vision of the Essay

Paul Lynch

PART THE FIRST

Recently, I taught a class called "Introduction to the Essay."[*] It was not a first year writing class, which most students are required to take, but a sophomore elective. For a long time, nobody signed up for the course. I didn't understand why. I was prepared to teach some great stuff: essays about love, sex, mashed potatoes, turtles, getting lost, getting drunk, getting migraine headaches, noise, things people hate, things people love, and deer antlers. (I'll explain this last one later.) When students finally did sign up, it was at the last minute, when all the other required English classes had already filled. Eventually, after I got to know my students and they got to know me, I felt comfortable enough to ask them why they had been reluctant to take the class. "To be honest," one student said, "it was the title. It just didn't sound that interesting." I asked them what they thought they'd be writing in the course. "School essays," they said. "The kind we've been writing all our lives."

Looking back, I'm surprised that I hadn't seen it coming. When I was a middle school teacher, I decided to cover the bare walls of my classroom with some posters. I went down to the supply closet, and I found one that immediately grabbed my attention: it was called "The Cheeseburger Essay." Maybe I grabbed it because I was hungry. Anyway, the poster pictured a triple-cheeseburger—I must have been really hungry—and each part of the sandwich was stamped with part of an essay. I'll bet that most of my "Intro to the Essay" students could have diagrammed the poster even without seeing it. The top bun was the introduction. The cheese was the thesis. Each of the three patties represented a reason that supported the thesis. And the bottom bun was the conclusion. So let's say I were asking my middle school students to write a "cheeseburger essay" about whether they should get homework every night:

> Students have always gotten a lot of homework. Teachers think it is important because it helps students, but the students do not like it because it is more work. Students should not get homework every night for three reasons. First, they have many extracurricular activities. Second, they should spend time with their families at night. Third, they should rest so they can be ready for school the next day.
>
> Students have many extracurricular activities. They do sports, music lessons, and art classes . . .

I'm sure you could write the rest of this essay in your sleep. (Perhaps you already have.) You know the rules, just like my students did. When I asked them what an essay was, they said the following. First, it has five paragraphs. Why five? I asked. Because you need one for your introduction, one for each of your three reasons, and one for your conclusion. What goes in the introduction? The thesis and the reasons. What else? Don't use the pronoun "I." Why not? Because you're supposed to be making arguments based on the support, and the support should prove the point. If you use "I," then it sounds like *you're* saying these things. Don't include your personal opinion because your opinion doesn't matter. Essays should speak for themselves. Don't use "you" either, they told me. It's too informal. And don't—I mean, *do not*—use contractions.

Whenever I teach college writing classes, I always ask how many students have been taught the five paragraph form. Almost every hand goes up every time. Why does everyone learn it? One, it's easy to remember. Two, it's easy to perform. If you're writing an SAT or AP exam, the five paragraph essay gives you a blueprint that you can re-produce quickly. To be honest, it's also easy to grade. A teacher can recognize the parts very quickly. Is there an intro? Check. A thesis? Check. Reason #1? Check, and so on. For a high school teacher with 125 students, being able to read and grade quickly is crucial. So there are some good reasons to teach the five paragraph essay. Many of your college writing classes, by the way, will be capped at twenty students; the idea is to make grading papers a little easier and giving feedback a little more worthwhile. Unfortunately, you might also have an adjunct professor who's teaching four or five sections, which means they might have as many students as your high school teachers. They may be in-clined to ask for these kinds of formal structures if only so they can keep their heads above water.

In any case, you may have noticed that I've just listed exactly three reasons why the five paragraph essay gets taught: "Students have al-ways been taught the five paragraph essay. Teachers teach it for three reasons. First, it is easy to remember. Second, it's easy to perform. Third, it's easy to grade. . . ." Once again, you can probably see how this very essay on the essay going to shape up. And the bad habit of slipping into the five paragraph structure also reminds me of my bad conscience. I hung that cheeseburger poster in my classroom and taught my students to follow its advice so that they would do well on our state-mandated standardized tests. ("Who is your hero? Give three reasons why.") Such advice isn't terrible, and I don't mean to pick on middle and secondary school teachers, not only because I was a middle and secondary school teacher, but also because the vast majority of my college students have been very well prepared by the time they get to my class. (Notice that I just offered *two* reasons for my opinion, and I used an "I." I even used the passive voice. *What will he do next?!?*) Third of all—damn . . . I *still* cannot get out of the habit of offering three reasons—the good old five paragrapher does feature the basics. Academic writing should make an argument; arguments should have reasons; reasons should be based on evidence. But as you can see, the form tends to straitjacket writing: it fits everyone, but once you're in it, you can't really move.

English teachers often complain that people think of us as the grammar police. (Introduce yourself as an English teacher, and you're sure to hear something like, "Oops, I better watch my grammar.") This gets old, but I suppose we have no one but ourselves to blame.

We spend a lot of our time marking grammatical errors and writing things like *AWK* (as in awkward), *CLARIFY, SPECIFY,* etc. Again, I feel guilty about this—I've written these kinds of comments more times than I can remember. But they're not very helpful, are they? I might as well scribble *Write better!* in the margins. Kind of like yelling *Kick it!* at a soccer game. A student might ask, "If I knew how to *CLARIFY, SPECIFY,* and avoid *AWK-ing,* then don't you think I would have done it already?" It seems as if we want student writing to be like clean glass: we should see right through it to what you're telling us. The writing should be as clear as crystal, easily understood, with no effort on the reader's part required. The writing should also be brief and concise. No unnecessary words. Sentences should be like assembly lines, with not a move wasted. No hemming or hawing. Our previous five paragraph example exemplifies this plain style: "Students have always gotten a lot of homework. Teachers think it is important because it gives students practice, but students do not like it because it is more work. . . ." Sure, it's clear, brief, and sincere, but it's also really dreary and boring. Would you write or talk like this in any other part of your life? Imagine a five paragraph love letter. It would start like this:

> Since the dawn of time, men have written love-notes to women. I find you attractive and would like to accompany you to the local Cineplex for three reasons. First, we share many of the same interests and hobbies. Second, we like the same kinds of movies. Third, your beauty causes me to perspire excessively.

This is clear and brief, and it's even got three reasons, but it's probably not going to win anyone's heart.

(By the way, that was the sixth paragraph of the present essay. I'm just saying.)

What if you wrote an introduction like this?

> Others form Man; I give an account of Man and sketch a picture of a particular one of them who is very badly formed and whom I would truly make very different from what he is if I had to fashion him afresh. But it is done now. The brush-strokes of my portrait do not go awry even though they change and vary. The world is but a perennial see-saw. Everything in it—the land, the mountains of the Caucasus, the pyramids of Egypt—all waver with a common motion

and their own. Constancy itself is nothing but a more lan-
guid rocking to and fro. I am unable to stabilize my subject: it
staggers confusedly along with a natural drunkenness. I grasp
it as it is now, at this moment when I am lingering over it. I
am not portraying being but becoming: not the passage from
one age to another (or, as the folk put it, from one seven-year
period to the next) but from day to day, from minute to minute. (Montaigne 907–08)

This introduction goes on for a while longer, but let's pause there for a
moment. It's easy enough to say already what's wrong. Lots of "I." In
fact, a lot of focus on the author himself. Thus, these sorts of pieces are
often called "personal essays." But even though this is a personal essay,
one focusing on the author, the author is still not sure exactly what he's
writing about. He is "unable to stabilize his subject." He is painting
his very own portrait, but he's not even sure how to do that: his brush-
strokes "change and vary," and his picture "staggers confusedly . . .
with a natural drunkenness." This is hardly an efficient way to write.
Indeed, the author is promising to wander haphazardly, even drunk-
enly. Not only is the author writing entirely about himself, he is also
suggesting that his self changes constantly. He doesn't worry about
contradicting himself, another no-no for the school essay. There is no
thesis statement of any kind. How could he offer a thesis if his subject
is himself and he's not even sure what that means? He's simply going to
record "varied and changing occurrences." If he could find something
more solid in himself, he would. He can't give the final word, only the
word of the moment.

Ironically enough, the paragraph I've just quoted was written by
the author who is traditionally considered the inventor of the essay—
Michel de Montaigne.

Montaigne was a sixteenth-century Frenchman who, upon his re-
tirement, began writing short prose pieces in which he explored his
thoughts and feelings on whatever subject occurred to him. He called
them his *essais,* which comes from the French word for "try" or "attempt." It is, of course, the root of our word "essay." Originally, then,
essay meant something like an experiment or an exploration. Montaigne's titles include "On Idleness," "On Liars," "On a Monstrous
Child," "On Sadness," "On Sleep," "On Drunkenness," and so on.
Often his main focus was himself. "Reader," he writes in his introduction to the *Essays,* "I myself am the subject of my book" (1). He

called them *essais* because he knew that he was simply testing out ideas. Later essayists would think of essays like going for walks, walks where the destination doesn't really matter. Virginia Woolf, a great novelist and essayist, wrote, "We should start without any fixed idea where we are going to spend the night, or when we propose to come back; the journey is everything" (65). In school essays, the destination is usually what matters. Personal essays, however, begin without a destination in mind. Basically, essayists like Montaigne and Woolf tried to understand the subjects that caught their interest by understanding their own thoughts and feelings about them. Today, we call this "writing to learn." It's the kind of writing in which the writer tries to figure out what she thinks *while* she's writing rather than doing so *before* she writes.

I hope the irony is becoming clear. I've just given examples from the inventor of the essay and one of its greatest twentieth-century practitioners. Yet, I'm not sure that most of their writing would have received passing grades in a standard first year writing class. Had they been graded in the usual first year writing class, the margins would have been filled with comments like *Focus!* and *Stick to the point!* Their written thought experiments didn't have traditional thesis statements that are supported with evidence. And in Montaigne's case, he was never finished with them. He revised and republished his essays twice, and his wife published a final version after his death. These new versions of his essays not only added new entries, but they also included revisions of his old entries. For Montaigne, it was perfectly natural to go back and change pieces that had already been published. Five centuries before computers and word processing, Montaigne was always rewriting.

Why did Montaigne write in this way? He had an unusual education, learning to read and write in Latin before he did so in his native French. He had read a lifetime's worth of classical literature when he was still very young. But this learning did not always console him. "I would like to suggest," he wrote, "that our minds are swamped by too much study and by too much matter" (151). With minds stuffed with knowledge, Montaigne argued, students did not learn to think for themselves. "We know how to say, 'This is what Cicero said'; 'This is morality for Plato'; 'These are the *ipissima verba* of Aristotle.' But what have *we* got to say? What judgments do *we* make? What are *we* doing? A parrot could talk as well as we do" (154). Montaigne also complained that the teachers of his day "keep us for four or five years learning to understand words and stitch them into sentences; as many more, to mold them into a great body, extending into four or five parts" (189). Sound familiar? As a student, Montaigne had learned the formal structures of classical rhetoricians, who also had their version of the five paragraph essay, and Montaigne came to hate it. Tired of having his head crammed with other people's words, and tired of the strict formalism he had been taught, Montaigne sought a way to write that was informal, skeptical, and unsure.

Montaigne wasn't the only person who wrote what we might call "essays." He may have coined the term in the sixteenth century, but even centuries before, people were writing short nonfiction pieces about their experiences and thoughts. In thirteenth-century Japan, for example, Kenko wrote *Essays in Idleness*. The original Japanese title reads, "With Nothing Better to Do" (29). "What a strange, demented feeling it gives me," he wrote, "when I realize I have spent whole days before this inkstone, with nothing better to do, jotting down at random whatever nonsensical thoughts have entered my head" (30). Kenko wrote about a wide range of topics, including sexual desire, longing for the past, board games, and parades. One of his shorter pieces makes the strange claim that one "should never put the new antlers of a deer to your nose and smell them. They have little insects that crawl into the nose and devour the brain" (36). I don't know whether this is true, but it shows that even before the term "essay" existed, some writers chose to "essay" about whatever floated into their minds.

In fact, essayists often write about small and minor things like mashed potatoes and ketchup, sidewalk chalk, going for walks, turtles, and even chasing after a hat that's blowing away in the wind. Other essayists take on more serious problems like alcoholism, migraine headaches, hunger, and other forms of suffering. Perhaps the only similarity that these essays share is that they recount the authors' own attempts to understand their experiences. In these essays, the writers don't start with their conclusion; they think through what's happening on the page. And while these essays have an organization, they are not organized in the usual thesis-plus-support system. The difference, according to Rutgers English professor Kurt Spellmeyer, is between writing that is "a means of achieving understanding" and writing that is a "demonstration of understanding" (270). The first is the kind of writing that Montaigne did: writing to achieve understanding, to try to figure out what he thought about what he read and saw and lived. The second is the kind of writing we've usually favored in school: writing to demonstrate understanding, to prove that you've learned the material or found the right answer to whatever question we asked you. William Covino, a professor of English at Fresno State in California, puts it this way: one kind of writing asks for "knowledge-as-information" and another asks for "knowledge-as-exploration" (54). School has usually sought the former; Montaigne and other essayists write the latter. Covino calls it "the art of wondering." And as Virginia Tech professor Paul Heilker points out, the word *essay* itself is "less a noun than a verb" (180). Again, the original word in French *was* a verb; Montaigne was naming more of an action than a thing.

At this point, you may be wondering how the school essay strayed so far from Montaigne's version. There are many reasons, but the simplest may be that "essay" is such a loose, baggy term that it eventually was used to describe almost any short nonfiction work (as opposed to novels or short stories, usually classified as fiction). Teachers just got in the habit of calling their assignments "essays," whether they were asking for research papers, book reports, critical reviews, or arguments. Now, perhaps unfortunately, "essays" refers to forms that Montaigne would not recognize (and conversely, Montaigne's works might not be recognizable as essays). We schoolmasters have tended to favor "demonstration of understanding" and "knowledge-as-information," so our notion of the essay has tended to ask students to show knowledge that they already have rather than asking them to discover knowledge that they don't have. We want students to prove, not wonder.

I can't help it, either. Look what I'm doing in this essay so far. It may not be five paragraphs long, but it's basically demonstrating information and proving what I know. Perhaps I needed to do that just to show that the word "essay" usually has referred to a much looser, wider, even wilder form of writing. But now enough of my point-making. We've walked the straight and narrow path of demonstration. Perhaps it's time to explore a little bit. Perhaps it's time to essay.

PART THE SECOND

If you've been teaching long enough, the schoolmaster habits can be hard to break. My initial intention for my "Intro to the Essay" class was to do the usual thing: analyze Montaigne-like essays and ask students to write pieces showing that they had understood the methods of analysis that I was trying to teach them. In other words, I was about to ask my students to write five paragraph essays about Montaigne essays. Sort of like teaching someone how to play the guitar out of a book (and without a guitar). You learn something, I guess, but you won't be able to make much music.

I could see very quickly that my students were not enthralled with my plans. So I asked them what they wanted to write, and they jumped at the chance to do something different, to imitate the personal essay rather than analyze it. "We already know how to write school essays," they said. I asked them whether they'd feel gypped. "This course," I said, "is supposed to teach you something useful. You know, how to analyze a text, how to use evidence. I'm afraid that what you're pro- posing won't be much help to you in your other classes." They assured me that they didn't care. "We've been writing theses for all of our other classes," they said. "It would be fun to do something different." So to relieve my boredom and theirs, we junked my plans to write more formal academic pieces. We decided to write the kind of essays we were reading: about love, sex, food, animals, getting lost, getting drunk, getting headaches, things people hate, things people love, or— if my students chose—deer antlers. (No one did finally choose to write about deer antlers or any other sort of antler, but they could have if they'd wanted to.)

It was a little strange at first, asking my students to write . . . well, whatever the hell they wanted. But that's what I had to do, at least if I were going to follow Montaigne's instincts. In fact, giving my students absolute free range was more than strange; it was downright frighten- ing. For me, at least. If you're a teacher and you're not . . . you know . . . *teaching*, then just what do you think you are doing? What happens when you have no idea what to expect?

It turns out that you can expect some really good, original writing, writing that made me forget to pick up my red pen. Take this opening, from my student Owen:

> I often have a strange feeling that there is some other place that I ought to be, and I do not know quite where it is. I am plagued with a vague suspicion that there is somewhere full of fascinating situations and events that were always meant to collide with my life and are waiting for me to stumble upon them but are slipping away into a void of hypotheticals while

I am miles or feet away doing nothing of any importance or
relevance to myself or anyone else. Thus my life slides away in
the most ordinary and horrible way possible.

Now *that's* an opening paragraph. Soon after I began reading Owen's
essay, I forgot that I was supposed to be "correcting" it. I was reading
it as though it were written by a peer rather than a student. I was reading it because I wanted to read it. Rereading it now, I'm struck by its
perfect Montaignian (that's a made-up adjective, but a good made-up
adjective can be impressive) quality. It makes the same "mistakes" that
Montaigne's essays make: it's all about the author—notice how often
that he uses "I"—and it focuses on the author's thoughts and experiences. It invites an identification between the reader and the writer. I
have felt this feeling, and perhaps you have, too. The writer speaks as
a companion, rather than as an expert.

The piece got better. Like Montaigne, Owen is a bit skeptical about
the benefits of formal education. School, he writes, "must convince the
student that boredom is an unavoidable and essential component of
life. If this were not accepted the 'real world' would fall apart." These
sentences made me glad that I had abandoned my original plan for the
course. Meanwhile, Owen's essay winds up to one of the best lines I
read all semester: "When I tell people I am an English major I am usually asked if I want to be a teacher. The idea is absolutely absurd to me.
How many inmates do you think apply for jobs as prison guards after
being released?" I say this is one of the best lines I read, but reading it
also made me uncomfortable since I had both been an English major
and become an English teacher. But it made me think, and it made
me wonder how often I have bored my students because I am guard-
ing in the same way I was guarded. I like to think that my teaching
"frees" students—from prejudice and ignorance. After Owen's essay,
though, I wondered whether I was freeing students or imprisoning
them. That's what the best essays do: they make you wonder.

Now, let's say he were writing this for a first year class that asked
for a research paper. Though our notion of the research paper is pretty
different from what Montaigne wrote, you will be asked to write formal research papers, and you may be wondering what the personal
essay has to do with the research paper. Fair enough question. The
answer begins with observing that Owen isn't just navel-gazing. He's
asking a serious question about whether education teaches us to toler-
ate boredom. In *Dumbing Us Down* (2005), for example, John Taylor

Gatto, former New York City Teacher of the Year and proponent of alternative schooling, has made a career about asking the very same question. Owen's wondering has led him to a question that also interests nationally-recognized educators, a question that one could do some research on and write about, a question that might be more interesting than whether you're for or against abortion, or gun control, or capital punishment.

Like Owen, Kathy begins with an experience to which her readers, including me, could easily relate: insomnia. (In fact, I'm drafting this essay at 1:14 a.m., so I can really relate to insomnia.)

> It is really a shame when one is not able to sleep. At least for me, it leaves me with nothing else to do but wrestle with my thoughts. I try to count sheep, hypnotize myself, concentrate on my breathing, and clear my head. All of these are techniques people have told me to try. None of them have worked for me so far. The problem lies in the fact that when I cannot sleep, I focus so much on trying to sleep, that it is nearly impossible.

The essayist here sounds like a peer or a friend rather than an expert or a professional. What's more, she takes a mundane experience and tries to turn it into something more serious, and thus she finds a subject that might interest her more than the standard research topics that demand us to be "for" something or "against" something. How many college students experience insomnia? Does it get worse as the semester goes on? How does it affect their grades? If you've ever found yourself wide awake in your dorm room all night, perhaps you've wondered about the answers to these questions. Writing about them in this essayistic, wondering/wandering way, you might be more likely to stumble across questions that really interest you.

Looking out her dorm window, Kathy sees our university's church, which leads her to recall attending services there. Though she planned on sleeping in most Sundays, now that she is away from home, a friend persuades her to go. And though she wakes up early only reluctantly, she does not regret going:

> The stained glass windows and architecture were amazing. I would continuously look up, for no other reason than to admire the way the golden arches on the off-white ceiling came together. The lights, pillars, candles, tabernacle, statues, es-

sentially everything in the cathedral, demanded my attention.
I was captivated by the beauty that surrounded me, and nothing could break my trance of sheer fascination.

Isn't that a lovely passage? Lovelier still is the way she begins the next
paragraph: "Back to reality, I am not in that gorgeous church anymore. Instead, I am stuck in this utterly boring dorm room." The contrast is wonderful. If the strength of the first image weren't enough,
Kathy sharpens our perspective by bringing us into her dorm room,
which she doesn't need to describe. You can picture it: cinderblock
walls painted flat white. It pales in comparison. But she tries to recon-
cile herself to her room. "After all," she writes, "this is the only space
in this city I have." I don't know if I would have gotten such strong
writing if I had given Kathy a formal assignment.

Jon decided to imitate Sei Shonagon, one of the great Japanese essayists, who wrote in the tenth century, long before Montaigne came
up with the word *essai*. Sei Shonagon liked to keep lists of her likes and
dislikes, and my class read one of those essays, titled "Hateful Things."
Though she wrote one thousand years ago, her dislikes can seem very
familiar: "A man who has nothing in particular to recommend him
but who speaks in an affected tone and poses as being elegant" (27).
Or, "Sometimes a person who is utterly devoid of charm will try to create a good impression by using very elegant language; yet he only succeeds in being ridiculous" (26). (In college, you may run into people
who use very elegant language but succeed only in being ridiculous.)

Jon kept his own list. "Since I am not in the greatest mood right
now," he writes, "I thought it appropriate to base this essay on Sei
Shonagon's 'Hateful Things.' I would just like to apologize in advance
for anyone I may inadvertently offend with the subsequent items." Already, I was primed simply to read this essay. How are you going to
"correct" what someone hates? Besides, I wanted to see how much, if
anything, Jon and I had in common. "The squirrels outside my window in the parking lot playing a friendly game of cat and mouse. The
freedom they have upsets me. While I sit in my room studying in order
to make something of my life, they run around without a care in the
world. Sometimes I wish I were as free as these squirrels, being able to
do whatever the hell I want whenever the hell I want." This is a very
common move in a personal essay: to take a mundane moment—for
example, watching squirrels play—and then to ask larger questions
about one's purpose in life. Something else Jon hates: "Having a ri-

diculous amount of work to do on Mardi Gras weekend. Where is the celebration in that? I believe there is a conspiracy among teachers to make as much work as possible due the week after what is known to be a busy weekend among college students." (Again, a question that might be worth exploring. Does homework increase near holiday and party weekends? How would you find out?) He continues, "I mean, I had big plans for this weekend, especially Saturday, I was going to get up early, go 'eat breakfast' at a friend's apartment, then go 'watch' the parade, come back and 'sleep' for a couple of hours, and go back to my friend's apartment to 'play some board games.'" This passage is interesting for a couple of reasons. First, it sounds like the author is writing his thoughts as they come to him. That gives the essay a lively tone. Second, the passage requires so much interpretation. As you can probably guess, Mardi Gras is not exactly the most wholesome event in the world, so the author's scare quotes make me wonder what he means exactly. I have a hard time believing that they're just going to be playing board games. I don't know for sure, but that's what makes it interesting.

Like Jon, Samantha followed a time-honored essay tradition, writing about the art of walking. We read Henry David Thoreau's essay on walking, and though Samantha didn't like it very much, she used as it inspiration for her own work:

> The reason I dislike Thoreau so much is because he consistently drifts far, very far, away from his intended idea. Then, when you try to figure out how he got to a certain point, it just confuses you more. He begins the piece by talking about the art of walking and by the end, he has wandered miles from the beginning idea and never returns to tie up loose ends. Is the reason I feel the need for the author to return because I simply have been trained that way? Throughout my life, I have been saddled with expectations that are supposed to teach me responsibility, obedience, control, and fluidity of thoughts. Eventually, I became accustomed to thinking everyone expected those of me and in turn I expect it from them.

What I like about this passage is the level of criticism. Sam isn't just saying she hates Thoreau's essay; she is also questioning why she has come to the conclusions that she has. She's wondering about her own interpretive principle. That makes this moment very Montaingian: it's not just the critique of another author but the critique and the personal reflection about that critique. Sam comes to wonder whether she reads because of how she's been trained, and that's a short step from wondering whether there are different ways of reading (and writing). These are questions that have troubled English professors for a long time. Is there a "right" way to read? Or do we just think that the way we happen to read is the "right" way? This is a serious question. Perhaps you've had the experience of being told that the books you like aren't literature, or that your interpretation of a poem isn't correct. Well, that all depends on what you mean by "literature" and "correct." There's a huge argument about this between scholars, but the truth is we usually don't share it in the classroom. It's sort of like the way parents try not to fight in front of the children. This condescension is obviously foolish: Samantha, who's not an English major, has found her way to a fundamental question simply by following her thoughts. Again, essays are more about exploring what's possible rather than demonstrating what's already known. (If it's already known, why demonstrate it?)

Speaking of exploring, I actually asked students to go for a walk one day, so they could practice wandering around aimlessly. This experience was strange for them, as it was for me. (I stayed behind to watch their stuff, and I can just imagine what someone who happened to look in might have thought. Were they all abducted by aliens?) Samantha wasn't quite sure what to do either. "When the class was told we were going for a walk," she writes, "I was expecting a kind of group walk around campus or, at least, some kind of structure. Never did I expect to just leave class and walk on my own. I was lost, and I believe, by the puzzled looks on the faces around me, the class was, too. The first thing that came to mind was *whom should I walk with so I don't look like a loser walking alone?*" This question suggests the same thing about school that Montaigne noticed and Sam has already noticed. School can so train you to think in certain ways that even taking a walk by yourself seems strange.

At this point, you may be wondering how to write such an essay. The truth is, I don't know. We just read some examples and went for it. Jon imitated a structure we'd read. Samantha took a theme and played with it. Owen captured the tone of Montaigne perfectly, and Kathy sat at her desk and imagined her entire world. Of course, we worked on these pieces throughout the semester, revising them to make them stronger, and proofing them at the end for any little errors. But the creativity came from the students, and its source was mysterious. In some ways, I did the least teaching that I have ever done in a semester. I just asked my students to read some essays and write essays like them.

I'm not trying to suggest that Montaigne's version of the essay is better than the formal school version. I'm simply arguing that there are other available ways of writing, ways that are as old and as important and valuable as the usual ways we're usually taught. You're still going to need to know how to write an argument with a thesis and with support. That's a good and useful thing to know. Moreover, it's not as if the personal essay and the school essay are diametrically opposed: the former can lead to the latter in interesting and compelling ways. The personal essay does not demand that you answer questions; it demands that you ask really interesting questions. Yes, these questions can lead to answers, but the better the question, the better the answer. At the very least, you now know that there is another way to write, one that allows you to wander far and wonder out loud.

DISCUSSION

1. If you could write about anything, what would you write about? If your writing teacher simply said, "Write what you want," where would you start?
2. What food would you write about? What animal? What girlfriend or boyfriend? What book? What strange event? What question?
3. If you weren't taught the five paragraph form, what kind of form(s) have you been taught? How have you been taught to structure essays? What reasons have you been given for structuring your essays in these ways?
4. Have you ever taken a walk to nowhere in particular? A drive to nowhere in particular? If not, why not?
5. Is there a piece of your own writing that you love but that has nothing to do with school?

FOR MORE ON THE ESSAY

If you want a really good and thorough introduction to the essay, I recommend Philip Lopate's *The Art of the Personal Essay: An Anthology from the Classical Era to the Present.* This book features a large collection of essays, starting with very early versions from the ancient world, continuing through Montaigne, and reaching all the way to the present day. Lopate also has a great list of books of essays and books on the essay, so you can probably find whatever you want by starting with Lopate. You can also check out John D'Agata's *The Lost Origins of the Essay,* which goes back in time even further than Lopate's collection. If you want to read Montaigne, you can read the M.A. Screech translation, which I've used here, or you can read the Donald Frame translation, which sometimes reads a little easier. You can also find a lot of essays online, especially of older essayists. If you google "Montaigne" and "Project Gutenberg" for example, you'll find a lot, though the translation is from seventeenth century. You can also find twentieth-century essayists online, including Virginia Woolf, George Orwell, and James Baldwin, among others. Many living essayists, however, still have their work copyrighted. Nevertheless, you may be able to find a lot of contemporary work on your library shelves and in your library electronic databases.

WORKS CITED

Covino, William A. *The Art of Wondering: A Revisionist Return to the History of Rhetoric.* Portsmouth, NH: Boynton/Cook, 1988. Print.

D'Agata, John. *The Lost Origins of the Essay.* St. Paul, MN: Graywolf Press, 2009. Print.

Gatto, John Taylor. *Dumbing Us Down: The Hidden Curriculum of Compulsory Schooling.* Gabriola Island, British Columbia: New Society Publishers, 2005. Print.

Heilker, Paul. *The Essay: Theory and Pedagogy for an Active Form.* Urbana, IL: NCTE, 1996. Print.

Kenko, "Essays in Idleness." Lopate 30–37.

Lopate, Phillip, ed. *The Art of the Personal Essay: An Anthology from the Classical Era to the Present.* NY: Anchor, 1995. Print.

Montaigne. *The Complete Essays.* Trans. M.A. Screech. New York: Penguin, 2003. Print.

Spellmeyer, Kurt. "A Common Ground: The Essay in the Academy." *College English* 51.3 (1989): 262–276. Print.

Sei Shonagon. "Hateful Things." Lopate 24–29.

Woolf, Virginia. "Montaigne." *The Common Reader: First Series.* Orlando, FL: Harvest, 1984. 58–68. Print.

Why Blog? Searching for Writing on the Web

Alex Reid

As Malcolm Gladwell and others have observed, it takes some 10,000 hours of dedication to a craft or profession to become an "expert."* Obviously this is a generalization that provokes as many questions as it answers, but the fairly self-evident bottom-line point here is that becoming good at anything worth becoming good at takes a lot of time. According to the 2008 National Survey of Student Engagement, the typical first year student writes 92 pages, while average college seniors write 146 pages (21). Given these statistics, we may assume that the average college student writes less than 500 pages during his or her academic career. It's difficult to equate pages with the hours in Gladwell's calculation, but I would think that even a student in a writing intensive major would not likely spend, on average, more than 1000 hours writing to get her degree. At that rate, 1000 hours of writing over four years, one would reach expertise (10,000 hours) in 36 more years. In other words, not even writing intensive courses are likely to ask students to commit the kind of time to their assigned writing that would be necessary to work towards expertise as Gladwell defines it. To make matters potentially worse, being an "expert" isn't necessarily all that it would seem to be. As one discovers with almost anything one dedicates one's time to, there is no ceiling, no final desti-

---

nation, on the path of mastery. There are always new challenges; there is always room for improvement. As I will discuss here, blogging is one good way to develop as a writer.

Of course, most students aren't interested in becoming expert writers. Does that sound like a condemnation of some kind? It shouldn't. I don't think there's anything wrong with not wanting to become an expert, professional writer, any more than there's anything wrong with not wanting to be a surgeon or a carpenter. On the other hand, unlike surgery or carpentry, college students pursuing professional careers will need some facility with writing. In other words, while most students will not take writing courses to become professional writers, they might take those courses to serve other goals and interests that benefit from good writing skills. Unfortunately, often the trappings of school curriculum can interfere with our ability to connect writing to our own goals and interests. General education requirements, credits, grades, and other potential rewards and punishments of academic life can crowd out our ability to find some intrinsic motivation. Even though instructors work hard to devise assignments that will inspire engaged student writing, they are also enmeshed in this same context of grades and GPAs. Students confronted with a syllabus or an assignment can find it difficult to get beyond the mindset of "what do I need to do to get an A?." Unfortunately, decades of research suggest that such extrinsic motivators can actually hurt our performance on challenging intellectual tasks like writing an essay.

What does this have to do with blogging? A great deal, at least in my view. A blog is an excellent opportunity for exploring and developing intrinsic motivations for writing. Course writing assignments are always imposed upon you. Often they come with requirements that you might find disagreeable: subject matter, length, format, due dates, etc. It can be difficult to establish intrinsic motivations in those contexts, even if your professor is willing to be flexible. On a blog, however, you control the subject matter, the length, the format, the timing of your posts, and all the other characteristics of your writing. You establish your own goals. For good or for bad, there are not likely to be many extrinsic motivations, like money, for your blogging, so your only reasons for continuing to blog will need to come from inside. Through blogging, you can discover such motivations not only for writing on your blog but for writing in general, and once you have some internal motivation for writing, you will find it easier to translate that motivation into your academic writing, and later into your writing as a professional.

As a student in a first year writing course, you may not envision yourself as a writer. It is understandable that you may not want to dedicate yourself to the 10,000-hour journey toward expertise. However, you might want to dedicate yourself to a more modest goal. You might want to be among the best writers in your major or among the applicants for the graduate school or job that you'll be pursuing when you graduate. Part of reaching that goal will be putting in time as a writer, and a blog can be an invaluable part of the time you spend. This essay is addressed to the composition student interested in pursuing blogging. It provides some history and technical background on the weblog. It discusses rhetorical strategies for getting started and finding success as a blogger. Finally, it offers some tips for designing your blog site and connecting your blog with the other social media applications you use.

WHAT IS A BLOG? OR BETTER, WHAT IS *YOUR* BLOG?

Defining blogs is difficult. Typically the first answer one imagines for this question refers to the *content* of blogs. One might think of blogs as public diaries or perhaps as amateur journalism or political, op-ed websites or maybe as celebrity gossip sites. The term web log or weblog (shortened to blog) is generally attributed to Jorn Barger in 1997. Barger had been a long time contributor to early net communities like newsgroups and e-mail lists and decided to create his weblog *Robot Wisdom* at this time (Rhodes). The term could be applied retroactively to earlier sites, but 1997 is as good a starting point as any. However, at that time, one needed knowledge of HTML in order to maintain a blog. It wasn't until 1999 that the first blogging application, Blogger, was created by Pyra Labs (Blogger is now owned by Google), which enabled a far larger group of people to begin blogging. Still, at this time, blogging was undertaken by a small number of mostly "techie" individuals, who wrote primarily to share information about the web. The events of September 11th, 2001 and the subsequent military actions led to an explosion of political blogging, mostly with conservative viewpoints ("Blog"). Today, political blogs on both sides of the aisle remain popular. However, many of the most popular blogs deal with specific interests from computers and automobiles to (allegedly) funny pictures of cats. The world of blogging has exploded this decade. Technorati.com, a site devoted to indexing blogs, has recorded 133 million blogs since 2002 representing an immense variety of interests and perspectives about what a blog can or should be.

A Sampling of Popular Blogs

According to Technorati.com, below are the top 25 blogs as of June 2010. As you will see, many deal with current events with either a liberal or conservative slant. Many others are focused on technology or entertainment. I am not suggesting that your blog needs to be or should be like any of these. However, they do represent some of the most successful blogging ventures and thus reveal something of how blogs can function. At Technorati, you can search for blogs in the specific subject areas that interest you.

1. The Huffington Post
http://www.huffingtonpost.com
News and editorial with a liberal perspective.

2. Mashable!
http://mashable.com
Social media and technology news.

3. TechCrunch
http://www.techcrunch.com
Technology business news.

4. Gizmodo
http://www.gizmodo.com
Technology reviews and news.

5. Engadget
http://www.engadget.com
Technology reviews and news.

6. Boing Boing
http://www.boingboing.net
A blog of "cultural curiosities and interesting technologies."

7. Gawker
http://www.gawker.com
New York news and gossip

8. The Corner on National Review …
http://corner.nationalreview.com
Blog for the conservative new magazine.

9. TMZ.com
http://www.tmz.com
Celebrity gossip.

10. Hot Air
http://hotair.com
Conservative news blog.

11. The Daily Beast
http://www.thedailybeast.com
News aggregator and liberal commentary.

11. The Daily Dish
http://andrewsullivan.theatlantic.com
Blog of conservative pundit, Andrew Sullivan.

13. Think Progress
http://thinkprogress.org
Current events from a liberal perspective.

14. ReadWriteWeb
http://www.readwriteweb.com
Technology news.

15. The Official Google Blog
http://googleblog.blogspot.com
Google's blog.

16. Kotaku
http://www.kotaku.com
Video-gaming blog.

17. Vulture
http://nymag.com/daily/entertainment
Entertainment and popular culture.

17. Jezebel
http://jezebel.com
Celebrity gossip and fashion.

19. The Onion
http://theonion.com
Comedy and news.

19. ArtsBeat
http://artsbeat.blogs.nytimes.com
Popular culture.

19. Business Insider
http://www.businessinsider.com
Business and economics.

22. Political Punch
http://blogs.abcnews.com/politicalpunch
ABC White House Correspondent Jake Tapper.

23. Mediaite
http://www.mediaite.com
Politics and news in the media industry.

24. RedState
http://www.redstate.com
Conservative editorial blog.

25. TPMMuckraker
http://tpmmuckraker.talkingpointsmemo.com
Conservative editorial blog.

✳ ✳ ✳

Instead of a definition based on content, you might attempt to provide a technical definition of a blog. While one might create and maintain a blog using only HTML, like a traditional web page, most blogs today operate on a web application (e.g., Blogger, WordPress, Ty-pepad, etc.). With such blogs, individual entries are saved in a database and those entries are then called up and published on the blog accord-ing to any criteria included in the database fields. For instance, you can publish entries chronologically, which is the convention for blogs. However, you could also publish them by category (also common on blogs) or by author (if there are multiple authors for the blog) or even alphabetically by title (which is certainly less common on blogs). Blog-ging applications make adding content to the web fairly easy, which is one reason why there are so many blogs. Perhaps because adding a blog post is easy, blogs originated with writers posting informal, daily observations about interesting websites. Informality remains a com-mon trait of blogging style, though certainly there are blogs with very formal prose as well.

Arguably, the practice of blogging has become so vast, including people from around the world, that any definition general enough to include everyone would be of little use in helping a new blogger in a composition course decide what to do. Instead, it is necessary to begin with identifying a narrower genre of blogging practices. In a sense, this is much like the more general advice I give to my composition students about writing. It isn't particularly useful to try to understand "how to write" in a general way. Instead, you need to learn how to identify the particular writing practices at work in the specific writing situa-tions that you face as a writer. That is, students in a literature course face different writing tasks from those in economics courses or biology courses, and writers in public relations firms face different tasks from technical writers in the computer industry or analysts at a bank. How-ever, any writer might begin with some fairly basic *rhetorical* questions:

1. Who is my audience? What do they expect from me? What do they already know about the subject of the text I am compos-ing? How will they react to my message?
2. What is my purpose? What is the exigency for this text? (i.e. what has motivated me to write this text?) What do I hope to achieve?
3. What is the genre in which I am writing? What are its conven-tions? (e.g., fairy tales being "Once upon a time . . . :" what are the familiar practices of this genre?) How are arguments made in this genre? What types of evidence will be found convincing?

These questions certainly apply to blogging. So when we ask "what is a blog?" the answer is shaped by who we wish to write to, what our purpose(s) might be, and how others with similar audiences and purposes already practice blogging. I know that when I began blogging, I didn't have a very strong idea of what my blog would be like. I knew that I would write about my professional-academic interests and experiences (as opposed to personal experiences or hobbies or pop culture). I also came to my decision to start blogging after having read the blogs of several colleagues, so I had some idea of what others with similar interests were doing. Most of all, I was already familiar with my intended audience (though, of course, on the public web, you never really control who reads what you write). I knew what other English professors and graduate students were like. I knew about their expectations for scholarly writing. That said, no one knew what academic blogging should be like, and arguably we still don't know for sure. So blogging was an experiment, an exploration into what that genre could do for me and other rhetoricians.

The specifics of my experience starting out as a blogger are likely quite different from what yours will be. However, there are some key commonalities that relate to the formation of intrinsic motivation. First was my sense of autonomy. As Daniel Pink points out, autonomy might be divided into four elements: task, technique, time, and team (94). I set myself the task of writing a blog and what the subject matter of my blog would be. I established my own technique: I decided I would write in a quasi-academic style. I wrote my posts when I wanted, and I decided to write an individual blog, though many others write blogs as a team and you might as well. As a blogger, you will have a similar autonomy over these decisions and the freedom to change as you see fit. Second was my engagement and desire to improve. The experience of autonomy when combined with a challenging task can create the optimal experience the psychologist Mihaly Csikszentmihalyi terms "flow" (4). The trick in creating a flow state is to set a task that is neither so hard as to create frustration or anxiety or so easy as to be boring. As such, it is essential that you discover a subject for your blog that truly engages you. Perhaps you might set goals of writing longer or more often or engaging more readers. Finally, as you develop as a blogger you will hopefully connect with a clear sense of a larger social or professional purpose. In the end, it is your autonomous pursuit of your own improvement as a blogger in service of this larger purpose that will help you to uncover your own intrinsic motivation. And maybe, in the end, it will be writing that interests you after all, or maybe writing will only be one small means toward a different purpose. Either way, the experience of blogging will have helped you to uncover something that really matters to you.

DISCOVERING WHAT TO WRITE

Since you are probably reading this as vvvvvvvvvvvpart of a composition class, there's a good chance that you will be asked to blog as part of the course. Within the context of a composition course there are a few general types of blogs that you might be asked to join. Certainly, the kind of blog you are asked to write will have some impact on what you decide to do, and unfortunately, the nearly inescapable carrots and sticks of the classroom can serve as an impediment to creative thinking. At the same time, as writers and creative thinkers, we always work within contexts that provide both unique constraints and opportunities. The task therefore is to gather whatever autonomy you can within the situation in order to customize your work in a way that will allow you to engage productively with your work and tap into some intrinsic motivation for writing.

Table 1. Types of course-assigned blogs.

Type	Characteristics
Class Blog	In a class blog, the students and the instructor post to a common blog on the subject of the course. Often students are asked to post new material and comment on their peers' posts.
Individual Reading or Learning Blog	Here, though you are keeping a solo blog, you are asked to write specifically about the topic of the course. Perhaps you will write in response to readings or other assignments in addition to reflecting on your learning experiences.
Class Team Blog	In some classes, students work on group projects and are asked to keep a blog that updates the class on their activities. Here you may have a wider degree of autonomy on the subject matter of your blog, depending on the particulars of the assignment you are given.

Type	Characteristics
Individual Blog	This type of blog would give you the greatest autonomy, which can also make it the most challenging kind of assignment. For example, I might ask students to post 20 times with posts that are at least 100 words in length over the course of a semester, but provide no assignment requirements beyond that.

As with all writing, perhaps the most challenging task is finding a subject on which to write, or what we rhetoricians term "invention." By claiming an interest and reading other bloggers with similar interests, hopefully you will find a worthwhile topic. Perhaps you have already declared a major. If so, that should give you a good place to start. If not, then you might have to get more creative in thinking about a subject that you would like to read and write about. As the educational theorist and activist, Sir Ken Robinson, explains, our talents and passions are sometimes hidden, submerged by well-intentioned but misguided schooling experiences (Robinson). Perhaps you can think about the moments when you find yourself in a state of flow. Csikszentmihalyi conducted an experiment where he paged people randomly 40 times during a week and had them write about what they were doing at that moment in an attempt to discover and describe flow experiences (4). You might do something similar. Wherever you experience flow, your interests are likely close by.

Once you've decided on a subject, you need to investigate other blogs with similar interests. Read a wide range of blogs—the most popular blogs on your subject, blogs by experts on your subject, blogs by those with amateur interests, and blogs by students like yourself. Reading is an essential part of blogging. Once one gets beyond the diary blog, it is quite common to blog about what one reads elsewhere on other blogs (aka the "blogosphere"). In fact, writing about other bloggers is one of the primary ways you can build an audience and community for a blog. Researching for blog writing is much like researching for course assignments. You can begin with a general search engine. Google allows you to search specifically for blogs, or you might try Technorati.com: a site that indexes blogs. The goal here is to find a handful of the most popular blogs in your area of interest. From there, things get trickier. Most blog sites include a list of links called a "blog roll" somewhere on their sidebars. This is a list of blogs that blogger also reads. Sampling the blog rolls of bloggers you like is a good strategy for finding other worthwhile blogs. I'm not suggesting that you have to do what everyone else does. To the contrary, one of the great things about blogging is the opportunity for autonomy the genre can provide. But reading other bloggers with similar interests can help you in understanding the kinds of choices you might make and will also aid you in finding an audience for your work.

Of course, knowing what to write about (and even what you might wish to say on the subject) and knowing how actually to compose your post are two different things. In my view, the fundamental challenges of blogging are not very different from those of any kind of writing. You require sufficient exigency to write. Where does this come from?

1. An urgency to the subject matter (e.g. a current event)
2. An important and reasonable purpose (e.g. writing a job letter to get a job)
3. A sense of authority, feeling qualified to write about a subject
4. A strong personal interest (e.g. creative writing, political writing)
5. An audience that will give you positive feedback

The familiar advice about brainstorming and free writing applies as much to blogging as other types of writing. However, blogging has a special relationship with serendipity and inspiration. As a blogger you have no deadlines. You are not required to write about anything in particular, and you're not required to write in a particular format or for a particular length. As such, you are free to write whatever and whenever you like. For example, maybe you are interested in graphic design. You take an interest in reading about graphic design and seeing examples of interesting design. You read an interesting article or see an image of an interesting design, so you write a brief post about it. You write something about what you saw and why it interested you, and you include the link. Perhaps you read something interesting in a design course or learn something during class discussion, and you blog about that. Before you know it, you've started to build a collection of brief posts. At some point, something will come of all that posting. You'll start to see a trend. You'll make connections, and suddenly you will have something longer to write. Over time, as you continue to blog, it is likely that different exigencies will emerge. More importantly, as you develop a writing habit, you begin to think less about needing a reason to write. Hopefully there is always some reason of course, but I think, as a writer, the act of responding to your experiences with writing becomes more natural or expected. It simply becomes what you do. As a regular writer or blogger you begin to trust that exigency or purpose will become clear through the act of writing.

This is the great advantage of blogging. Out of necessity, classroom writing assignments are short-lived. They usually take place over a few weeks and then you might never write on that subject again. You take another class with new writing assignments, and there is little or no relationship between those assignments and the ones from the semester before. Blogging gives you the opportunity to write many, informal, short posts over a long period of time. As a blogger you might commit to spending 10–20 minutes, two or three times a week, for a year. In the end, you'll have 100 or more posts chronicling your thoughts and interests. Even if you don't end up writing longer posts, your blog could serve as a reservoir of ideas and links for writing assignments, especially if you choose to blog about your academic interests. Ideally though, the regular writing practice of blogging will help you discover some intrinsic motivation for writing. Outside of the extrinsic carrots and sticks of classroom assignments, you might find some value in writing itself, a value that you can then bring to your assignments.

So my advice to you is to give blogging a try. It's easy. It's free. And if you give it a decent try, you might discover some tremendous benefits that will carry you through college and into your career.

Some Technical Advice on Building a Blog

There are now many websites that allow users to create and maintain free blogs. Often these sites will place advertising on your blog instead of asking you to pay. Usually there is a pay option if you prefer to have a blog without ads. Two of the more commonly used sites at this point are Blogger.com and WordPress.com. Both sites are fairly easy to use, offer step-by-step instructions for getting started, and a range of templates for the layout and design of your blog. Later, when you become more confident with your blogging, you might want to learn about CSS (cascading style sheets) and other elements of web design that will allow you to customize your site even further, but the choices offered by either of these sites will be more than enough to get you started. The first decisions you will have to make are the name and URL (i.e. your web address) of your blog. These are an important decisions, especially the URL. Once you create your URL, Google and other search engines will use it to link to your site. Other bloggers will use it to link to your pages. If you change your URL later, it will break all those links. The title of your blog and your URL will also be two of the main ways that your blog will be indexed by search engines. Therefore, if you want your blog to be found by readers, you should include words they might use in searching for you. For example, because I wanted my blog to by an extension of my professional, academic identity, I chose to use my name for my URL, alexreid.typepad.com. I named my blog Digital Digs because I knew I was going to be writing about digital media. Changing the name of your blog later is not a big deal, but you might want to give some careful thought to your URL (also keep in mind that many popular URLs will already be taken).

The next step will be selecting a layout and design for your blog. Here the decision you make should reflect your ideas about what the content of your blog will be. The good news is that it is easy to change the template you are using without losing any of your content, so you can always change your mind later. There are different templates that are made to accommodate different blogging styles.

- Will you write frequent short posts, maybe posted from your phone or other mobile device? Or will you write longer, less frequent posts? If you plan the former, maybe you want to have 10 or more of your most recent posts on the first page. If you are planning the latter, maybe you'll only want two or three. The length of your average post might also inform your choices for the size of the font you use and the width of the text column. Again, these are things with which you can experiment.
- Will you include many images? Some blogs are primarily collections of photos. There are some blog templates designed to allow you to display images in a grid-like fashion.
- How about video or audio podcasts? You should consider including a range of media. Maybe you will want to record your own video or audio, or maybe you'll just want to embed media you find on YouTube or similar sites. If so, you will want to make sure that you pick a template that has a wide enough text column to include the video player.

Most templates will include default font and color choices that you can customize. It's important to keep readability in mind. If you are following my suggestion and creating a blog that will address your professional or academic interests, you should make design choices that reflect that professionalism. In other words, no crazy color combinations! Of course, you should feel free to experiment, but, generally speaking, dark text on a light background is the easiest to read. Clear text is especially important if your posts will be longer than a short paragraph.

As you can see, questions of design and layout are interrelated with questions of content. The content of your regular blog posts is likely the most important part of your site, but you should also consider the content of your *sidebar*. Most blogs include one or two narrow columns with a variety of information. The advertising that appears on free blogs will appear in the sidebar. However, the contemporary blogger has the opportunity to provide a variety of media and opportunities for interaction through widgets. Popular widgets allow bloggers to include information form other social media such as Facebook, Twitter, YouTube, and Flickr (a photo-sharing site). Sites like Widgetbox. com offer millions of free widgets that are easy to add to a blog.

My own blog is a fairly typical example of blog design. As can be seen in this image of my current site (see fig. 1), the blog has three basic parts: a banner, a sidebar, and the main text column.

The banner is your opportunity to create a strong identity for your site. As you can see in the other images here (see figs. 2–6), I have gone through several banner images during the years I have run my blog.

The colors that dominate your banner will then inform the color choices that you make elsewhere. For example, the blues and grays in the banner image appear as font and background colors in the sidebar. My sidebar includes several widgets. There's Tungle, which is a web application where my students can make appointments to meet with me. I also have my Twitter feed and a "blog roll" (a list of blogs I read), which is powered by Delicious. In addition, I have a list of recent comments posted to my blog (see more on commenting below). Though my blogging application, like all blogging applications, has its own commenting system, I use Disqus, another social media site, which allows commenters to create identities that they can carry from one blog to another (wherever Disqus is used). Finally, the primary part of the blog is the main text column. I have taken my own advice and

Fig. 1. A screen capture of my current blog, www.alex-reid.net.

digital digs

an archaeology of the future

alex reid, associate professor
english & professional writing
state university of new york
college at cortland

reida@cortland.edu
607.753. 2069
web.cortland.edu/reida

digging up the past, digging the future

Figs. 2–6. Examples of different banners I have used for my blog.

used dark text on a light background. You should experiment with font, font size, and spacing. Because my posts tend to be long, I have emphasized readability by selecting a simple font and adding some additional spacing between the lines (i.e., more than single-spaced).

The final major step is deciding how your readers will access and interact with your blog. You will have the option of creating an RSS feed. RSS stands for "real simple syndication." As I mentioned, blogging applications like Blogger and WordPress work by creating a database of your posts. Using this database they can also create an RSS feed, which is a file that is automatically updated every time you post something new. Your readers can subscribe to this file using any number of desktop and web-based applications. This way, they will be able to check easily whether or not you've posted a new entry. People who read blogs often keep track of a number of their favorites. It would be difficult to do this if one had to visit each site to see if there was new material. By subscribing to blogs using what is called a "blog aggregator," you only have to check in one place to see which of one's favorite blogs have fresh material. Since, as a blogger, you will probably be reading many blogs in your field, I suggest you create a free account at one of these blog aggregator sites for yourself. Google Reader is a popular web-based aggregator.

An RSS feed will allow your readers to interact with your blog in a wider range of contexts, including reading your posts on mobile devices. The other key element of interactivity is your blog's comment function. As you may have noticed from blogs you have visited, most sites allow readers to post comments on posts. Commenting is an important social aspect of blogging. Not only do comments allow you to learn what your readers are thinking, they also provide a way to strengthen your relationship with your readers and keep them coming back. Of course, comments also have their drawbacks. The most obvious of these is comment spam. Much like email spam, comment spam are random comments on your posts that include links to (often questionable) websites. Most blogging applications include filters to try to keep out spam, but you will still need to be vigilant. One option is to turn on comment moderation, which means you will have to approve messages before they get posted. However, this is sometimes discouraging to genuine commenters. You'll have to make that decision for yourself. Also, you may have to make a decision at some point about what to do with critical and/or belligerent comments. Should you delete them? Should you try to block that poster from making further comments? Should you respond or ignore them? There are no easy answers to these questions, and it may be that you'll not face this problem as a blogger. In the end you will have to decide what is and isn't appropriate for your blog. For example, if you start blogging in your class and a classmate comments in disagreement with you, what will be the fallout of deciding to delete or ignore the comment? As you will discover, the choices we make as bloggers reflect upon our identity and reputation. Of course, this is often the case with writing; blogging is a great place to learn how this works.

FINALLY, GIVE YOURSELF A MONTH

If you decide to start blogging, give yourself a month to try it out. Start out easy by using one of the templates offered on whichever blogging application you decide to go with. If you already are invested in other social media sites like Twitter or YouTube, and you want to share those things in your sidebar, that's fine, but if you aren't, that's fine as well. Just focus on blogging. The main task of every blogger is to seek out interesting topics and write posts about them. Set an ambitious but reasonable goal for yourself that reflects your interests. Maybe you want to post at least one short message every day. Maybe your goal is to get two longer posts each week. Once you've set that goal, stick to it for a month at least. It takes time to develop positive habits. I often think of writing as I do running. As a runner, it took me a while to recognize how running feels and what I was capable of doing. Eventually I realized I could run regularly and that, though I would exert myself, I could consistently meet my goals. Similarly, a blogging regimen may seem intimidating at first, but if you meet your goals for a month, you will have direct evidence of your ability as a writer. And though blogging may not ultimately be the kind of writing you really need to do as a student or a professional, the experience of a regular writing practice will form a strong foundation for meeting your future writing challenges.

WORKS CITED

"Blog." *Wikipedia*. Web. 13 Oct 2010.

Csikszentmihalyi, Mihaly. *Flow: The Psychology of Optimal Experience*. New York: Harper, 1991. Print.

Gladwell, Malcolm. *Outliers: The Story of Success*. New York: Little, Brown and Company, 2008. Print.

Indiana University Center for Post Secondary Research. *National Survey of Student Engagement*. 2008. Print.

Pink, Daniel H. *Drive: The Surprising Truth About What Motivates Us*. New York: Riverhead, 2010. Print

Rhodes, John S. "The Human Behind Robot Wisdom: An interview with the power behind Robot Wisdom, Jorn Barger." *WebWord*. WebWord, 27 Sept. 1999. Web. 10 Sept. 2009.

Robinson, Ken. "Ken Robinson says schools kill creativity." *TED*. TED. 2006. Web.

—. "Sir Ken Robinson: Bring on the learning revolution!" *TED*. TED. 2010. Web

A Student's Guide to Collaborative Writing Technologies

Matt Barton and Karl Klint

Have you ever been asked to write a group paper or collaborate with your peers on an essay or research project?* Many students dread these assignments, knowing all too well the difficulties of scheduling meetings and making sure that each member does his or her fair share of the work. In the past, these assignments could be very difficult, but modern students have access to useful software that makes group work much easier to manage, even if your group members are unable to meet in person outside of class.

This chapter presents a scenario in which students use Web 2.0 social media technologies at each stage of the writing process. After the scenario, we give a breakdown of each tool and where to download it.

Scenario: The Research Paper

Madison and Dakota are first-year students at a community college. Their professor, Dr. Gonzales, has asked them to collaborate on a 12–15 page research paper on a "hot button issue" of their choice.

Dr. Gonzales has asked them to cite at least eight different sources and include a Works Cited page using MLA format.

Unfortunately, Madison and Dakota are commuters from different towns, and their full-time job schedules prevent their meeting in person outside of class. However, both of them have computers at home with Internet access.

When Dakota gets home late that evening, he logs into his Twitter account and begins to micro-blog on the topic. During the drive home he was listening to National Public Radio (NPR) and heard an interesting discussion about health care reform. His first post, or Tweet on the topic goes something like this: "All this talk about health care on the news—great topic for paper." Since Dakota is using Twitter, his messages must be short—only 140 characters! However, he can Tweet as often as he likes, so just before bed he adds another post: "I work full time and go to school. I am uninsured."

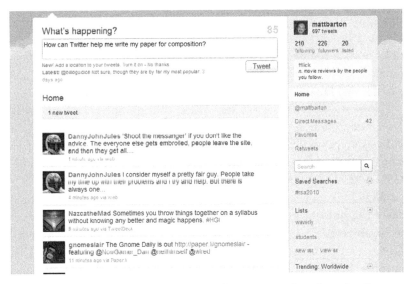

Fig. 1. Twitter is a great way to send brief messages to friends and colleagues. Many students use it to share information with their friends and classmates about their hobbies, social activities, classes, and assignments.

The next morning, Madison checks her email and finds an invitation from Dakota to join Twitter. Madison completes the registration process and selects the option to "follow" Dakota, so she will be notified when Dakota posts any more Tweets. She also notices the

RSS logo on Dakota's Twitter homepage, so she adds the feed to her Google Reader account. Now Dakota's Tweets will show up alongside her daily dose of news and blog posts. Since she has to go to work soon, Madison downloads the Twitter application for her mobile phone so that she can respond to Dakota during her breaks. For now, though, she replies to Dakota's Tweet with, "That sounds great! My mom has breast cancer and the family is really struggling."

Later that day Dakota sees Madison's response to his Tweet and also several replies from his other friends. One of them is Brittney, a friend at another school who plans to apply to medical school next year. Brittney tells him that the topic is very controversial and sends him a link to her blog that discusses the pros and cons of the "public option."

Dakota logs into his Facebook account and updates his status to read, "I am doing a paper on health care reform. Please help!" One of his friends, Darrin, is also online at the moment and pages him through Facebook chat. "Try Google Scholar to find sources for it! Here's a link." Dakota clicks on the link and finds all sorts of articles from academic journals about health care reform—and also how many times each of them has been cited. There are over a million and a half links! He soon realizes that he will need to narrow his topic.

However, Madison is one step ahead of him. She is now on break and finds time to send Dakota another Tweet: "Let's do it on why the bill needs a public option." Dakota tries another Google Scholar search using "public option" and finds fewer, yet more relevant articles. He replies, "Sounds good. I will work on finding articles."

Now Dakota needs a way to share articles with Madison. He could email the links or put them in his Tweets, but he wants a better way to organize them. He remembers Dr. Gonzales telling him about a Firefox extension called Zotero, which is designed for precisely that purpose. It will even generate a Works Cited page when they are done! Dakota installs the application. Now he is able to save the articles he finds on Google Scholar into Zotero and share them with whomever he wants. Dakota creates a public group on Zotero called "health care reform" and gives everyone permission to join it. This way, anyone on Zotero interested in the topic can add items to the group's library of citations.

Even though they've only talked face-to-face a few times, Dakota and Madison's research into public options is going well. The sheer

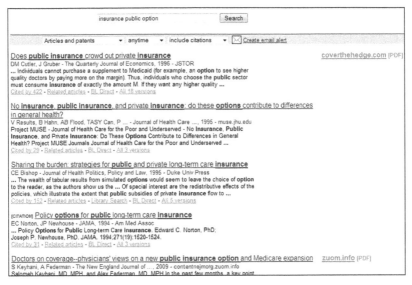

Fig. 2. Google Scholar is a lot like Google, but it searches academic, government, and legal documents. Some of the links it finds are freely or cheaply available online, but others are available only to paying members or subscribers. Before paying for access to an article, you should check to see if it is available at your school's library.

number of Tweets Dakota sends out is, unfortunately, starting to overwhelm Madison. Madison sends Dakota a Tweet that says, "Overwhelmed need to meet driving past your town thurs. U use doodle?"

Dakota hasn't used Doodle before, but discovers that this site is able to accomplish two things Dakota needs to do. First, Doodle helps people administer polls. Dakota has been looking for a way to set up polls at school for his disc golf league. He found a park between himself and campus that could fit a 12-hole disc golf course, but without any statistics to back up his claim that the area needs a disc golf course, the local park and recreational department won't even discuss the idea. Dakota also finds that Doodle connects to Microsoft Outlook, an email and calendar management tool used at many colleges. Dakota isn't a big fan of expensive software, but perhaps the Outlook connectivity will come in handy.

Outside of the polling option within Doodle, Dakota discovers where Madison was going with that last Tweet. Doodle offers a daily and weekly scheduler that can be accessed by many people. This is great because Dakota doesn't really want classmates to view his Outlook schedule. Up until this point, most of Madison and Dakota's interaction has been online and asynchronous. Asynchronous just means that they are communicating, but not at the same moment. Also, Madison's mom has started cancer treatment, and the hospital is near Dakota's apartment. Madison will be driving her mom to treatments at least once a week, but the appointments won't always be at the same time. Even though their school has a really nice course management system (such as Blackboard, D2L, Sakai, or Moodle), a synchronous Facebook chat helps Madison and Dakota decide to use Doodle to schedule meetings. This works wonderfully for both of them because they are able to share each other's schedule in detail. In short, Dakota was worried he might have to miss his Thursday night disc golf league, but he's able to show his league on the schedule. This eases his mind a bit.

Dakota and Madison now have a good idea of what they want to write about, but how will they draft their document? Dakota decides to open a Google Document. Google Docs is a tool that makes it easy to draft and collaborate online. Dakota shares the new file with Madison, and now they can draft and edit the document together. However, Dakota tries drafting an introduction and thesis statement, but ends up with a case of writer's block. He sends out another Tweet asking for help organizing his thoughts.

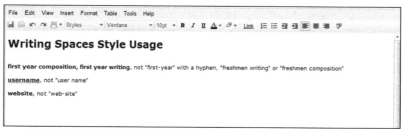

Fig. 3. Google Docs is a free, easy-to-use word processor that stores your documents online. You can then share them with friends and classmates. It's a much better solution for collaborative writing than emailing documents back and forth between group members.

Darrin sees the Tweet and suggests that Dakota use Mindomo, a free online mind-mapping tool. Mind maps will allow Dakota to see how his ideas are connected, and possibly find new ways they are related. Furthermore, he will be able to share his map with whomever he wants, and get feedback too. For the next few hours, Dakota works on a map, making topics and subtopics. He's having lots of fun, and eventually gets an idea—the debate over the public option seems to have a lot to do with business and politics. Some of the articles Dakota read argued that such a move would amount to socialism, with the government interfering in free trade. However, his research showed that similar arguments were made about Medicare and Social Security, which turned out to be very popular programs.

Dakota sends a link to his map to Madison. Later, Madison looks at the map and agrees with Dakota. Madison pulls up the Google Doc and drafts the thesis statement: "Congress should include a public option in its health care reform plan because similar policies worked out well in the past." She then expands the introduction by talking about the reform plan in general, then focuses on the arguments about the public option. She sets up the paper by mentioning Medicare and Social Security and how they faced similar opposition in Congress.

Madison needs some facts and quotations to support these arguments, so she pulls up Zotero and syncs with Dakota's links. When she logs in to Zotero, though, she finds that someone from Washington, D.C. has been there and suggested several new articles for the group to consider. The links all seem to be against the public option, but Madison still finds a few that may be useful for the project. She drafts long into the night.

When Dakota looks at the document the next morning, Madison has already drafted six pages. Now that they have a definite direction and good research, Dakota is easily able to finish up the draft. Using Zotero, he is able to add a correctly formatted MLA Works Cited page in just a few clicks.

After Madison and Dakota have gone through the draft to correct errors and smooth out the style, they decide to see if anyone else will review their paper. A few more eyes, after all, can only help iron out hidden issues they may have overlooked. Darrin replies to a Tweet that says, "Editing help wanted. Fresh eyes needed." He directs Madison and Dakota to the school's writing center. Neither had been aware of this, but the writing center's webpage lists online consultations as a type of service provided to students. Excited about this oportunity, Madison calls the writing center. She asks if she can email the paper to a tutor for review. Following writing center practices, the tutor explains that the staff won't necessarily correct a paper, but if Madison is willing to set up an online meeting, the tutor is willing to discuss the paper (and any errors they find) while talking. Also, this writing center uses an online document system that combines all the communication techniques found in both Google Docs and Skype. Though many different programs like this exist, this writing center is using Wimba.

While at the hospital, during one of her mom's appointments, Madison meets with Dakota so they can both sit in on the tutorial session. Besides allowing them to talk with the tutor, Wimba also allows the tutor, Dakota, and Madison to make marks, highlights, and changes to the paper. Though the tutor didn't correct the paper, useful comments are offered that cover everything from organization to grammar. Also, the tutor has been trained to refrain from giving compliments about student papers (tutors are taught to not pass judgment), but only minor stylistic and grammatical changes show up during the tutorial. In the beginning, both Dakota and Madison had doubts about working online to construct this paper. Now, all those worries are gone.

While online with the writing center tutor, Dakota checks Doodle and notices that Madison will be driving her mom to four more medical appointments this week. He tells Madison he will make the needed changes and submit the final draft. Their instructor, Dr. Gonzales, has set up a dropbox using the college's course management system, so after considering the tutor's suggestions, and giving the paper one last edit and proofread, Dakota submits the file.

A week later, Dr. Gonzales returns their now graded paper through the course management system. Madison and Dakota have earned an A on their paper! It wasn't easy, but taking the time to learn so many useful tools made the difference. Dakota couldn't wait to get home and send a Tweet out about their achievement.

Now let's break down the tools Madison and Dakota used at each stage of their writing process.

PREWRITING TOOLS

Dakota and Madison used all sorts of social media tools to plan their paper. Remember that an important part of writing happens before you actually start drafting. Discussing your project and ideas with other people can help you overcome writer's block and begin visualizing what your paper will look like.

The first tool Dakota and Madison employed was Twitter, a free microblogging tool (http://twitter.com). The definition of blog varies, but it's easy to think of a blog as a sort of online diary or journal that you share with your friends (or the wider world). Blogs vary widely in content and style, and individual posts range from a few sentences to several pages, though many people stop reading blog entries after about three to five paragraphs because of the way in which weblogs are laid out on the screen. In short, it is easier to move on to another webpage then scroll down through a five-page blog entry.

Twitter, which limits posts to only 140 characters, is a microblogging tool. Whereas a typical blog post might take several minutes to an hour to compose, a post—or Tweet—on Twitter should only take a minute or less to compose, even if you're composing on a mobile phone. Twitter has a large community, and many choose to "follow," or receive updates, of other Twitter users. This ability is especially handy if you follow people in your areas of interest, such as fellow skateboarders or *Twilight* fans. Since these folks will probably be Tweeting about these topics, you can find them with Twitter's built-in search tool. Likewise, if you Tweet on certain topics, chances are others will find and follow you. For obvious reasons, Twitter works best for quick updates and short messages, such as where you are or what you are doing at the moment.

Madison took advantage of RSS feeds to kept tabs on Twitter and several other applications Dakota was using. An RSS feed is a list of updates automatically generated by a blog or website. RSS feeds are handy because they save you time. Instead of having to visit a bunch of different blogs and websites to stay current, you can subscribe to all of their RSS feeds and have them fed into an application like Google Reader (http://www.google.com/reader). Google Reader is a free RSS feed manager that keeps track of your feeds for you. You can use tools like Google Reader to stay abreast of activities occurring across a very broad array of online applications. Most modern sites offer RSS feeds, and some offer many specialized feeds. In most cases, subscribing to them is as simple as clicking on the bright orange RSS icon.

Dakota also used Facebook (http://facebook.com), a popular social networking site originally designed for college students. While many students use Facebook to keep in touch with friends or to find parties, you can also use it to find study partners or to get help with your homework. You can do this by posting status updates or messages to

Fig. 4. Google Reader is an RSS Feed Reader with a large variety of features. You can use it to quickly find and share blog posts and news items with your friends and classmates, as well as take notes and organize important information.

your wall (or your friends' walls). Facebook Chat is a synchronous tool, which means that you have to be online at the same time as your friend to use it. There are many other tools that allow for synchronous chatting, such as AOL Instant Messenger (AIM) or Google Talk. If you have a webcam and a microphone you could use a program such as Skype (http://skype.com) to connect through a VOIP-based (Voice Over Internet Protocol) system. VOIP-based programs like Skype will allow you see each other, talk to each other, and also do basic instant messaging, if you have a high-speed Internet connection.

The duo also used Zotero (http://zotero.org), a free plugin for Firefox, an Internet browser. Zotero is a great tool for writing research papers because it helps you find sources, track them, and correctly cite them in your paper. The new version of Zotero lets you sync your sources online, so that you can access them from any computer (and share access with your friends or anyone else). Thus, if you wrote a paper using Zotero, you could easily share the fruits of your research with other students—or, find other people doing similar work and borrow their sources. Zotero makes research easier because you aren't just doing all the work yourself. Sharing makes life easier for everyone!

When scheduling became an issue, Dakota and Madison turned to Doodle (http://www.doodle.com/). In addition to allowing Dakota and Madison to gain a cohesive working schedule off campus, Doodle would have allowed them to generate statistics through simple polls. An alternative calendar option would have been Google Calendar, another free tool that lets you create a calendar of events and share it with whomever you want. If a team is using the same calendar, the members can not only see the schedule, but can also add their own events and details. Calendars such as these can alleviate stress by allowing users to easily see the times everyone else is available.

Finally, Dakota and Madison needed a way to collaboratively brainstorm, or to map out their ideas. They could have relied on text to do this, but decided instead to use Mindomo (http://mindomo. com), one of many freely available mind-mapping tools. Such tools allow you to put your ideas in small boxes, then connect other boxes and boxes on those. The idea is to organize your ideas, studying the relationships and discovering connections that you might not have realized. Although mind maps may not help everyone, they can be quite effective for people who prefer to think visually. One advantage of Mindomo is that it is hosted online and has built-in features for sharing and collaboration, making it ideal for group projects.

DRAFTING AND EDITING TOOLS: GOOGLE DOCS, ETHERPAD, AND ZOTERO

One approach to drafting the essay might have been for each of the writers to take turns, drafting a paragraph or two and then emailing the document back and forth. However, this approach creates bottlenecks, or periods during which one of the authors is sitting around waiting for the other author to get done. There is also a problem of making sure each author is working with the latest version of the document; it's easy to get mixed up.

Google Docs (http://docs.google.com) solves these problems by hosting documents online. This feature allows authors to share their documents, either with the world or with particular people, who can be invited strictly as viewers (able to read but not edit) or as co-authors. Authors using Google Docs can work on a document at any time, without worrying about bottlenecks or whether they're working on the latest version.

The tutor at the writing center was able to work with Madison and Dakota's paper in this way. Though this writing center used Wimba to connect with students online, other writing centers may use different programs that allow for the same tutor-client connections. Instead of using Google Docs, writing centers often pay for a similar service because a program like Wimba may also generate tutor session statistics for the writing center. This helps prove that the tutors are indeed a useful university offering. For the needs of most people, though, Google Docs will easily fulfill your collaborative writing needs.

It is possible to download a Google Document in a format suitable for word processors, like Microsoft Word (.docx) or Open Office (.odt), as well as more universal formats like .rtf and .pdf. You should always check with your teacher to see which file formats are acceptable.

There are, of course, alternatives to Google Docs, such as Buzzword (http://www.adobe.com/acom/buzzword/), Zoho (http://www.zoho.com/), and Etherpad (http://etherpad.com). Etherpad allows users to edit a document in real-time; that is, whatever you type will instantly show up on your partner's computer. Each partner's text is a different color, making it easy to keep each other's contributions straight. Etherpad would be a good choice if your group members wanted to work on a document simultaneously. The original Etherpad site has been shutdown, but Google has acquired the code and released it as open source. Now you can access Etherpad on several sites, including http://piratepad.net and http://typewith.me.

Zotero is a great tool for finding and keeping track of your outside sources, but it can also generate a Works Cited page or bibliography for you. There are also Zotero plugins for Microsoft Word and Open Office that will manage your in-text citations or footnotes.

Concluding Thoughts

Not all students are as tech savvy as Dakota and Madison, and everyone finds some tools more useful than others. Hopefully this chapter has given you some ideas and encouraged you to experiment with social media tools on your next writing assignment. The key thing to remember about these tools is their social nature—instead of working alone, you will be part of a vast network of other writers. Many of these writers will happily share their ideas or research with you, and many others might enjoy or benefit from seeing your work. In any case, remember to treat others with respect and follow any posted rules of conduct. Be friendly, polite, and helpful to others, even if you know you will never meet them in person.

Learning to write as a group can be a daunting and frustrating process, but social media tools can make a difference. Madison and Dakota were both hard working students who wanted to earn an A on their project. You may have a group member or two who cares much less about success. Social media tools like Google Docs can track individual contributions, so at the end of the process you will have a record of who did what. Sometimes, just being able to see what the other group members are doing (as well as receiving regular updates via email) is enough to spur a deadweight partner into action. If all else fails, though, at least you will have solid proof of your partner's lack of effort.

When you are done with your project, you might want to consider sharing your work with others. A simple way to do that would be to share your Google Doc with the world, so that other students (or anyone else) can find and read it. Zotero will let you share your research. Indeed, almost every tool we discussed in this chapter has a sharing feature. Although it's possible to keep everything private, or just between you and your group members, sharing your work is a good way to enrich the community and make new friends.

There are new social media tools, features, and concepts being developed every day, and chances are that by the time you read this chapter, many things will have changed. However, you shouldn't let that fact prevent you from experimenting with new tools or seeking ways to enhance or simplify your writing. Take the time to learn about new tools and be willing to experiment with them.

DISCUSSION

1. Security is always an issue when using any website or online software. What are some good habits and strategies you can use to safeguard private information when using sites like Twitter and Facebook?

2. By the time you read this, there will probably be many new and exciting writing and collaboration technologies. What are some convenient ways to stay current?

3. Collaboration can be challenging even under ideal circumstances. What are some good ways to avoid losing work to

power outages, corrupt files, or interruptions in your Internet service?

4. Not all students are tech savvy, but that doesn't mean they can't be good group members. What are some good ways to bridge the gap between the tech experts and novices in a group?

SOFTWARE REFERENCED

Doodle. Doodle AG. Available at http://www.doodle.com/.

Etherpad. Google. Available at http://etherpad.org/.

Facebook. Facebook, Inc. Available at http://facebook.com/.

Google Docs. Google. Available at http://docs.google.com/.

Google Reader. Google. Available at http://reader.google.com/.

Google Scholar Beta. Google. Available at http://scholar.google.com/.

Mindomo. Expert Software Applications. Available at http://www.mindomo.com/.

Twitter. Twitter, Inc. Available at http://twitter.com/.

Zotero. Center for History and New Media at George Mason University. Available at http://zotero.org/.

Beyond Black on White: Document Design and Formatting in the Writing Classroom

Michael J. Klein and Kristi L. Shackelford

You've received your first assignment in a college writing course.[*] You've created an outline, done the necessary research, and written a first draft of your paper. Now it's time for you to revise your work so you can submit the paper. However, writing a paper for a course involves more than simply generating content and turning it into your instructor. Equally important as the words you write is how the appearance of your document influences the way readers interpret your ideas.

Most people think of design as the arrangement of images on the page. This is only half true: Graphics can convey concepts that you can't express in writing. If you were writing an article about an oil spill and the damage it caused, one powerful photograph could make your point more persuasively than pages of writing. Good document design integrates the words on the page with appropriate imagery to fully illustrate your meaning. An image of the Deep Horizon oil spill won't have the same impact if the image isn't coupled with a sentence about the scope of the spill.

An often-overlooked element of design is the visual treatment of text itself. In this definition of text, text does not include your word choice or the structure of your argument. Instead, it refers to the look of the words on the page. Are all the fonts the same? Are key ideas written in a text larger than other text? Are some words in bold? All of these choices influence the way your document looks and is perceived by your readers. Depending on the type of paper your instructor has assigned and the preparation rules or style guide required, subtle variations in text might be your only design option.

In a typical first year writing course, you'll be focusing—of course—on writing. If the intent of writing is to communicate an idea, the way you present your writing is also important. You can greatly improve a standard research paper on climate change with the addition of an image showing differences in ice caps over a period of years. You can strengthen data supporting your position in an opinion paper if you present it in a graph rather than a narrative format. However, include graphics in written assignments with care: they should supplement, not replace, your writing. When you are creating, don't think of design features as only images. Remember that visual design applies to the style of the text you use to convey ideas. The remainder of this chapter focuses on the use of text as a design element.

What You Should Know about Design Choices and Elements

You can talk about design in a multitude of ways. What some designers call white space, for example, others call negative space. In both cases, they are referring to areas of a page free from text or objects, such as the white space that makes up the margins around the text of this paragraph. A designer may talk about the use of alignment in a design, while someone else will describe how textual elements "line up" on a page. All theories and methods of design include the same basic ideas, just expressed in different terms. The names of elements on a page are much less important than their function. The definitions below will help you understand the way we use these terms.

Text and Type

Typeface refers to the look of your text. It typically includes the font family (e.g., Times New Roman), the type size (e.g., 12 point) and type emphasis (e.g., bold). Spacing is the amount of space around a line of text within a document. The amount of space between lines of text is called leading (pronounced *led*) or line spacing. Leading is typically the size of the font plus two points. For example, standard leading for 12-point type is 14 points, indicated as 12/14 point; this paragraph uses 11 point Adobe Garamond Pro with 13.2 point leading. Increasing the amount of leading, or size of line spacing, can increase readability. Large amounts of text are often set with a leading of twice the text (12/24 point), also called double-spacing.

Images

The visual elements of a design range from simple boxes to the use of color photographs. Designers often use the term "images" to refer to the wide range of visual elements available—photographs, line drawings, technical illustrations, graphs, charts, and so on. Not all images are appropriate for all uses. A color photo of the beach, for instance, may have more persuasive power than a black-and-white drawing because the photograph evokes a more complete and personal reaction. A technical illustration that allows a reader to see the inside of a device can demonstrate the proper assembly of equipment in more detail than an actual photograph. In some cases, though, images can distract from the meaning of your text. You should not include random clip art of a tree, for example, to supplement a paper on the importance of environmental sustainability. In contrast, you may strengthen your position on environmental sustainability with a graph showing the cumulative effects of non-recycled materials.

Design Elements

Like the combination of text and images, the integration of four key design elements—Contrast, Repetition, Alignment and Proximity— gives a design power. You can remember these elements by the acronym CRAP. Don't let the name influence you, though—following these principles is one of the best ways to ensure your document looks its best. It is sometimes difficult to differentiate among these concepts because they influence each other.

Contrast

Contrast refers to the visual differences in elements on a page. These differences highlight the significance of the individual items, as well as draw the reader's attention to different areas of a page. In a magazine layout, for example, the largest photograph is more noticeable because of its larger size in comparison to others on a spread. Color in a design can also provide noticeable contrast.

In text, you see contrast through different uses of formatting options. This might include choosing different typefaces to visually separate headings from your main text. Contrast may also be visible in the differing sizes or emphasis applied to a text. If you apply bold formatting to keywords in your document, they stand out from others and indicate that they are significant. If every other word in your document is bold, however, the effect of the contrast is lost. A similar effect occurs when you overuse a highlighter when marking a textbook: important information gets lost rather than being easier to find.

Look at the first page of this chapter. You can immediately see the name "Document Design" and recognize that it is the title of the chapter. Your eye is immediately drawn to it because it is the biggest item on the page. Just below the title, the authors' names are in smaller, italicized text. The contrast between the size and emphasis in the two lines of text quickly illustrates that they are providing different information.

Repetition

Repetition involves the use of consistency to visually group multiple items that express similar ideas or are somehow related. You can apply this design element to graphics, including the use of shapes and color. For example, many of your textbooks may include a section summarizing key ideas from the text. By placing all summaries in a similarly shaped box or highlighted by the same color, you can tell that these items have something in common. Once you realize that all summaries in your political science textbook are in green boxes, you can find them at glance.

You can apply repetition simply by formatting text in different ways. When you look at a restaurant menu, you'll see that the larger categories—like "Appetizers" and "Desserts"—are presented in the same font and size as each other, which is different from the listing of the food items themselves. This repeated format shows that those categories are equivalent. It also indicates that a new section is beginning, as do the headings that divide sections of this chapter. In papers written for a class, you express repetition in text primarily through placement, such as always putting page numbers in the same place on the page. On a Works Cited page, the organization of citation materials (such as the author's name and book title) makes information easier to locate. Repetition makes your intent more obvious to readers.

Repetition lets you quickly glance through this book and find information, even in sections you haven't already read. To find the first page of a chapter, you look for a large title with lots of white space above it. If you're looking for a specific page in the book, you know to look at the outside corners to locate the page numbers.

Alignment

In design, alignment refers to the placement of elements on a page. While everything on a page is aligned in that it has been placed somewhere, some alignment strategies are better than others. You can think of it as asking a sick friend, "Do you have a temperature?" Of course, everyone has a temperature; what you're asking is if your friend has an elevated or abnormal temperature. In the same way, when document designers talk about alignment, they typically mean consistent alignment. For example, text that is left justified or graphics that run along the edge of the page are considered properly aligned.

Aligning elements creates a cleaner, more attractive design and emphasizes the consistency of information on a page. Alignment also helps readers access and process information in a publication. Appropriately aligned text clarifies for the reader where ideas begin and end. It also increases readability by allowing the reader's eye to return to a consistent location on the page while reading. Breaking the alignment scheme is also a valuable design tool. When a block quote is indented, it is quickly apparent that the text has a slightly different meaning than the text above and below it.

The text alignment throughout this chapter indicates when a topic is changing and how a large piece of text (the chapter) can be broken into smaller chunks (the sections). Main headings within the text are centered over justified body text. To find the idea you're looking for, you can look for the centered text and know that a new idea is being introduced.

Proximity

Proximity is the grouping of elements that have something in common. Often a layout involves a single idea, and the designer uses the entire page to place thematically related text and graphics. When multiple ideas are included on a single page, the reader can tell which are related based on how close—or far—they are from each other. An obvious example is a box including a photo and its caption.

In academic writing and formatting, the placement of text often illustrates proximity. You place headings that identify the content of a section directly above that section, cuing the reader to a shift. This proximity also allows readers to quickly find related information based on the heading of a section.

Look at the image labeled as Fig. 1. As soon as you see the graphic, you can look immediately below it, see what it is named and why it is included. What if that label was on the next page? Placing related elements together is an efficient way to make sure they are properly understood.

For More Information

Design texts aren't just for professional designers! You can find examples of the principles discussed here in a variety of design books. Look for a basic book that covers designing with images and text to learn more. A good one to start with is Robin Williams *Non-Designer's Design Book;* many of the ideas in this chapter are based on ones presented in her book.

How You Can Apply These Design Principles

Incorporating design principles into a publication has an immediate and compelling effect. Even text-heavy documents, such as academic papers or resumes, become more appealing and comprehensible with even minor restructuring.

The example in Fig. 1 shows an unformatted resume. The lack of repetition, contrast, alignment, and proximity make the document unattractive as well as difficult to follow. There is no way to easily distinguish important information, like the applicant's name and contact information. Sections run together, and no key ideas are clear.

Fig. 2 shows the same content using the previously discussed design elements. The document is more visually appealing as well as being easier to review. Each individual design principle is involved, and their combination leads to a stronger design.

Matthew J. Kraft
225 Ingram Road
Harrisonburg, VA 22807
kraft@hotmail.com
555-555-4321

Education2008 – Bachelor of Arts, University of Arizona, Tucson, AZ Major: Creative
Writing   Minor in Political Science
Courses: Creative Writing Workshop, Genre Theories, Technology and Writing,
Publication Management

2004 – Honors Diploma
University High School, Phoenix, AZ

Employment2007 – current   Editorial Assistant, *Political Science Summary*,
Tucson, AZ
                                Managed day-to-day activities of a monthly journal in political
                                science. Tracked manuscript submissions and kept in contact with
                                authors and publisher.
2006 – 2007   Graphic Design Intern, University of Arizona Marketing and
Communications, Tucson, AZ
                                Designed and produced marketing brochures, pamphlets, and
                                catalogs. Maintained web sites for participating clients.
2002 – 2004   Server, Phoenix Café, Phoenix, AZ
                                Took customer orders, managed nightly restaurant closing,
                                prepared bank deposits

Software Skills

Adobe: InDesign, Illustrator, Dreamweaver

Microsoft: Word, Excel, PowerPoint

Operating Systems: Macintosh and Windows

Clubs and Organizations

Alpha Beta Fraternity (President)

Student Ambassadors

Fig. 1. An unformatted resume.

Repetition is shown through the consistent emphasis and text used in the various sections of the resume. There is contrast between the size of the author's name and the contact information, clearly highlighting the most significant information. School and business names shown in bold create strong contrast within lines of text. Text is firmly and consistently aligned. Text is easy to read from the left justification, and the author's name is highlighted as the only centered text on the page. Proximity makes finding information simple, as section headings are placed directly above their supporting information.

Mathew J. Kraft

225 Ingram Road   kraft@hotmail.com
Harrisonburg, VA 22807   555-555-4321

Education

2008 – Bachelor of Arts, **University of Arizona**, Tucson, AZ
    Major: Creative Writing   Minor: Political Science
    Courses: Creative Writing Workshop, Genre Theories, Technology and Writing,
    Publication Management

2004 – Honors Diploma, **University High School**, Phoenix, AZ

Employment

2007 – current   Editorial Assistant, **Political Science Summary**, Tucson, AZ
    • Managed day-to-day activities of a monthly journal in political
      science.
    • Tracked manuscript submissions and kept in contact with authors
      and publisher.

2006 – 2007   Graphic Design Intern, **University of Arizona Marketing and
                   Communications**, Tucson, AZ
    • Designed and produced marketing brochures, pamphlets, and
      catalogs.
    • Maintained web sites for participating clients.

2002 – 2004   Server, **Phoenix Café**, Phoenix, AZ
    • Took customer orders
    • Managed nightly restaurant closing
    • Prepared bank deposits

Software Skills

    Adobe: InDesign, Illustrator, Dreamweaver
    Microsoft: Word, Excel, PowerPoint
    Operating Systems: Macintosh and Windows

Clubs and Organizations

    • Alpha Beta Fraternity (President)
    • Student Ambassadors

Fig. 2. A formatted resume.

The Basics of Style Guides

Style guides are collections of conventions on everything from word choice to format gathered into one place and used in writing. Their primary purpose is to ensure that all documents in a given environment adhere to a certain look and consistent use of language, but they serve a much broader purpose.

Style guides eliminate the guesswork in areas of writing that have multiple options. For example, both advisor and adviser are accurate spellings of a word; a style guide specifies which instance is preferred for the document you are writing. Style guides assure consistency in an organization's publications, such as placing the titles and page numbers in the same area of the page for all documents. Finally, they make reading and comprehension easier for the audience by presenting similar information in similar ways. Readers who want to view the source material you've used in a paper, for example, will refer to your list of authors and publications. The format and even the title of this section will vary depending on the style guide you've chosen. The "Works Cited" or "Reference" pages provide the information on all referenced documents in a presentation different from the main text, making it easy to identify.

Most academic disciplines follow a style guide. In addition, many companies and academic institutions establish their own style guides to supplement established style guides. In most writing courses, as well as other courses in the humanities, we use the Modern Language Association (MLA) style.

A Primer on MLA Style

The Modern Language Association produced their first "MLA style sheet" in 1951 as a way to ensure consistency within documents shared in the academic community. The style sheet evolved into the first edition of the *MLA Handbook* in 1977. Now in its seventh edition, the *MLA Handbook* is the primary source for stylistic choices made in writing for the humanities.

Style guides reflect the items of importance in writing for a particular community. The types and structure in information shown in the MLA style guide differ from those in other disciplines. For example, the American Psychological Association (APA)—used by many of the sciences—has its own style guide. Even popular media, including newspapers and magazines have their own style guide: the Associate Press (AP) guide.

Writers using a specific style guide will emphasize different pieces of information. For example, citations in MLA emphasize the author as primary focus, while the APA style guide features dates (see Fig. 3).

Style guides are dynamic documents, and they change to reflect evolutions in technology for both research and production. When MLA style was first developed, it did not include a style for referencing

MLA Style In-Text Citation

Johnson felt that "there was a lack of trust amongst people when it came to money" (234).

Some researchers argue that money creates "a lack of trust amongst people" (Johnson 234).

MLA Style Works Cited

Crowley, Sharon, and Debra Hawhee. *Ancient Rhetorics for Contemporary Students*. 3rd ed. New York: Pearson Education, 2004.

APA Style In-Text Citation

Johnson (2003) felt that "there was a lack of trust amongst people when it came to money" (p. 234).

Some researchers argue that money creates "a lack of trust amongst people" (Johnson, 2003, p.234).

APA Style Reference

Crowley, S. & Hawhee, D. (2004). *Ancient rhetorics for contemporary students*. (3rd ed.) New York, NY: Pearson Education.

Fig. 3. MLA and APA emphasize different citation elements.

Internet sources. As online media became an increasingly significant means of sharing resources, the style guide was adapted to incorporate references for Web sites, online journals, and print journals retrieved online. Changes in production options for writers and publishers also influenced changes to style guides. When authors typed papers using traditional typewriters, they were unable to use italics to indicate the name of a publication; instead, the underlining of text indicated these documents. Modern word processing programs allow the author to control type at a much more precise level, allowing italics as well as control of spacing and line breaks.

Like most style guides, MLA style changes over time. The guidelines presented here are appropriate for the seventh edition of the MLA Style Guide. You should check to make sure you are using the most current version. In the college courses you take, your individual instructors may impose additional style choices or ones that conflict with the style guide for the academic discipline. Be sure to follow the special style instructions for the assignments in that course.

APPLYING MLA STYLE IN YOUR OWN PAPERS

The way you use words and place text on a page influence the audience's ability to comprehend information. Much the way the shape of a stop sign indicates the same meaning as "STOP" to a driver, readers understand information in part through its placement and format. As a result, there is consistency among the papers submitted within a writing classroom and established journals in an academic field. This consistency allows readers to become accustomed to certain conventions and increases readability. When a professor reviews multiple papers formatted in the same way, for example, she can easily find the author's name and class section on all of the papers. Likewise, students in an English class will be able to find a source from the information given in an academic journal because they can understand in-text citation and bibliographic reference.

MLA-formatted papers for a class rarely include graphic elements, like illustrations or tables. In fact, MLA style limits the use of design in formatting to ensure that the focus remains on the text. Settings specified by MLA incorporate the design principles reviewed above. The remainder of the chapter discusses MLA formatting of academic papers, like the research papers you'll develop in your writing classes, as opposed to writing for publication, such as professional journals.

The primary use of repetition in MLA format is to indicate that text formatted in the same way throughout a paper signifies a similar use. Contrast is important in separating distinct sections of a paper from one another. Alignment in MLA increases readability by providing a common starting point for the reader. Proximity helps readers follow related ideas. For example, section headers are located directly over the text they introduce, allowing readers to quickly find information.

Margins

Margins are the distance from the edge of the paper to where the text starts. They define the amount of white space around the text on the page. They are important because they emphasize the text through contrast (black text on a white page) and increase readability through consistent alignment (headings and text line up to the left margin). Margins also contribute to readability by providing a place for the reader's eyes to rest: they ensure appropriate white space to prevent a page from becoming too dense with text.

The MLA style guide requires specific margins of one inch (1") on all four sides of a page (see Fig. 4).

See section 4.1 of the *MLA Handbook* for information on margins.

Fig. 4. The first page of a paper formatted according to MLA style.

Typeface and Spacing

Appropriate typeface usage involves all design elements. The repetition of a single font throughout a document shows the reader that each section of the paper is part of a single whole. The strong visual color contrast of black text on a white background increases readability. Black text, for example, is easier to read than gray text, a difference you may notice when your printer is low on ink. Alignment indicates a separation of ideas or the introduction of a new concept. The title of the paper centered over the left-aligned text shows the beginning of the paper's content. The placement of section titles illustrates proximity. Each one is adjacent to its respective text directly above the first paragraph of a section.

MLA requires a serif font (like Times New Roman) in 12-point type. A serif font is one that has edges or "feet" on the ends of letters. A sans-serif font (like Arial) is straighter, without edges or flares as part of its shape. Serif fonts are traditionally easier to read, though this distinction has decreased as desktop publishing programs and font qualities have improved.

All text, from the initial header through the reference page, must be double-spaced (see Fig. 5). There is no additional spacing before or after headings. Each new paragraph is indented by ½ inch. The consistent spacing within the document makes reading easier as well as providing a reviewer with room for notes. The indention of each paragraph clearly indicates the beginning of a new idea.

See section 4.2 of the *MLA Handbook* for information on typeface and spacing.

Title and Headings

A title and internal headings help to separate the body of the paper into smaller, more specific, sections. They break text into shorter, more readable sections, or chunk information in the paper into reasonable portions. In addition, headings allow the reader to quickly skim through a document in search of specific ideas. Headings are described in levels, meaning their hierarchal structure in the paper. A second level heading must follow a first level heading. For example, after reading this entire chapter, you can easily find information on a specific element by looking for the appropriate heading.

Within MLA style, the title refers to the entire paper, while headings refer to individual sections within the paper. The contrast in MLA titles and headings comes mainly from alignment. Both students writing in the classroom and professionals writing for publication use MLA style. Limiting the amount of formatting—like adding italics or bold for emphasis—and focusing on alignment helps ensure that headings remain consistent when different fonts are used. The title is centered over the main text; headings are left justified over body text that is indented (see Fig. 5).

See section 4.3 of the *MLA Handbook* for information on titles and headings.

Fig. 5. A page formatted in MLA style showing double-spacing and a section heading.

Headers and Page Numbers

Headers are a user service, providing information to readers regarding their location in the text. The header includes the author's last name and the page number (see Fig. 4). Because the header information is formatted consistently and placed in the exact location on each page, this use of repetition helps readers easily find and identify document information.

On the initial page of a research paper, the header also includes the author's name, the date of submission, course instructor's name and course designation, usually left justified (see Fig. 4). This information, but not its placement, may vary depending on your course. Always check with your professor or refer to handouts provided in class for specifics.

Subsequent pages of the paper require that the author's last name and page number be placed in the upper, right-hand corner of the page, one-half inch (0.5") from the top edge of the page and one inch (1") from the right edge of the paper.

See section 4.4 of the *MLA Handbook* for information on page numbers.

Illustrations

Illustrations, including photographs, line drawings, maps, or graphs, help your readers better understand the information you are communicating. Sometimes illustrations support the function of the text. For example, we use the illustrations in this chapter to help you better understand the concepts we are writing about. Understanding the importance of graphics would be much harder with no illustrations as support. In other instances, the illustrations themselves are the primary pieces of information. For instance, a simple graph can be far more dramatic and comprehensible than a long paragraph full of numbers and percentages.

With MLA style, illustrations should be labeled *Figure* (usually abbreviated as *Fig.*), numbered consecutively, and given a brief caption following the label. As we have done with the illustrations in this chapter, the caption should readily identify the key feature of the illustration. Place the illustration as close as possible to the text where you first reference it to help readers understand why you included it.

Writers frequently use illustrations created by others to supplement their writing. If you find an image on a website, you cannot use it without permission. And while some websites explicitly give permission to use their images, you must still cite the source in your own work.

While you can use others' properly attributed illustrations, sometimes you will create the illustrations yourself. For example, you may want to capture an image of your computer's desktop to add to a document about computer systems. To copy a screen shot of your computer to the clipboard, press <Ctrl-Shift-Command> (Apple)-3 on Mac OS X or <Print Screen> on Windows. Once on the clipboard, the image will be available for you to manipulate with an image editing software or paste unaltered into almost any type of graphics program.

While some images may already be exactly the way you need them, most of the time you will need to make changes to images before you can use them. Two free image editing software packages are GIMP—the GNU Image Manipulation Program—for Mac OS X and Windows systems (available at <http://www.gimp.org/>) and Paint.NET for use only on Windows systems (available at <getpaint.net>).

Other things to remember when using illustrations:

- *Always use visuals of good quality.* A bad illustration can distract your reader and lessen the credibility of your argument.
- *Don't distort the image.* Keep the image in proportion by holding the <Shift> key as you are adjusting the image in your word processor.
- *Make sure the image is of the right quality and resolution.* An image that looks great on a website may not look as good when printed. Check the resolution of the image before enlarging it so there is no loss of quality.
- *Use the image at the appropriate size.* Don't try to force a full-page PowerPoint slide into a one-inch square space.
- *Crop images to remove extraneous material.* Keep the focus on the important part of the illustration, just like you do with text. For example, if including a web browser screenshot of a web page in a paper, readers do not need to see the browser window frame or your favorites/bookmarks menu in the visual used in the document.
- See section 4.5 of the *MLA Handbook* for information on working with illustrations.

Conclusion

While not every class, assignment or topic lends itself to the inclusion of graphics, you can still design your documents to be appealing to your reader. Good design choices can also make your document more accessible to your readers. A clean design with graphic and typographical indicators of content gives your readers more opportunities to engage with and understand your intention.

Style guides define typographical and design rules for you as a writer and a reader. MLA is the most commonly used style guide in first year writing, but most disciplines have their own. All style guides answer the questions you commonly encounter as a writer—Should page numbers be at the top or bottom of the page? How do I cite an article from a magazine's Web site? When you answer these questions, you can concentrate on the writing itself and developing your ideas. As a reader, you will be able to identify an established style and use it to your advantage. Finding the information you want (paper topics, authors cited) is easier when you know where to look (headings, reference pages). While the reasoning behind the rules in a style guide may not be intuitive, following them leads to better-designed documents.

DISCUSSION

1. What style guides have you used in the past? How did following a style guide influence your writing? In what different writing situations do you think a style guide would be most effective? Least effective?
2. In what ways does the appearance of a document affect your perception of the message and of the author?
3. How can you integrate the design elements of contrast, repetition, alignment and proximity into class assignments? What documents would benefit most from good design principles?
4. How much value does including an image add to a traditional academic paper? What types of images do you think are appropriate? In what ways can images detract from the impact or intent of an academic paper?

WORKS CITED

Modern Language Association of America. *The MLA Handbook for Writers of Research Papers.* 7th ed. New York: MLA, 2009. Print.

Contributors

Matt Barton, Associate Professor of English at St. Cloud State University, teaches courses in composition, rhetoric, and new media. He has published three books: *Dungeons & Desktops*, *Vintage Games* (co-authored with Bill Loguidice), and *Wiki Writing* (co-edited with Bob Cummings).

Janet Boyd, Assistant Professor in the Writing Program at Fairleigh Dickinson, teaches first year writing and serves as the coordinator of both the writing studio and the developmental writing courses. She has published in the *Journal of Basic Writing*.

Michael Bunn has a PhD from the joint program in English & Education at the University of Michigan and an MFA in Creative Writing from the University of Pittsburgh. He has been teaching a variety of collegiate writing classes for ten years and is particularly interested in the intersections between the processes of reading and writing.

Colin Charlton, Assistant Professor of Rhetoric & Composition and the Developmental English Coordinator at the University of Texas Pan American, teaches classes in first year writing, rhetorical theory and invention, and innovative technology. He also runs an iPad-based reading & writing studio.

Gita DasBender, Senior Faculty Associate and Coordinator for Second Language Writing in the English Department's Writing Program at Seton Hall University, teaches freshman and advanced writing. Her research interests include second language writing assessment, assignment sequencing, language and literacy history of generation 1.5 students, and directed self-placement.

Dana Lynn Driscoll, Assistant Professor in Writing and Rhetoric at Oakland University, teaches first year composition and upper division courses in peer tutoring, global rhetoric, research, and literacy and technology. Her research interests include research methods, transfer of learning, and metacognitive aspects of learning to write.

William Duffy is a PhD candidate in English at the University of North Carolina at Greensboro. His most recent essay, about the rhetoric of settlement worker Jane Addams, is forthcoming in *Rhetoric Review.*

Cynthia R. Haller is an associate professor of English at York College, City University of New York. She has also served as acting dean of humanities and social sciences, writing across the curriculum coordinator, and writing center director. Her research has appeared in *Written Communication, Technical Communication Quarterly,* and the *Journal of Engineering Education.* Currently, she is engaged with projects on student research writing and the rhetoric of agriculture, food studies, and the environment.

Rebecca Ingalls, Assistant Professor in the Department of English and Philosophy at Drexel University, specializes in composition and rhetoric. Her work may be found in *The Review of Education, Pedagogy, and Cultural Studies; Academe; inventio; The Journal of Teaching Writing* (forthcoming); *POROI* (forthcoming); and *The Journal of Popular Culture* (forthcoming). She is currently working with colleagues on an edited collection on plagiarism.

Seth Kahn, Associate Professor of English at West Chester University of Pennsylvania, has published articles on ethnographic writing pedagogy in *Composition Studies and Lore: An E-Journal for Teachers of Writing* and served for several years as co-chair of the qualitative research network at Conference on College Composition and Communication. His most recent publication is a co-edited collection titled *Activism and Rhetoric: Theories and Contexts for Political Engagement* (Routledge 2010).

Michael J. Klein, Assistant Professor of Writing, Rhetoric, and Technical Communication at James Madison University, teaches courses in first year composition, technical communication, and publications management.

Karl Russell Klint, a recent addition to the realm of higher education instruction, currently teaches face-to-face composition classes for Ridgewater College. He also teaches English, online, for North Dakota State University. His research focus is split between his two rhetorical passions. First, how does computer coding and visual design affect writing practices within online writing spaces? And, how does the hierarchy of the contemporary University design affect the financial support given to non-credit generating entities, such as writing centers?

Steven D. Krause is a professor in the Department of English Language and Literature at Eastern Michigan University. His research and teaching explore the connections between writing and technology.

Paul Lynch, Assistant Professor of English at Saint Louis University, teaches courses in composition, the history of rhetoric, and the essay. His work on St. Patrick of Ireland has appeared in *Rhetoric Review* and the recent collection *Rhetoric in the Rest of the West*. He has also published articles in *College Composition and Communication* and *KB Journal.*

Randall McClure is an associate professor at Georgia Southern University and chair of the Department of Writing and Linguistics. His essays have appeared in *WPA: Writing Program Administration, portal: Libraries and the Academy, Computers and Composition Online, Composition Studies, Academic Exchange Quarterly,* and the *Journal of Literacy and Technology.*

Catherine Ramsdell, Professor of Writing at Savannah College of Art and Design Atlanta, teaches courses in composition, business and professional writing, promotional writing, writing for the web, and writing for new media. She holds a PhD from Auburn University and is on the books staff of *Popmatters.com,* an online magazine dedicated to cultural criticism.

Alex Reid, Associate Professor and Director of Composition and Teaching Fellows at State University New York Buffalo, studies digital media and rhetoric. His book, *The Two Virtuals: New Media and Composition,* received honorable mention for the W. Ross Winterowd award for best book in composition theory, and his blog, *Digital Digs* (http://www.alex-reid. net), received the John Lovas Memorial Weblog Award for contributions to the field of rhetoric and composition.

E. Shelley Reid, Associate Professor of English and the Director of the Composition Program at George Mason University, has published articles in *College Composition and Communication, Pedagogy,* and *Composition Studies.* She teaches writing and editing classes and helps prepare graduate students to teach composition.

Karen Rosenberg directs the Writing Center at the University of Washington Bothell. Her research and teaching focus on feminist discourse analysis, social inequalities, and storytelling as a tool for social change. Her publications include articles in *Signs: Journal of Women in Culture and Society, Teaching Sociology,* and *Feminist Teacher.*

Catherine Savini, Associate Professor at Westfield State University in Massachusetts, teaches writing courses and serves as the writing center director and writing across the curriculum coordinator.

Kristi L. Shackelford, the Director of Academic Policy and Curriculum Development at James Madison University, teaches courses for the School of Writing, Rhetoric and Technical Communication including editing and publication management.

Nathalie Singh-Corcoran, Clinical Assistant Professor at West Virginia University, directs the writing center. She is also the vice president of the International Writing Centers Association. Her publications have largely been in the areas of writing center administration and writing center connections to undergraduate writing programs.

Kyle D. Stedman, a doctoral candidate at the University of South Florida, teaches composition and professional writing and works as technology coordinator for the first year composition program. His dissertation is on music composition and the rhetoric of sound. In 2010, he won the Conference on College Composition and Communication Chairs' Memorial Scholarship.

Janice R. Walker, Professor of Writing and Linguistics at Georgia Southern University, has published journal articles and book chapters about online research, documentation, and writing, in addition to her two most recent books, *The Columbia Guide to Online Style* (Columbia UP 2006) and *Bookmarks: A Guide to Writing and Research* (Longman 2006). She is founder and coordinator of the Graduate Research Network at the annual Computers and Writing conference, and co-coordinator for the Georgia Conference on Information Literacy hosted by Georgia Southern University.

CPSIA information can be obtained
at www.ICGtesting.com
Printed in the USA
FFHW020709271218
49996017-54712FF

9 781602 351967